WITHDRAWN

AN INTERPRETIVE APPROACH TO *TOUR GUIDING*

Enriching the Experience

AN INTERPRETIVE APPROACH TO **TOUR GUIDING**

Enriching the Experience

Kirby LRC
Middlesbrough College
Roman Road
Middlesbrough
TS5 5PJ

John Pastorelli

Hospitality
Press

Pearson Education Australia
Unit 4, Level 2
14 Aquatic Drive
Frenchs Forest NSW 2086

www.pearsoned.com.au

Publisher: David Cunningham
Senior Project Editor: Natasha Dupont
Copy Editor: Valerie Marlborough
Cover and internal design by Ingo Voss
Illustrations by Andrew Hore
Typeset by Midland Typesetters, Maryborough, Vic.

Printed in Malaysia

1 2 3 4 5 06 05 04 03

National Library of Australia
Cataloguing-in-Publication Data

Pastorelli, John, 1962– .
  Enriching the experience : an interpretive approach to tour
  guiding.

  Bibliography.
  Includes index.
  ISBN 1 86250 522 5.

  1. Tourism – Australia. 2. Tour guides (Persons) –
  Training of – Australia. I. Title.

338.479102394

An imprint of Pearson Education

Foreword

I have learnt that life is the natural teacher and experience is the outcome. Because in living we often face the hardest teacher of all—it starts out by giving us the test and you learn later from the experience.

It is in this vein that I first came across the concept of 'Interpretation' while working as a Park Ranger with the NSW National Parks and Wildlife Service. It formed the cornerstone of my thinking about the overwhelming power of experience and gave such delight when I discovered evidence confirming my beliefs in nature and my own cultural spirituality.

So too are visitors and tourists alike seeking the same enrichment—something that inspires passion, and that affirms a greater faith in nature.

I would hope that this book provides a simple but significant contribution to this quest. One which recognises that the way in which we deliver this structured experience is part of an ever-changing marketplace of needs and trends and the refinement of choices against more discerning preferences of the individual.

Key to this must be our Tour Guides: the dedicated people who play an essential role in the initiation and pursuit of our experience. These are the individuals who lever the everyday, ordinary aspects of our lives to give us a viable, alternative and healthy addition to our experiences.

In short, Tour Guides are there to provide the positive and sustainable by assisting us in making those choices and remembering those experiences long after the day is over.

I hope this book provides a better understanding of the experience and more importantly provides Tour Guides with the skills to fulfil their roles in this quest.

In closing, savour the moment and live twice through the experience.

Aden Ridgeway
Senator for NSW

Contents

Chapter 6—Planning and developing tour activities

Chapter 7—Your tour commentary

Chapter 8—Working with tour groups

Chapter 9—Extended tours

Chapter 10—Working with stories

Appendixes

Bibliography

Index

Preface

The one thing I remember from my first experience of leading a tour was that it was not particularly successful. However, it served as a huge learning experience. The tour was conducted in one of the national parks around Sydney and was due to run for three hours. After two hours we had walked all of 300 metres, of a planned five kilometre walk. My intention was to ensure that I imparted as much information as possible to the tour participants. They had no option but to listen politely as I recalled spiels of plant and bird names, flipped between soil types and habitat characteristics, and inserted numerous dates and events relating to the area's history. At the end of the tour everyone seemed okay—there were thanks all round and comments such as 'That was great' and 'We'll be back'. However, upon reflection something didn't click—a degree of conviction was lacking in those parting hand-shakes and waves of farewell.

Over the ensuing months I researched, tried, tested, experimented and evaluated a vast variety of techniques and approaches until that conviction resounded with a stronger degree of sincerity. This journey led me to realise that tours went far beyond just facts and sharing information, and that tours comprised an experience created, evoked and driven by an immense variety of elements. It dawned on me that I facilitated the journey for people in that transition from observation and exploring, to experiencing and discovering, and to understanding and appreciation. And that this journey and its ensuing memories remain infinite.

I learnt that tours require structure, varying degrees of entertainment value, central messages and themes, periods for reflection and staging, and communication principles for building healthy rapport with people. I also learnt that the content and style of the tour were as much determined by the needs of the audience as they were by my needs and those of the organisation for whom I was working.

Collectively I refer to these elements as 'an interpretive approach to guiding', which is the principal focus for this book. It brings together the ideas, thoughts and concepts which I have learnt (and continue to learn) over the years through both my own work and that of others.

In many ways, leading a tour is much like sharing a story with people—stories of people, places, events, items and objects. When leading a tour the Guide needs to share the same 'space' as everyone on that tour, a space which extends beyond the physical to the emotive and intellectual. Those people who come along to an interpretive activity need to be provoked and encouraged to think. They need to be emotionally moved so that they leave with both intellectual and emotional memories.

An interpretive approach to guiding is about promoting this guiding effort so that it promotes significance and uniqueness. What makes one event unique compared to another almost identical event? What makes two historic houses side-by-side different?

Or two adjacent art pieces? Why are you, 'the Guide', bringing focus to a particular object or event or to some other point of interest?

What about the array of interconnected processes, activities, events, tangible objects, and the ensuing relationships that lie in the stories of people, places and events?

With an interpretive approach, the Guide needs to be clear about what it is he or she wants the audience to learn, and about what message and experience he or she wants people to take away. Guides also need to be aware that there is an increasing need amongst visitors for an educational component to their tour experience.

An interpretive approach moves away from a scripted approach that can polarise everything we do to the extent that there is no discovery left in the grey areas. It promotes flexibility to take advantage of shifting needs and environmental opportunities, and any opportunities to incorporate spontaneous elements.

I have always held the belief that guiding is not for everyone. In the same way that not all of us would be suited to working as a mechanic, CEO or sports person, not all of us would be suited to working as a Guide. It is a frontline occupation that requires a professional attitude of the highest order. Although it can be glamorous, fun and exciting, guiding also involves a lot of hard work.

For such a skilled profession there are no national or even state awards for Guides. There are moves afoot to bring some consistency and minimum standards of practice to the guiding industry, such as the EcoGuide Program pioneered by Alice Crabtree and Betty Weiler (Appendix 4), and in-house certification and accreditation programs like those of Savannah Guides in the northern parts of Australia.

Such programs provide useful models for raising the profile of guiding, and for ensuring its professionalism and sustainability; an endeavour which needs to attract the collective effort of all levels of government, industry operators and individuals.

This book has been written as a reference for the competency-based training of Guides within the Vocational Education and Training sector. However it is hoped that Guides throughout Australia will find it useful in providing ideas, concepts and techniques which they can incorporate into their tours. It includes activities, case studies, and contributions from leading interpreters and Guides throughout Australia. I have tried my best to keep the book practical and skills-based with ideas and techniques that could be applied immediately.

In this respect the book does not delve with any great depth into the managerial and strategic aspects of working with Interpretation. There are a vast variety of references and resources available to assist people with this specific interest (contact the Interpretation Australia Association for further information).

I believe Interpretation operates within a framework of curiosity, respect and flexibility. Being curious to learn and find out more; respect for yourself, your audience and your environment, and flexibility to ensure that what you do remains relevant to the situation at hand.

I also believe that one of the outcomes of an interpretive process is an increased level of wisdom, a wisdom that supports a deeper and stronger relationship with the social, cultural and natural values of this world.

They say that to seek wisdom consult a wise person. They also say that when we meet such a person we often hear them yet fall short of listening to them. But in those times when we do go beyond the hearing and allow ourselves to listen, we soon discover that the wise person lies within us. Listen to them, learn from them, love them. Share and encourage the same in others. I hope this book helps in this journey.

AUTHOR ACKNOWLEDGEMENTS

To Mark Wilson who provided my original interpretive experience and thereafter served as an inspiration.

To Steve King and Christine O'Brien—thanks for my first professional interpretive position.

To Jokki—thanks for your support and inspiration, and for the memories which will always remain precious.

To all those people who contributed text and/or provided permission to include text, thank you: Rosemary Black, Cath Renwick, Alice Crabtree, Bernie Cavanagh, Genelle Sharrock, Steve McAuley, Gil Field, Robin MacGillvray, Lee Adendorff, Lynne McLoughlin, Rachel Faggeter, Bill Nethery, Peter Lehmann, Jo Pillinger, Vicki Longmuir, Jenny Manning, Mirah Lambert, Vince Scarcella, Rosie Williams, Brian McDonald, Guy Patching, Janine McLeod, Sabina Douglas-Hill, Raffety Fynn, Sandra O'Neil, David Newton, Di Eva, Kevin Coate, Nadia Lalak, Jonathon Woods, Dan Grieve, Bernice McCarthy, Nicholas Hall, Keith Williams, Gill Anderson, and Jan and Jeremy from WA (maybe next time). Thanks Andrew Hore for the great cartoons.

Thanks also Peter and Pat Dargin, and Gil Field for reviewing the text, and to the anonymous reviewers of the text organised by the publishers—thanks for your great comments and support for the concept.

For the opportunity to share the ideas and principles discussed in this book within training workshops thanks to: Liz Keirs and the crew at the Australian War Memorial, Wendy Haylock and the interpretive staff on Kangaroo Island, Sarah Breheny, Susan Davies, Pat Hall, Kerry Robinson, Sharon Lane, Rhonda Brown, Cath Renwick, Karen Kearnes, Jenny Bolwell, Rebecca Brown, Penny Wise, Lorraine Barlow, Roger Mills, Barbara Webster, Colin Beckett and the team at Agtours, Donna Edwards, Faye Gardiner, Dave Paton, Camille Dunsford, Katrina Cashman, Rachel Ely, Jane Latief, Briony Edwards, Anja Simpson, Robyn Bushell, Suzanne Ackermann, Sara Williams, Chris Grundoff, Paul Green, and to Rebecca, Aletha and Mirah from the Museums and Galleries Foundation (NSW). Thanks also to Karen Jack, Kirsty Almond, and to Fergus and Kerry Hides-Pearson from the environmental education training company *terra cordis*. To the teachers and staff at Ultimo and Crows Nest TAFE—Meaghan, Dana, Amanda, Gary, Mary Ann, Sue and Janine.

To all those people working within the field of Interpretation and who I've met along the way and have made the journey of Interpretation all the more fun, exciting and rewarding. A very special thanks to Gill Slocum.

For inspirational interpretive learning opportunities thanks to: Sam Ham, Mike Watson, Dave Dahlen, Adrienne Williams, Nigel Sutton, Jane James, Julie Hudspeth, Alan Nurthern, Bob Crombie. Thanks Anne and the crew at Impromtu Theatrix.

To Bill Smallwood and Todd Coates for the opportunity to be part of the start-up team at BridgeClimb; and to Kim Wilkinson and the first team of Climb Leaders (wherever you are) thanks for a stack of great memories. For the opportunities to continue being a part of BridgeClimb thanks to Rachel Martyn, David Barnes, Tricia Siva, Loreley De Los Santos, Carolyn Doherty, and to Natalie and Renata. For the original referrals thanks to Margo Homersham and Craig Edmonson for your faith in my ability 'sight unseen'.

To the CHASE ALIVE team thanks for the memories, for the infinite periods of enjoyment and for all you taught me in the years when I was managing the program. Thanks to Patrick Holland and Sharon Sullivan for the initial opportunity and to Bob Conroy for the latitude and trust to allow the program to breathe despite some radical manoeuvring. To the so many friends and colleagues from the CHASE ALIVE program thanks—you know who you are.

To Ken Griffiths and all those people involved in the Urban Wildlife Survey, especially those who assisted with running tours throughout the state of NSW.

For your support when needed, thanks to: Kirsten Daly, Kathy Miller, Lesley Neil, John Lavarack, Penny Ewing, Simon McArthur and Isabel Sebastian, Ashle Tucano, Jenny Biggin. For your support and training opportunities relating to my creativity workshops thanks to: Colin Sharp, Anthony Mitchell, Colin Wise, Graham Mackie, and to Liz Griffin and Karin Gieroszynski and the team at Ernst and Young.

To the following friends who with their empathetic ear kept providing me with support during 2001 and 2002—a huge thanks for being there: David Purvis-Smith, Jane Dawborn, Rod and Kim Sharples, Paul Bateson, Kevin Wale, Susan Huxley, Lorraine Smith, Janine McLeod, Julie Bourne, Chris and Naomi Keyzer, Jamie Shaw, Elizabeth, Susie Danos, Benny (wherever you are), Terry Forster, Sarah Breheny, and Chontarle Pitulej (thanks for listening and helping out, bro!). A huge thanks also to my brothers and parents.

Thanks to the participants and trainers of the original gathering and to Jo Davies.

Thanks to Matthew Coxhill from Pearson Education who took the chance and said 'Yes!' To Natasha, thanks for your patience when I constantly pushed the deadlines.

Once this book goes off to press there will be only one thing to keep me awake at night—I hope I didn't forget anyone. If I did accept my apologies and it'll be my shout next time we meet.

1

Guiding—an interpretive approach

What are the learning outcomes for this chapter?

By the end of this chapter you should be able to:
- Define Interpretation.
- Identify the principles of an interpretive approach to guiding.
- Identify a variety of tourism industry sectors.
- Outline trends within the tourism industry.
- List a variety of tour activities.

THE GUIDING ENVIRONMENT

A tour can be thought of as comprising three components: the audience, the environment and the Guide. Together these make up the guiding environment.

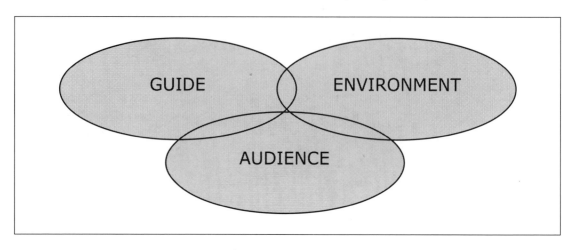

THE GUIDE

Guides play a significant role in facilitating and managing the tour experience. Guides work in a variety of locales including museums, historic sites, galleries, national parks, cities and suburbs, marine environments and desert landscapes. They conduct tours which can last from 30 minutes to several weeks. They work on a volunteer, employee, freelance or contract basis, and as owner-operator Guides.

THE AUDIENCE

Your audience are your clients and customers. They might be visitors from other suburbs or towns, tourists from another country, or anyone else coming along on a tour. They are of all ages and demographic backgrounds, and come with different and unique interests, expectations, motivations and needs. Your audience can arrive as individuals, couples or in groups of three people to tens of people.

THE ENVIRONMENT

The environment is where the tour takes place (e.g. historic house, national park, museum, bushland area or cityscape) plus all the elements relevant to that place, which can include stories, settings, objects and processes. It also includes all aspects related to the logistics of the tour including organisational policies and practices, relationships with colleagues, and any other elements which can influence the tour experience.

THE TOUR EXPERIENCE

The tour experience involves the Guide, an audience and the environment. This is when all three components of a tour interact at the same point in space and time and share the same focus. That is, they share the same journey for a period of time.

During this period a myriad of relationships take place—between audience and environment, between audience and Guide, between Guide and environment, and between all three. Guides should manage these relationships with the aim of ensuring a positive experience for the visitor, a sustainable experience for the environment and a rewarding experience for themselves.

AN INTERPRETIVE APPROACH TO GUIDING

WHAT IS INTERPRETATION?

Interpretation is one of a number of communication disciplines which seeks to generate an increased understanding and appreciation of our environment. These disciplines include environmental education, museum education and community education.

The word 'interpretation' is derived from the Latin *interpretari*, which means to explain, to translate. In its traditional usage interpretation is connected to the verb 'to interpret' and relates to the translation of languages—that is, a person of one culture requires an interpreter to translate languages.

Your role as a Guide is to explain and translate the features and characteristics of a site, feature and/or event in such a way that it means something to people. From an interpretive perspective it is hoped that through this process people will then attribute a greater sense of meaning and significance to the site, feature and/or event which is the focus of the tour experience.

Within this book Interpretation will be defined as 'A learning experience which seeks to enrich the meaningful relationships we hold with our world, and to foster and build a set of values which supports these relationships'.

 ACTIVITY: The practice of interpretation follows a set of principles. Consider the following definitions of interpretation and list what you consider to be the most important principles. (Once you have completed these, also refer to the principles of Freeman Tilden in Appendix 1.)

An educational activity which aims to reveal meanings and relationships through the use of original objects, by first-hand experience, and by illustrative media, rather than simply to communicate factual information.
Freeman Tilden (1977)

Interpretation is a means of communicating ideas and feelings which helps people enrich their understanding and appreciation of the world and their role within it.
Interpretation Australia Association newsletter, used with permission

The essence of good interpretation is that it reveals a new insight into what makes a place special. It gives people new understanding.
Carter (1997)

The interpreter is at his best when he discusses facts so that they appeal to the imagination and to reason, gives flesh and blood to cold facts, makes life stories of inanimate objects . . . gives biographies, rather than classifications.
Enos Mills

What we do in the world flows from how we interpret the world . . . and how we interpret the world is closely linked to our values, to what we hold to be important and what is right . . . they define our relationships and mould our identities, beliefs and goals.
Charles Birch

The task of interpreters is to share the meaning and significance of a place with our visitors: to link them with the site's spaces and places, its objects, the experiences which it provides, and its ideas and stories. We do this because as custodians of the community's heritage, it is our democratic duty to do so, but

we also hope that our visitors will understand more, enrich their lives and in the process become participants and advocates for the conservation process.
Rachel Faggetter

Some of the principles of Interpretation we can summarise from these definitions include:

● Interpretation is a process of learning and gaining deeper understanding.
● Interpretation seeks to provoke thought and reveal meaning.
● Interpretation involves communication.
● Interpretation aims to stimulate an appreciation of our natural and cultural heritage.
● Interpretation aims to bring items and events to life.

Traditionally Interpretation has been practised by natural and cultural heritage based organisations. In particular Interpretation has strong roots in the national parks and land management sectors where it is used to foster a greater understanding and appreciation of the role and values of national parks, and to complement the management activities within national parks.

ACTIVITY: A local reporter phones you after hearing about this concept called Interpretation. She asks for your definition of Interpretation. What definition would you provide?

PRINCIPLES OF AN INTERPRETIVE APPROACH

As outlined above, Interpretation involves a learning experience which seeks to enrich the meaningful relationships we hold with our world, and to foster and build a set of values which supports these relationships. An interpretive approach to guiding seeks to foster the development of such relationships, and to enrich the experience for both your audience and yourself. The following principles underpin this interpretive approach.

● This approach captures, engages and involves your audience by:
　—being relevant, interesting, enjoyable and interactive;
　—stimulating people and provoking thought;
　—evoking curiosity and a willingness to find out more;
　—bringing the tour experience to life 　　　　　　　　　g a landscape
　　　rather than sterilising it;
　—incorporating effective communicatio
● This approach reveals the meaning and 　　　　　　　　　nt, site and/or place by:
　—letting people know the wider conte 　　　　　　　　　meaning and

significance of what you're sharing, and by addressing the whole picture and not an isolated element;

—ensuring learning opportunities for your audience;

—building relationships between the audience and the environment;

—being based on a structure which includes a commentary that contains a message, is based on a theme and follows a story-line.

● This approach works to a framework that is ethical, legal and respectful. Such qualities are consistent with all relationships and imply that the activity:

—will be conducted with an honest and open attitude on the part of the Guide;

—respects and promotes the value and significance of an area's natural, social and cultural heritage;

—implements, whenever possible, minimal impact and sustainable tourism practices;

—respects local people and communities, and observes any rules and regulations of the governing/managing organisation.

Those in your audience create their own memory of each and every tour—as a Guide you need to make sure that you work towards assisting people to create positive memories, and that you escalate a tour from a simple outing to a memorable experience.

WHY DO WE NEED AN INTERPRETIVE APPROACH?
From a guiding-industry perspective

An interpretive approach is seen as one way to raise the standard of guiding within Australia, and set in place a benchmark for best practice. This helps ensure a rich and positive experience for the visitor, which in turn would benefit the tourism industry.

Interpretation is increasingly being introduced as a licensing, accreditation and legislative requirement within tour operations. It is also becoming an integral component of Guide-training programs, and is a competency unit within both the Certificate III and IV in Tourism (Guiding) qualifications.

From a visitor's perspective

Although the majority of visitors do not know what Interpretation is, they are nevertheless seeking the experience generated by an interpretive approach—that is, one which is enjoyable, relevant, interesting and meaningful. Interpretive activities satisfy the increasing trend among visitors seeking educational experiences.

From a Guide's perspective

Being involved with interpretive activities encourages Guides to continually update their skills and knowledge. It also helps to make their guiding enjoyable, stimulating and fresh, and to keep them in step with the increasing industry requirement to incorporate interpretive principles into their operations.

As outlined above, interpretive activities can benefit visitors. This can have a positive flow-on effect for Guides, for example repeat business and promotional opportunities, accolades and peer/industry recognition.

FACE-TO-FACE INTERPRETATION AND INTERPRETIVE MEDIA

The applications of Interpretation techniques are often categorised into either face-to-face Interpretation or interpretive media (sometimes referred to as non-face-to-face Interpretation). Websites are a mix of both of these.

Face-to-face Interpretation

Face-to-face interpretive techniques are associated with any activity where the interpreter interacts directly with an audience. Typical venues include national parks, museums, galleries, visitor and tourist information centres, and historic sites. People who might practise face-to-face interpretive techniques include visitor services staff, national park rangers, Tourist Guides, public contact officers, interpretive officers and education officers.

This book focuses on face-to-face Interpretation and, in particular, its applications within the field of tour guiding.

Interpretive media

Interpretive media involves the use of a medium between the interpreter and audience. These media include brochures, publications, displays, dioramas, books, audiovisual equipment and audiotapes, as well as signs and exhibits.

Websites

Websites are an interesting mix of face-to-face Interpretation and interpretive media. Some sites are interactive and provide the opportunity to liaise directly with a person to obtain additional information. An example of such a site is the Australian Museums and Galleries Online site (www.amol.org.au), which is one of the most comprehensive websites focusing on Australia's cultural heritage. This website will be used as a reference and resource site for later chapters. More and more people are spending an increasing amount of time researching the locale, site and/or event they will be visiting. As a Guide leading tours for these people you also need to ensure your knowledge is extensive, current and accurate. Websites such as Australian Museums and Galleries Online (AMOL) are an excellent resource for such endeavours.

Special Focus

A brief history of Interpretation and its association with the related disciplines of environmental education and museum education

Lynne McLoughlin
Graduate School of the Environment
Macquarie University, NSW

Interpretation is an activity conducted at a place or in the presence of an object, which aims to reveal the significance, meanings and associations connected with that place or object in ways which engage the visitor/viewer/listener and provoke ongoing thought and interest.

Guides have been showing people how to find their way to and around unknown places for centuries and many of those wayfinders undoubtedly whiled away the time on the journey with stories about the places they passed through and the people who lived, loved and died there. However, Enos Mills, a Nature Guide in the Rocky Mountains in the United States from 1889 to 1922, is generally regarded as the founder of the present field of Interpretation, developing its first principles and techniques as a Guide, teacher and writer. His success in convincing the National Parks Service to license two of his best pupils as Interpretive Guides in the Rocky Mountains National Park began a long commitment of the US National Parks Service to the development of Interpretation in its parks.

As a result, Interpretation has always been involved with the visiting public in their leisure time, with its philosophy based on enriching visitors' experience at a site, satisfying their curiosity, and increasing their understanding and awareness. By promoting understanding and appreciation of places and their values, it has also often been considered an important tool in promoting preservation and conservation of heritage, particularly in natural areas. In more recent years Interpretation of the natural environment has developed more focused environmental education elements, as environmental problems have become more obvious and the need for everyone to consider the impacts of their actions on the environment has been more broadly recognised.

In 1957 and 1967 Freeman Tilden, an author, playwright and much-travelled visitor to national parks and historic sites in the United States, defined the basic philosophy and guiding principles of Interpretation with passion and gentle humour in *Interpreting Our Heritage*. Although written for US national parks and now dated in style, this work remains Interpretation's 'classic' work, expressing the very essence of the interpreter's art and rationale. When the various Australian states set up their national park systems in the 1970s and 1980s, many aspects of the US National Parks Service organisation, including Interpretation, were brought into Australia's national parks. Interpretation has since spread here to many different types of sites managed by many different organisations.

ENVIRONMENTAL EDUCATION

Environmental education as a separate field began mainly in schools, although different to the older environmentally related fields of nature study, biology, ecology and geography. Part of the awakening of protest and community participation in the 1960s, environmental education sprang from a growing awareness of environmental problems and the degradation of our world environment. Along with scientific and technological developments, education was seen as an important social aspect to solving the environmental crisis and developing new ways of interacting with the environment.

Environmental education emerged first in the United States in the mid-1960s, and was formally recognised in Australia in 1970. It remained strongly associated with schools until the early 1990s, although mass communication and public campaigns were being widely used by the conservation movement to gain public support for conservation causes through this period. In 1992 Agenda 21, a policy framework for international action on the environment based on the principles of ecologically sustainable development, emerged from the United Nations Earth Summit at Rio de Janeiro and began to be adopted around the world. With increasing recognition of the scale of environmental impacts and the urgent need for better environmental practices in all spheres of society, community-based environmental education initiatives began to proliferate.

Some of these programs have essentially been marketing initiatives, whereby information regarding environmental problems and the ways people can assist in solutions to those problems are promoted using the mass media. However, in its broadest sense, environmental education is a process that engages and empowers people to protect their environments and improve quality of life. It develops awareness, knowledge, values and action skills to enable people to form judgments about sustainable lifestyles and to take action to protect the environment. By engaging visitors' interest and helping them understand environmental issues in a specific place, well-constructed interpretation is a tool that can play an important role in the environmental education process.

MUSEUM EDUCATION

A third associated professional field is museum education. Traditionally, a museum's primary role was to collect, preserve and present objects. Education grew from a desire to provide information for the public about the displayed collections, so that museum education was originally about objects and the general goal was learning and personal enrichment, rather than acquisition of practical information or skills, or an answer to wider community or environmental problems.

Two trends have broadened museum education approaches and focus. As Interpretation has spread, its techniques and approaches have been incorporated into the ways museums present their collections, with the goal of attracting and engaging larger audiences at a time when there are so many competing demands for visitors' time. Exhibitions have also broadened to include general subject matter related to a museum's collections, such as the environmental issues and threats to species displayed in a natural history museum, although the emphasis is still on the objects and an experience of 'the real thing'.

A WRAP!

Despite the increasing similarity of objectives and desirable methods in Interpretation and environmental education and their absorption into museums, there are three separate professional associations in Australia for each of these fields. Each has its own literature and set of current practices.

Differences in objectives and the ways educators and interpreters see themselves and their task inevitably make a significant difference to their approach and the likely outcomes of their programs. Some practitioners belong to more than one of these organisations and bring together elements from the various fields within their programs.

Despite the somewhat artificial division into different fields, they are all still dealing in the communication of messages about the environment. They are all interacting with people, variously described as visitors or learners, in leisure time in non-formal environments, markedly different from formal (school, TAFE, university) learning environments. Visitor attention is entirely voluntary, dependent on the visitors' intrinsic interest in the subject matter, the quality of the Interpretation, exhibition or tour being presented and the visitors' social environment at the time.

This book is designed to help you capture the attention of those visitors, to hold it through your tour, give them a memorable experience and enable them to take away some important messages about the place they have visited.

A TOURISM INDUSTRY OVERVIEW

Travel has always been a part of the human experience with explorers, traders, scientists, navigators, religious followers and indigenous people travelling between locales for their own unique reasons. Today people travel for a variety of reasons including fun, leisure, the visiting of relatives and friends, education, business and as means for cultural exchange. All aspects of travel are catered for by the broad tourism industry.

Tourism is the range of activities, services and infrastructure which caters for people involved in travelling for leisure and pleasure away from their normal place of residence. This definition could also be extended to those people who travel primarily to visit friends and relatives (the VFR market), and to those who travel for business purposes as these people often incorporate leisure-related activities into their travels.

Tour operations is considered to be a sector within the tourism industry, and it is often complemented by services and products provided by other industry sectors such as those illustrated in the following diagram. A great deal of liaison can take place between these various sectors during the planning and implementation of tours.

TOURISM SECTORS
There are many different sectors in the tourism industry.

Tour operators and wholesalers
Tour wholesalers are those organisations that package a range of tourism products and services into a single entity for a consumer. They bring together a range of related

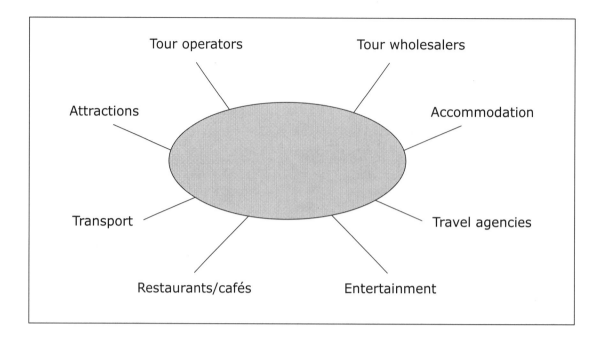

tourism services and products including accommodation, entertainment, transport, attractions and tour-based activities. Tour operators can take on similar roles but are also involved in promotional, planning and other logistical details of making a tour happen. This can include coach transfers and reconfirmation of tour details, and managing several tour managers and/or Tourist Guides.

Transport
Transport can include coaches, airlines, cruise-liners and other watercraft, cars, bicycles, horses and rail. Of these coaches and airlines are the most popular modes of mass transport used in tour-based activities.

The primary role of Guides when working with airlines and cruise-lines is to provide a transfer-assist service, which includes both a meet-and-greet upon arrival and a departure-assist upon leaving. Guides also work with airlines for the transport of tour groups between different legs of their tour. When working with these transport providers Guides need to have a working knowledge of:

● departure and arrival procedures including check-ins;
● customs and immigration procedures;
● the layout of transport terminals including the location of arrival and departure gates, and facilities such as toilets, phones, transport and car/bus pick-up zones, car hire and automatic teller machines (ATMs).

Watercraft are used for coastal tours such as marine mammal watching (whales, seals, dolphins and dugongs), birdwatching and reef tours (especially in the Great Barrier Reef).

Coaches are a popular mode of transport involved with tour operations and are used to provide an immense variety of tours from half-day sightseeing tours to weekend get-aways to extended tours of several weeks. Characteristics of coach travel include the following:

- The route of travel is normally predetermined to maximise the opportunities to visit relevant and interesting attractions, services and other sites.
- The same group of people are generally included for the whole tour.
- The group is generally accompanied by the same tour manager throughout the tour.
- For extended tours, accommodation and most meals are normally included as part of any coach-tour package.

Retail travel agencies

Retail travel agencies are often involved in providing a link between an audience and a tour. They are responsible for making tour bookings and travel arrangements, and liaising with inbound tour operators. Some travel agencies are also tour wholesalers who develop tour packages for retail sales, as well as receiving tour packages from wholesalers.

Attractions

Attractions are either the main focus of a tour or can be provided as optional extras. They can include:

- purpose-built attractions such as theme, entertainment and adventure parks;
- structures such as the Sydney Opera House, Sydney Harbour Bridge, Stockman's Hall of Fame, museums and historic houses;
- natural features and phenomena such as the Great Barrier Reef, Uluru, the Kimberley Ranges, mass bird migrations and the flooding of Lake Eyre;
- cultural/social activities such as indigenous events and festivals, Mardi Gras, the Melbourne Comedy Festival, World Music Festival (Adelaide), Perth Festival of the Arts, Todd River Boat Races (Alice Springs) and the Tamworth Country Music Festival.

Hospitality industry

The hospitality industry is part of the broader tourism industry and includes such sectors as accommodation; cafés, restaurants and other food outlets; entertainment; and conferences and conventions.

Accommodation

Accommodation is an essential requirement for all people who travel. People often use accommodation establishments as a base from which to explore an area or region.

In these situations Guides frequently interact with the establishments at meeting and drop-off points for tours. During extended tours people often use a vast array of different accommodation types during their trip including motels, self-contained units and camp grounds.

Guides can also be involved in meet-and-greets and in transfer-assists, during which they assist the transport of people between a transport node (e.g. airport) and their place of accommodation.

Staff at accommodation establishments are often involved in referring tour programs to their guests, in assisting with transport arrangements to attend tours, and in liaising with tour operations staff to confirm relevant details. This is sometimes undertaken by Guides who assist at accommodation information desks within certain establishments, especially during extended tours when they might staff the hospitality desk in the mornings to provide relevant information to people from their tour group.

Some of the styles of accommodation are:

● hotels and motels;
● self-contained apartments;
● camp grounds;
● cruise ships and yachts;
● resorts;
● farm stays and bed & breakfasts.

Guides should be familiar enough with the accommodation provider to give the following information:

● style and standard of accommodation;
● location, which can include distance to shopping areas and other attractions/points of interest, and availability of public transport;
● security of personal belongings;
● facilities and amenities;
● what's included as part of the stay of your audience;
● any interesting information and/or stories about that particular accommodation establishment which can be shared with your audience.

Cafés, restaurants and other food outlets

Guides often liaise with food outlets as either an impromptu food stop, or when providing meals as an inclusive element of a package tour. An idea of what food will be provided is useful information, especially with the varying expectations of different nationalities. Also, an idea of how the food will be served is needed, for example set menu, buffet or à la carte.

Guides are sometimes involved in dine-outs in which dining in a restaurant is included as part of the tour or is sometimes the principal focus of the tour.

Entertainment

People love to have fun when travelling, and to see as much as possible of the places they visit. Entertainment venues include nightclubs, casinos and the good old Aussie pub.

Conventions and conferences

Tours are often included in these events as part of the delegate's package. These tours can be an optional extra or an essential session of the conference such as a field trip. Conventions and conferences fall within the MICE tourism sector—meetings, incentives, conventions and exhibitions.

ACTIVITY: Collect promotional material from each of the tourism sectors discussed in this chapter and design a collage to illustrate the relationships they have with each other.

INTERNATIONAL AND DOMESTIC TOURISM

The world tourism industry has grown quite significantly over the past few decades with greater transport options, larger disposable income, more leisure time, increased preferences for people to travel, and more marketing and promotional campaigns.

The World Tourism Organisation has estimated that the number of international tourists has increased 28-fold since the 1950s to recent times with 698 million arrivals in the year 2000. As an example, in the mid-1970s one in thirteen people travelled from an industrialised country to a developing country. In recent years this has increased to one in five (Mastny 2001). Within Australia international tourism accounts for approximately 25 per cent of all tourism activity, with the remaining 75 per cent being attributed to domestic tourism—that is, travel by Australian residents within Australia.

This increase in tourism activity has had a significant impact on the tour operations sector with a greater diversity of people attending tours, a higher demand for tours and an increased need for appropriate attractions and destinations.

The strengths of Australia as a destination include:

● friendly people;
● vastness of the landscapes;
● unique flora and fauna;
● relatively safe environment;
● pleasant climate.

Some of the trends within the tourism industry include the following:

- The preference has increased for travellers to visit less crowded destinations and take part in special-interest activities. This includes the increased demand in people seeking regional tourism opportunities as a way of 'escaping' the stress of urban life.
- There has been a move away from mass tourism, leading to a growth of niche industries such as ecotourism and other heritage-based activities in which people can find out more about the natural, social and cultural heritage of places they visit.
- The shift in tourist characteristics is influenced by:
  —greater access to information through cable TV and its associated documentaries and world events, the Internet, and magazines and papers from around the world;
  —higher standards of living leading to increased affluence and spending power in seeking out unique experiences.

Some of the tourism markets relevant to guiding with definitions provided in Appendix 1 are:

- heritage tourism;
- adventure-based tourism;
- cultural tourism;
- indigenous tourism;
- nature-based tourism and ecotourism.

Other markets include:

- outback;
- wine tourism;
- MICE.

TYPES OF TOURS

There are many types of tours including those that are based on a particular site, a special interest, or on a type of transport.

Site-based tours include:

- museums and galleries;
- zoos and wildlife parks;
- indigenous sites;
- botanic gardens;
- factories, mines and other work sites;
- waste-transfer stations, dams, power stations and sewerage plants;
- historic houses and significant buildings.

Special-interest tours include:

- sporting tours;

- photography tours;
- wildlife trips, for example birdwatching (including ornithology trips and penguin tours) and marine mammal watching (including dolphin, seal and whale watching);
- wine tours;
- regional tours of rural areas;

- scientific and educational-based tours;
- garden tours.

Vehicle-based tours include:

- four-wheel drive (4WD) tours;
- coach tours ranging from a couple of hours to extended tours of several weeks;
- aircraft tours—seaplane tours, land-based scenic flights and helicopter tours;
- car rallies.

Water based tours include:

- snorkelling and scuba diving;
- canyoning, canoeing and kayaking;
- cruise boating and yachting;
- marine mammal watching, birdwatching and fishing tours.

Tours can also include:

- suburban and city-sights walking tours;
- city family tours which begin with a meet-and-greet at the airport and end at the hotel foyer;
- cycling and mountain-bike tours;
- camel and horse-riding tours;
- hiking and bushwalking trips through government-managed bushland areas (e.g. national parks, local government bushland areas and crown reserves);
- wilderness camping expeditions.

ACTIVITY: List any tours you have participated in or have seen advertised, and identify which of the above categories the tours would fit into.

Special Focus

Interpreting Aboriginal heritage

Vince Scarcella
New South Wales Heritage Office

Interpretation of an object or place or event is about telling stories. Interpreting Aboriginal heritage is no different in that it's still about telling a story; however, there are many variables that often make the interpretation of Aboriginal heritage more of a challenge.

Prior to European settlement Joanne Schmider in *Working with Aboriginal Peoples* suggests that there were 270 separate Aboriginal languages in Australia and between 600 and 700 dialects of language. There were many cultures, many traditions and many different countries. The term 'country' is often used by Aboriginal people to describe their culture. Country is more than just the land and is talked about in the same way in which most Australians would talk about a person. Aboriginal people talk to country, sing to country, visit country. The country hears and talks and feels. Country is not an undefined type of place but rather an integral part of a living culture; it is nourishment for the body, mind and spirit.

Tour operators or guides in telling stories about Aboriginal country are defining the livelihood of Aboriginal people, and the sites all tell a story of part of that country. At times there is conflicting advice on what story a particular site holds. This does not mean someone is right or wrong but rather that neighbouring countries have different stories about the same site.

In dealing with interpreting Aboriginal heritage there are a series of what are called 'culturally appropriate behaviours' that should be addressed in order to ensure the information you are relaying not only is an accurate account but also is culturally appropriate.

'Knowledge is local and strangers often know little or nothing' is a phrase often used to describe Aboriginal site knowledge. Although in most states of Australia, Aboriginal sites are owned or managed by government agencies, the reality is that the only true knowledge holders are the local Aboriginal community themselves. Ownership of country and knowledge is deeply embedded in many Aboriginal communities with only a recognised few able to tell the stories of their country. Before deciding to visit or take a group to an Aboriginal heritage site you must have the appropriate approval and knowledge given by the local Aboriginal community; otherwise, the story you are telling is your own. This is also a sign of respect and an indication that you honour their country.

The following suggestions will help you when trying to seek knowledge to interpret Aboriginal sites:

- *Confidentiality*. Information that is gained must be used in the way it was intended by the relevant Aboriginal community. A lack of trust among Aboriginal communities in Australia today is evident and exists as a result of past information seekers obtaining the information and using it in an inappropriate way. Any concessions made on restrictions of information or portrayal of information must be followed to the absolute degree.
- *Community representation*. It is true that Aboriginal communities are often disjoined and with little similar form from one community to the next. Often this is seen as part of the 'Aboriginal problem' or the problem in liaising with Aboriginal groups. It should be remembered that a vast majority of these factions have been made through various government policies that have shifted Aboriginal individuals and communities from their country onto others.

Early settlement patterns moved Aboriginal communities west, north and south from the east coast of Australia. Protection and assimilation policies moved Aboriginal communities and individuals to different 'country'. Land Rights Acts and other recent government initiatives have provided artificial boundaries for Aboriginal communities which are outside their own country.

All of these changes coupled with traditional localised cultures have led to problems associated with Aboriginal community representation. While seeking information it's important to remember that in order to obtain accurate information it's not your job to filter information into accurate and inaccurate categories. The same Aboriginal community can have differing views on the interpretation of their heritage, both of which may be correct for their individual group.

- *Confidence on home ground.* If seeking information from the Aboriginal community about a particular site, always discuss it at on-site meetings. Aboriginal sites not only are what you see as evidence in front of you but also are a reflection of a series of relationships between Aboriginal community, environment and often their relationship to Aboriginal people or other Aboriginal heritage sites in the vicinity. An Aboriginal site by itself has no meaning without the story of the culture and the people.
- *Communication.* Be aware of culturally appropriate behaviours. Some Aboriginal people have individual aspects of culture that you will not be familiar with. Some Aboriginal people rarely establish eye contact when talking and, although seen as a lack of respect in European cultures, is seen as a mark of respect in some Aboriginal cultures. Be aware of any such aspects of cultural diversity and appropriately accept these behaviours as simply different, rather than as wrong or bad mannered.
- *Relationship.* With most Aboriginals, communities' relationship comes before anything else. If individuals cannot form a strong relationship with communities then often their efforts in obtaining information is frustrated. Having an ongoing relationship prior to seeking any knowledge from an Aboriginal person or community is usually beneficial as the transferral of information is only made once respect is established. In some Aboriginal communities, before you can be fully accepted, the community may need to work out exactly where you fit into their community or kinship structure before giving information.
- *Decision making.* Different communities will have different approaches to meetings, consultations and the sharing of cultural knowledge. It's important to try to understand the local expectations and to avoid being seen as too demanding when seeking any type of information.
- *Information and research.* When undertaking any kind of Aboriginal community analysis it's important to think about the best approach from an Aboriginal community viewpoint. Questionnaires will often gain little response. More effective approaches include personal or informal meetings or discussions involving the Aboriginal community or elected individuals (that is, elected by the Aboriginal community not yourself).

A good starting point for all Aboriginal community consultation involves obtaining a series of essential contacts and asking your contacts where to find the appropriate information. Ownership of information and knowledge relating to Aboriginal heritage is through a series of rights. Finding the right persons to contact, finding the right information and behaving in the right way.

Aboriginal people rarely say 'no', provided what is being asked is in keeping with what is appropriate for a given place or place usage. They do however insist on being asked and therefore having the right to say 'yes' or 'no' where one is counted as a newcomer to country.

ABORIGINAL HERITAGE TYPES

The following categories are the main Aboriginal site types that are found in Australia. This list is by no means definitive, as different countries will have different sites and stories and so it is to be used only as a guide.

Understanding the different site types does not enable a tour operator or Guide to understand Aboriginal culture. It gives you an understanding of the type of sites Aboriginal communities are talking about when describing their country. These sites are of very little interpretive importance without the knowledge of stories. These stories can only be learnt from the Aboriginal knowledge holders themselves.

Aboriginal heritage can be loosely broken up into two different categories: Aboriginal sites and Aboriginal places.

Aboriginal sites

Aboriginal sites are those areas and relics that demonstrate Aboriginal occupation of a certain area. These sites include the following:

Rock engravings. Rock engravings, carvings or pickings are pictures carved into rocks. They are usually on open, flat surfaces of rock, although some engravings have been found in rock shelters and on vertical rock faces.

Like paintings, rock engravings provide important information about Aboriginal material culture and social life. Many sites are regarded as being of sacred or ceremonial significance to Aboriginal people, and they should not be visited without the permission of the Aboriginal community.

Rock paintings. Rock paintings are pictures which have been painted onto a rock surface, usually in a rock shelter or near the mouth of a cave. The 'paints' used were made from materials found locally or traded from another source.

Red and yellow ochre, white pipe clay, gypsum (copi) and charcoal were the most commonly used elements. These were ground up and mixed with water to make a paste. The paste was applied to the rock surface with 'brushes' made of chewed twigs or with the fingers. Sometimes dry pieces of ochre or charcoal were rubbed on the wall, making a drawing rather than a painting.

Stone artefacts. An artefact is anything which has been made or modified by humans. The term 'stone artefact' includes both the finished implement and the debris which is a by-product of its manufacture.

Stone artefacts are the most common form of archaeological evidence found in Australia. In areas where the landscape has not been drastically altered by European settlement, such artefacts can be found lying on the surface, often in quite large numbers or exposed by erosion, road works, ploughing and other activities.

Open sites. Open sites are Aboriginal habitation sites found in the open. They are the places where people lived and contain evidence of Aboriginal activities such as the manufacture of stone tools.

Open sites usually consist of scatters of stone artefacts although they may be associated with food debris, charcoal and implements of shell or bone. Often they have the remains of a cooking fire or earth oven.

A range of activities were carried out at open sites, such as the preparation and cooking of food and the production of wooden implements.

Shell middens. The word 'midden' means rubbish dump and a shell midden is a place where debris from eating shellfish has accumulated. Shell middens can also contain such things as the bones of fish, birds and mammals used for food, and tools made from stone, shell or bone.

Shell middens provide a lot of information about Aboriginal activities in the past. The types of shells present can indicate the season and the aquatic habitat being used when the site was occupied. Different types of shells can indicate different habitats being used or changes in the diet over time.

Scarred trees. Aboriginal people used trees extensively. Trees which show evidence of Aboriginal occupation are known as scarred trees. Some trees are still living and so the scar is still changing.

Scarred trees can be divided into three main categories: trees from which bark has been removed for use; trees from which wood has been removed for use; and trees that show evidence of hunting or climbing.

Bark and wood removal was important for making canoes, tools and weapons, shelters, coffins, shields and items to carry water or resources (often referred to as coolamons).

Aboriginal places

Aboriginal places are those places that are of contemporary or spiritual importance to Aboriginal peoples according to Aboriginal custom or culture. Such places may include:

- land containing Aboriginal burials;
- places that are identified by Aboriginal stories or celebrated through ceremonies;
- land that was once an Aboriginal reserve or mission or other post-settlement living area;
- land known from archival or historical records or from the Aboriginal community to have been the site of an important historical event such as a massacre;
- areas that contain one or more relics or a combination of cultural landscape including culturally important plant or animal species;
- archaeological sites that are of significance to Aboriginal people;
- land, buildings or places that are significant to Aboriginal culture post-1788.

ABORIGINAL HERITAGE

Aboriginal heritage is an important non-renewable resource that provides all Australians with an opportunity to learn about our past. While we can often find out more about the recent past in books and through the media, Aboriginal heritage is not afforded that same luxury.

Aboriginal heritage should be protected by all to ensure that this valuable resource is kept for future generations of Australians, and to ensure that Aboriginal culture continues to live on through current and future Aboriginal generations together with their stories.

With all Aboriginal heritage Aboriginal people are the cultural owners and managers of information relating to their heritage. Information relating to Aboriginal heritage provided by members of Aboriginal communities is to be treated with respect, and any agreements regarding access and/or confidentiality in information sharing is to be honoured.

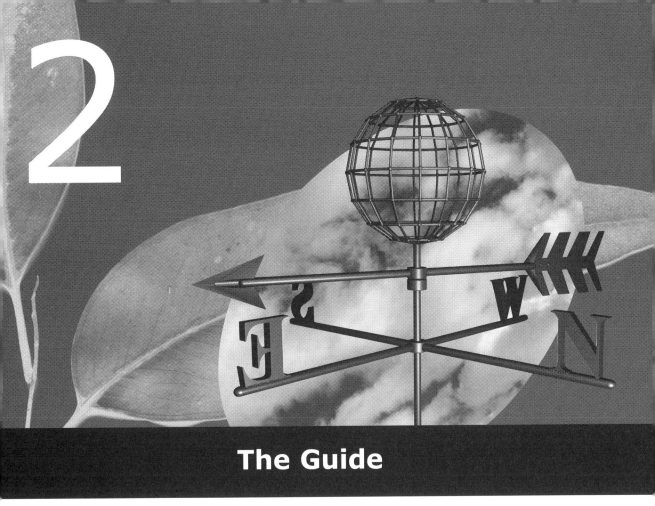

2

The Guide

What are the learning outcomes for this chapter?

By the end of this chapter you should be able to:
● Describe the working environment of a Guide.
● Identify the roles and responsibilities of a Guide.
● Identify the key skills and qualities of a Guide.

TOURIST GUIDES—A SKILLED GROUP OF PROFESSIONALS

Tourist Guides are an extremely resourceful group of professionals whose vocation requires an amazing array of skills, subject knowledge and personal attributes. Being a Tourist Guide is arguably one of the most demanding professions—whether undertaken on a paid or volunteer basis.

WHO IS A TOURIST GUIDE?

 ACTIVITY: Consider the following perspectives of a Tourist Guide and write your definition of the role of a Guide.

A tour guide is a person who guides groups or individual visitors from abroad or from the home country around the monuments, sites and museums of a city or region: to interpret in an inspiring and entertaining manner, in the language of the visitor's choice, the cultural and natural heritage and environment.
International Association of Tour Managers and the European Federation of Tourist Guide Associations

A guide is a person with an effective combination of enthusiasm, knowledge, personality qualities and high standards of conduct and ethics who leads groups to the important sites (in our city), while providing interpretation and commentary.
Professional Tour Guide Association of San Antonio

ATTRIBUTES OF A TOURIST GUIDE
Some of the key skills required by Tourist Guides include:

- communication—listening, negotiation, conflict resolution and Interpretation;
- leadership and group management;
- creative and strategic thinking;
- research, planning, design, implementation and evaluation;
- emergency and incident management, first aid and ability to implement occupational health and safety (OHS) procedures;
- navigation;
- improvisation and flexibility.

In fact, a Guide wears many hats.

Guides also require sound subject knowledge to support their commentaries, to satisfy question–answer sessions and for general interaction with their audience.

For example, if conducting a tour of a historic site a Guide might need to know about historic periods and significant dates in the site's development, and characteristics of this period with regard to building and architectural styles, education, work practices, government policies, dress and other cultural specifics.

Guides also need to develop an understanding of the relationships between different subjects. For example, they might need to know about plants and their relationship with soil types, or the role of the transport routes in suburban development or the context of a particular period in history. Tourist Guides working for organisations might need to know mission statements and relevant policies.

Beyond skills and knowledge Guides are also expected to possess a range of personal attributes such as enthusiasm, empathy, respect, diplomacy, curiosity and endurance, and cultural and environmental awareness. They need to be professional while being friendly, they need to ensure the safety of a group while being relaxed, and they need to be serious while having fun. These attributes shape the personality of a Guide and are extremely important to any tour experience. It is these qualities of a Guide which people remember most about any experience. The importance of personal attributes is highlighted by the recruitment adage 'Recruit on attitude, train on skills'.

 ACTIVITY: What do you think are the most important qualities of a Tourist Guide? Rank these qualities from most important to least important.

A tourist guide is someone who can tune into the moment, the occasion. They are spontaneous, humorous, and knowledgeable. They have an in-depth knowledge but select this knowledge to what is important and relevant to their audience. They respect and validate their audience and the subjective experience of their audience, and build the tour around this.
Guy Patching, freelance Sydney-based Guide

One of the most demanding parts of guiding is making sure everyone has a great time. This means managing individual needs and expectations, being able to give a 'great tour' in all weather conditions, being able to give your all even if you have just finished a full-day tour the day before and are feeling quite tired, managing unexpected delays and mishaps, being a storehouse of information, and having an in-depth knowledge of what it is you are talking about. No wonder guiding can be so exhausting.
Janine McLeod, freelance Sydney-based Guide

Special Focus
What's in a name? The Tourist Guide

Rosemary Black
Lecturer, Charles Sturt University

Guides come with a variety of names—Tour Guide, Tourist Guide, Tour Leader, Group Leader, Tour Manager, Local Guide, City Guide, Step-on Guide, Driver-Guide, Interpretive Officer, Adventure Guide, Interpretive Guide and Ecoguide. While there is considerable overlap in the responsibilities of Guides working under different names, these names also reflect unique responsibilities.

The term 'Tourist Guide' is used by the Institute of Australian Tourist Guides and is preferred by many Guides in Australia. It is also the term used throughout Europe including the United Kingdom.

These names can vary from region to region, between the public and private sectors, and within different sectors of the tourism industry. They reflect the immense variety in the types of guiding responsibilities, locations and perceptions of stakeholders such as other Guides, tour operators and visitors.

Education and training levels of Guides are also quite varied. Some Guides may have a postgraduate qualification in their specialist area, and others may have an industry certificate such as a scuba diving instructors certificate. Some Guides have no formal training but are people who are familiar with their local area and have the skills and attitudes needed to be an effective Guide.

SOME DEFINITIONS OF A GUIDE

The Oxford English Dictionary defines a 'guide' as 'one who leads or shows the way, especially to a traveller in a strange country; spec. one who is hired to conduct a traveller or tourist (e.g. over a mountain, through a forest, or over a city or building) and to point out objects of interest' and 'one who directs a person in his ways or conduct'.

There are many different definitions given for Tourist Guides. One simple definition provided by the Australian Standard Classification of Occupations is a person who 'escorts people on sightseeing, educational and other tours and describes and explains points of interest'. However, this term does not include any reference to the type of employer such as inbound tour operator, period of tour, whether any travel is involved or the location of tour.

THE DIFFERENCE BETWEEN A TOURIST GUIDE, TOUR MANAGER AND TOUR OPERATOR

People often confuse the terms Tourist Guide, tour manager, tour operator and inbound tour operator—and although there are opportunities for overlap they also have quite distinct responsibilities.

Tourist Guides: accompany visitors on local tours and services and guide within a specific country, region, area, city or site. They provide special information on matters relating to such things as history, archaeology, monuments and works of art, the environment, culture, natural and built attractions, places of interest and any general matter of interest to the visitor. The Guide's main role is to interpret and deliver localised information in the language of the visitor. They can provide a range of services which may include offering arrival and departure assistance at the destination and coordinating prearranged touring details. Tourist Guides may recommend products and sell optional tours to the visitor and may receive commissions on any sales generated.
Australian Tourism Export Council/Tourism Queensland (2001b)

In contrast a *tour manager* is usually responsible for the operational aspects of managing the tour, and is sometimes known as the tour organiser, tour director, tour leader or tour escort. The tour manager is usually the overall coordinator as the tour progresses, especially for extended tours. The tour manager is also the on-site representative of the tour company and is responsible for organising and coordinating the tour. A tour manager will often accompany an inbound tour group, especially if arriving from Asian countries. (In these situations they are often referred to as a tour leader.)

Traditionally, while a tour manager accompanies the group, that person will utilise the skills and expertise of a Guide to provide commentary. Within extended tours, these roles experience a considerable degree of overlap and if responsibility falls on the one person, that person spends a lot of time wearing a multitude of hats.

The role of *tour operators* focuses on the promotional, planning and other logistical details of making a tour happen. In this role they often provide a package for the visitor by bringing together a range of related tourism services and products including accommodation, entertainment, transport, attractions, activities, coach transfers, reconfirmation of tour details and food. A tour operator will usually be responsible for managing several tour managers and/or Tourist Guides, who are responsible for leading and/or managing the actual tour experience.

Inbound tour operators are one of the major players in attracting overseas tourists to Australia, as they promote their packaged products to the inbound (overseas) market through their relationships with overseas markets.

The Australian Tourism Export Council defines an inbound tour operator as an entity who facilitates the purchase of an Australian tourism product or products by the international travel trade through activities including but not limited to:

- creating itineraries and packages;
- providing a booking service to the international travel trade as a primary business;
- managing visitors when in Australia; and
- marketing travel products and services.

WHERE DO GUIDES WORK?

Guides work in a wide range of environments and sites and their expertise and knowledge vary enormously. Guides lead tours which last for a few hours or lead extended tours which might last for several days or even weeks. They may be freelance city Guides undertaking city tours, Ecotour Guides taking people on bushwalks, or Site-based Guides working in museums, national parks or attractions. Some work as freelance Guides and others are employees of government agencies.

Guides work within a variety of employment situations including:

- employees of government organisations, for example national park and land management agencies, state and national museums and galleries;
- employees of private companies, for example wildlife parks and Savannah Guides (northern Australia);
- freelance Guides who tend to work with either one or several commercial tour operators (which can include both inbound and outbound operations), coach companies and/or tour managers;
- contract Guides for either a short-term or an extended period, for example some Guides might be employed on contract for the length of a shipping cruise season;
- self-employed Guides within their own tour operations company;
- volunteer Guides (there would arguably be more volunteer Guides than paid Guides working in Australia), for example the National Maritime Museum of Australia in Darling Harbour has over 250 Guides, and the NSW National Parks and Wildlife Service's CHASE ALIVE program based at Ku-ring-gai Chase National Park has over 100 Guides.

Some industries and businesses employ Guides to conduct tours of their facilities with the aim of educating visitors, promoting their business and/or enhancing their public image. For example, some wineries have Guides who conduct tours of their vineyards and offer wine tasting. Mining companies employ Guides for leading tours associated with site-based visits and inspections. Waste-transfer stations also employ Guides to lead educational and technical tours of their sites.

THE ROLES OF A GUIDE

Guides play a vital role in the tourism or visitor experience and are at the front line. They perform a wide variety of roles that can include interpreting, communicating, role-modelling appropriate behaviour, navigating, leading, managing the group, integrating the group, keeping good humour and morale, and entertaining group members.

They are always in a position of responsibility, ensuring the safety and security of the group, especially when leading the group through unfamiliar areas or countries, and/or through difficult terrain.

As a leader the Guide might also have other skills in areas such as business, administration, project management, catering and camp-ground skills. They may also have dual responsibility for operating a water vessel such as a boat or canoe, or for driving 4WDs, coaches and buses, and other vehicles.

The roles that Guides play in the tourism experience will depend on a number of factors including the setting of the tour, the purpose of the tour, the motivation and experience of the tourists and the characteristics and motivation of the Guides themselves, and the expectations of the tour company or employer.

KEY ROLES OF THE TOURIST GUIDE

Some of the key roles of the tourist guide are as follows.

Information provider

A number of studies have identified the role of information giver (Holloway 1981; Cohen 1985; Weiler & Davis 1993). In her study of Guides leading tours of Aboriginal and Torres Strait Islander communities in Northern Queensland, Hughes (1991) finds that the tour participants regarded the dissemination of information as the most important role of the Guide. She discovered that the more positive the evaluation of the Guide's commentary, the greater the visitor's satisfaction of the tour.

Robin Aiello (1998) also highlights a number of situations in which knowledgeable Guides have been responsible for significant and positive levels of tourist satisfaction.

Social facilitator

More than most other tourism workers, Guides have the opportunity to interact at a more personal level with tour groups. Guides have an important social role within the group in which the Guide is a social catalyst, encouraging interaction between group members, and generally facilitating a positive social setting for the tour experience. Pond (1993) uses the role of host to describe the social roles of the Guide, and considers that this role is faceted and can take many forms.

Cultural host

In this role the Guide facilitates a relationship between tourists and a host community/culture. This might involve language interpretation through to cultural interpretation, and providing information on appropriate social behaviour and social norms, along with local customs. Within such situations the Guide is obviously responsible for respecting the rights of the host community, and ensuring the appropriate behaviour of the tour group.

Guides are responsible for members of their tour group behaving in an appropriate manner, without causing any damage to the area or interfering with the activities of the local community. In this way Guides are both role-modelling appropriate behaviour and shouldering responsibility for the behaviour of the group, which might involve the Guide incorporating discipline measures and conflict-resolution skills.

Motivator of appropriate conservation values

This role of motivator of environmentally responsible behaviour and conservation values has been particularly identified among Ecotour and Nature-based Guides (Weiler & Davis 1993; Haig 1997). This role reflects the recent interest in nature-based tourism and ecotourism, and the concern of the tourism industry and general community with the environment, and with the environmental and cultural impacts of tourism (Weiler & Davis 1993; Hawkins & Lamoureux 2001; Dowling 2001). In this role Guides are seen as playing an important role in 'educating people about the vulnerabilities of their regions and the ways in which visitors can play a role in preserving them' (Pond 1993, p. 79). Guides are seen as having some responsibility for the host environment, encouraging the appropriate use of resources for tourism, and a responsibility to monitor and minimise the adverse effects of visitor activities on the environment so that natural ecosystems are used in a sustainable manner (Weiler & Davis 1993).

Interpreter of the natural and cultural environment

Many studies have identified the role of interpreter, which suggests it is universally acknowledged as a key role of a Guide irrespective of the tour setting.

According to Schmidt (1979), 'An ideal Guide should be competent in both knowledge and presentation, integrating and involving the tourists into the scene, role-playing, and giving the tourists a feel for the place. Part of this role is to tell stories, myths and local legends and translate the unfamiliar'. Holloway (1981) suggests that a feature of successful tours depends on the 'dramaturgical' skills of the guide to make a routine tour or experience come alive for the tourists. This results in 'shared personal experiences' among the group, which can often be a memorable highlight of a tour or holiday. Many of the skills such as role-playing, telling stories, relating to the group and using drama are part of what are now commonly referred to as interpretive skills. These skills are considered an important part of a Tourist Guide's role (Ham 1992; Weiler & Ham 2001).

The increased use of Interpretation, both face-to-face and non-face-to-face, by managers of natural and cultural environments aims to encourage visitors to gain a greater level of understanding and appreciation of a particular site or event, and a resultant behaviour which supports its value and significance. For example, an interpretive activity conducted within a national park might focus on encouraging a level of understanding and appreciation of the park's significance, and hence long-term support for its conservation.

People mover

This includes the range of duties Guides undertake to assist people moving between varying locales such as meet-and-greets at airports and major transport terminuses, transfers to and from hotels and places of accommodation, assisting with check-ins, and organising and/or confirming travel details. Such duties are particularly relevant for extended tours, especially if the Guide's duties extend to those of tour manager and tour leader.

Other roles and responsibilities of Guides include:

● teacher or instructor;
● safety officer;
● ambassador for one's country;
● public relations representative/company representative;
● entertainer;
● problem solver;
● confidant and counsellor;

- navigator;
- record keeper and administrator.

THE GUIDE'S INFLUENCE ON VISITOR SATISFACTION

Visitor satisfaction is arguably one of the ultimate measures of a successful tour. Guides need to recognise that they are in an influential and significant position to have an effect on visitor satisfaction.

One of the few studies that attempts to assess the effectiveness of the Tourist Guide from the visitor's perspective was undertaken by Hughes (1991) on Palm Island in North Queensland. In this study she invited the tourists to evaluate the Tourist Guides on the information they provided, on their interactions with the tour group and on their general organisational skills. With regard to the information provided by Guides, Hughes found that the level of tourist satisfaction was highest when the commentaries connected tourists' past experience, interests and knowledge with the features of the area; that is, when Guides were able to assess the requirements of both the tour group and the tourist environment, and adjust their guiding style accordingly.

Hughes also found that her tourists sought a participatory rather than an observer role. The skills of the Guide in 'connecting' with the visitors, providing a 'meaningful' and 'participatory' tour, and of bringing these elements together into a smooth running tour were those of an effective interpreter.

As well as influencing visitor satisfaction, providing good-quality Guides has other advantages for the tour operators. Arnould et al. (1998) in their study of US White Water Rafting Guides argue that the level of skills and knowledge of the Guide were important in influencing the behaviour of the tour group and might be a factor in differentiating tours between competitors. Aiello (1998) likewise draws similar conclusions.

THE ROLE OF THE GUIDE—A WRAP!

Providing a high-quality visitor experience is vital to ensure the sustainability of the tourism industry and individual operators. This industry, perhaps more than many others, is customer-focused and relies heavily on personnel who can deliver a high standard of service and who have excellent communication, interpretive and interpersonal skills. All these qualities are fostered in an interpretive approach to guiding.

 ACTIVITY: You are a tour operator who wants to employ more Guides. Write a relevant job advertisement of at least 100 words outlining the skills and knowledge you would be keen to seek.

Special Focus

A day in the life of a tourist guide

Brian McDonald
(Brian received the Institute of Australian Tourist Guides (IATG) Best
Specialist Guide Award in 1997 for his tour of the Quarantine Station,
upon which he has based this article.)

Gliding through the corridor of sleep to reality. Dreams become thoughts. Thoughts merge slowly into validity. Today is the day! Today is judgment day!

Today the magnifying glasses of 30 Tourists Guides will focus on my each and every word; my every movement and every turn of phrase—my every action.

In what year did the ship *Bussorah Merchant* arrive? What year did the NSW National Parks and Wildlife Service acquire the Quarantine Station? How many people came through the station? How many did not leave and are buried here? Above all—how do you convey the anguish, pain and suffering during 156 years of the Quarantine Station at North Head to 30 Tourist Guides . . . with magnifying glasses . . . watching my every action; listening for every mistake; ready to do battle with inaccuracies; their ears and eyes targeting in to every . . . wait . . . calm down . . . relax!

Breathe deeply. That's it. Now, let's walk through the tour. First of all—the greeting—be friendly but confident. First impressions are important. Take control but don't be too bossy—people don't want to be treated like children.

Let them know the guidelines (pardon the pun), the regulations governing the site. Let them know from the beginning what is expected from them. Don't be too 'teacher like'. This would be a good time to throw in some humour. Let them know I'm not too stuffy . . . this tour could be fun.

Oh, my name! Don't forget to introduce myself. It's embarrassing when you're asked for your name halfway through the tour. And besides, they have to know my name to write those letters of praise . . . or the other type of letters!

Introduce the site. Give an overview of the tour . . . what they will see . . . why it was built . . . how it was utilised . . . who came here. Don't get too complicated! Confusion produces frustration. Frustration builds barriers. A good introduction leads the group to a general understanding but leaves them asking questions.

And when questions are asked—make sure to include the group. Private conversations can frustrate the group. Another frustrating thing is not knowing the question you're answering! Repeat the question before answering—the inquisitive person's voice is not as powerful as mine (I hope!).

No question is a silly question! Others in the group may think otherwise, but always be positive with my answers—it encourages others.

Remain confident. If I'm feeding them interesting information, interspersed with fascinating pieces of trivia, I'll keep their attention. 'Trivia'—the Tourist Guides tools of trade! Read and reread Rabbi Brasch's books.

The more knowledge the better. But don't try to tell them everything! Overload! A babbling brook trying to be a waterfall! Keep the knowledge to yourself—it feels really good to be able to satisfy a person's question.

But above all else during the tour—*be enthusiastic!* Enthusiastic about the site, enthusiastic about our history and heritage, enthusiastic about Australia's unique past. Enthusiastic about my career—I have the best job in the world! For all Guides, present your tour with the zeal you have for our country and make every presentation seem like the first.

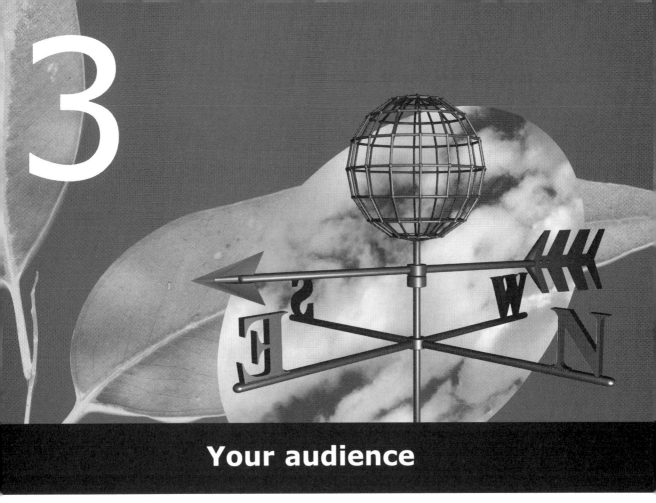

3

Your audience

What are the learning outcomes for this chapter?

By the end of this chapter you should be able to:
● Identify the main groups of people attending tours.
● Identify the needs, expectations and motivations of people attending tours.
● Identify means of finding out about your audience.
● Outline the principles for conducting tours.

GETTING TO KNOW YOUR AUDIENCE

Your audience includes people from a vast array of cultural backgrounds, with a variety of motivations, expectations, interests and needs. These people are often referred to as tourists, visitors, guests or clients.

Your audience might include:

- international tourists on a package tour of Australia;
- international tourists visiting Australia as independent travellers;
- domestic tourists travelling on a package tour of their state;
- a young family touring in a campervan;
- budget travellers;
- retired couples;
- honeymoon couples;
- single people;
- special-interest groups, for example study groups visiting a specific gallery;
- people visiting a museum or gallery within their own town or city;
- campers at a camp site attending in-situ holiday tour programs;
- people on educational excursions such as school groups and conference delegates.

One of the most important characteristics of any interpretive tour is that it is as relevant as possible to the audience. Finding out as much as possible about your audience is an essential part of planning and delivering interpretive tours.

In getting to know your audience you begin by asking questions:

- Who are they?
- Why are they joining your tour?
- What are their expectations?
- What are their needs?

With responses to these questions you can begin to develop a perspective which will be specific to the planned activity.

WHO ARE THEY?

Your visitors vary in ages, social demographics, cultural backgrounds, and in physical and intellectual abilities. You need to be aware of all these elements. The following characteristics of your audience provide an overview and possible areas for research. Use other sections of this book to apply your relevant skills when working with people from varying backgrounds.

Age

The age of people can vary immensely as can the composition of age-specific groups such as seniors, young people and young families. Specific tours attract corresponding age groups, for example Contiki caters for the 18–35 market.

ACTIVITY: Consider the following scenario involving two tours within a historic site. Both tours attracted a group of approximately 16 people, made up of children (aged from 7 to 12 years) and their parents, an adult couple and a few single adults. The Guide leading Tour A adjusted her tour to cater for the children as well as the adults. The Guide leading Tour B simply directed her tour at the adults.

What do you think was the outcome for each tour? How might the Guide in Tour A have catered for the children?

Where do they come from?

Most people on your tour can be considered to belong to one of the following tourist markets: international tourists and domestic tourists. There is some overlap between these and people not considered to be tourists—e.g. local people, groups or organisations visiting local sites.

International tourists

These tourists are people whose place of residence is outside Australia. When travelling to Australia they are referred to as inbound tourists. The key Australian inbound markets are:

- New Zealand;
- United States;
- United Kingdom and Ireland;
- Europe—Germany, Italy, Scandinavia, Switzerland, France;
- Japan;
- Asia—Hong Kong/China, Korea, Taiwan, Singapore and Malaysia.

There are unique segments within the inbound tourist market, for example backpackers and those on packaged tours. Backpackers are normally independent travellers from countries such as Germany, Scandinavia, Ireland, the United Kingdom and Canada (although there is an increase in the number of backpackers arriving from Korea and Japan). People on packaged tours often come from Japan, Italy and North America.

Domestic tourists

These tourists are people whose place of residence is within Australia and who are travelling within Australia. They are referred to as either interstate tourists (when they travel outside their state of residence) or intrastate tourists (when they travel within their own state of residence).

Each group will have unique characteristics when attending tours, which may include a shared culture, language and way of relating with other people.

ACTIVITY: Identify a popular tourist attraction in your area, and research where the visitors come from. What percentage are intrastate (local and regional), interstate and international?

Cultural considerations

Culture is how people think and feel as a community. Culture defines values and the perceptions shared by people. It defines the constructs and concepts people hold of their environment, and of the accepted behaviour among a group of people. The latter elements can include music, dance, beliefs and ways of living. Culture is often a reflection of shared history.

Some cultural characteristics relevant to people on tours include:

● ways of greeting and communicating;
● personal space;
● mannerisms and other characteristic types of behaviour;
● language;
● dress;
● status;
● ways of eating and types of food eaten;
● religious beliefs and practices;
● attitudes regarding protocol and etiquette;
● sexual preferences;
● expressions of emotion.

While we often consider culture to be associated with people from other countries, Australia has significant cultural variations. We can have not only macrocultural differences between migrant groups but also microcultural variations between age groups from different suburbs within the same city. Take the suburban train in Sydney from the central business district (CBD) along any of the suburban lines and you will notice significant changes in cultural groups between suburbs.

Even within the same ethnic group we can have microcultures; for example, first generation Italians are of a different culture from that of their parents who migrated in the 1950s. Likewise, young Koreans have a different culture from that of their elders. The main reason for this is living in Australian society and being infused with the surrounding culture. Family disputes often arise when these age-based microcultures clash and there is apparent disrespect for either culture.

With domestic tourism being such a significant market within Australian tourism, and given the increasing ethnicity of our Australian cultural make-up, the multicultural element within your tours could well comprise recent immigrants, first generation Australians and/or second generation Australians travelling as domestic tourists.

Socioeconomic considerations

The socioeconomic background of your audience might influence the level of disposable income they have. People on tighter budgets require different recommendations from affluent people, which means you need to have information on a range of options including types of activities, food and dining locations.

Psychographics

Psychographics refers to people's attitudes, values, concept of self, opinions and personality traits. Attitudes among people can vary immensely towards learning opportunities, the challenge of a new experience, physical activity and intellectual pursuits. People can also vary with reference to levels of politeness, appropriate behaviour and attention span.

What would they like to know?

The existing and desired knowledge of your audience affects the commentaries which you provide to your audience. With special-interest tours it is always best to check the knowledge they expect to gain from the tour and their anticipated activities, and then tailor your tour as best as possible to these requirements.

In finding out about their requirements try to also find out about their existing levels of knowledge. For example, a tour catering for history students would most likely require a far different approach from one catering for professional 19th century historians. If the request is beyond your level of expertise, liaise with other colleagues who might have the relevant knowledge to either accompany you or, if necessary, lead the tour.

How many people are there and how much time do they have?

Most tours work to expectations created by promotional material, and therefore most tour participants have a rough idea of how long the tour will take. You need to ensure that your tour meets these expectations.

At the same time if you were planning tours, you would need to be aware of how much time your target audience has and plan your tour accordingly. It would be pointless planning a tour which lasts for a few hours if the majority of visitors have only one hour.

You also need to consider your environmental constraints, for example it might be best not to organise tours along a narrow bush track when you know the majority of visitors arrive in large groups.

People travelling alone or in groups

It is often useful to find out whether your audience belongs to the same group—that is, some tours might be dominated by a group booking. These might be religious, political, family, business or gender groups. In such cases there might be a common interest among its members which you can foster and promote, while not leaving out other members of your tour. Each tour will have its own characteristics and might even feature people who take on group roles, for example the clown, the stirrer, the troublemaker or the organiser. An example of these groups includes business associates joining a tour being provided by their employer (e.g. BridgeClimb receive a number of group bookings made as part of incentive and team-building staff programs). Such tours can also be quite challenging in that these people might not want any great lengths of commentary—they just want to have a fun and entertaining time. Thus, you will need to assess the group and adjust your style accordingly.

WHY ARE PEOPLE JOINING YOUR TOUR?

Motivations are those unique individual elements which get people moving and doing something. What motivates people to attend a tour will often be a mix of factors including their needs, wants and interests. Whatever they are, most people *want* to be on your tour, which is a great thought to have when you start your activity. Possible exceptions might be when people are travelling as part of an overall tour package and are obliged to take part in all tours, even those they do not like, and when people are brought along by their partners or children are brought along by their parents.

Often the motivations of your audience are linked to their expectations and it is up to you to meet these expectations.

Some of the reasons people take part in tours include:

● to satisfy a special interest, for example a birdwatching tour of central Australia;
● as a leisure activity, for relaxation and/or as a social outing;
● for exercise, for example bushwalking and extended hiking trips;
● to learn about a particular subject—the opportunity to learn is an increasing motivation for people to attend tours (Jan Packer (from Queensland University of Technology) in her PhD research on interpretive experiences found that 50 per cent of visitors to a range of educational leisure settings, including museums, tourist centres and guided tours, indicated that discovering new things, expanding their knowledge and being better informed were extremely important as reasons for their visit. Such items were second in importance only to enjoying themselves);
● for fun and adventure;
● out of curiosity—perhaps people in your audience saw a brochure which excited their level of curiosity to the point where they had to take part in the promised experience.

WHAT ARE THEIR EXPECTATIONS?

The expectations of your audience can be extremely varied. Expectations can be generated through brochures, word of mouth and other promotional sources. People can also create expectations based on previous experiences. This is particularly relevant to people who are frequent visitors to attractions, for example people with a particular interest in museums or historic towns.

People are motivated to attends tours because of some specific and often unique set of reasons—some of which are stated and some implied. In attending a tour your audience would expect these reasons to be satisfied. For example, a person might be motivated to attend an activity because of their interest in Australia's maritime heritage. The expectations of this person would obviously include the opportunity to learn about this topic, but could also include that they will be part of a group of like-minded people, and that the tour lasts for the advertised time.

The Parks and Wildlife Commission of the Northern Territory (PWCNT) offers a seasonal 'Parks Alive' walks and talks program. The promotion of this program aims to develop in travellers the expectation that quality walks and talks on a variety of themes are available in parks throughout the Territory. To meet this expectation, the PWCNT endeavours to provide the necessary support for staff and infrastructure.

People also bring expectations of what tours are like. These can include negative perceptions of tours for the following reasons:

- They are too structured and regimented.
- On coach tours people are cramped into a coach for hours on end.
- They are an uncomfortable social situation in which people have to talk and socialise with others.
- There is limited freedom to do what you want.

 ACTIVITY: What would be some of your expectations if you were about to attend a tour of a historic house in a major city? If you were the guide leading this activity, how could you ensure these expectations were met?

Alternatively, people could have the following positive perceptions of tours:

- a cost-effective way to see particular areas;
- an opportunity to meet like-minded people;
- an opportunity to learn, and perhaps see out-of-the-way places;
- safety and security provided;
- organisation of all logistical matters;
- all decision making taken care of;
- usually the provision of translator services for people from a non-English-speaking background (when relevant).

Expectations are a reference which people often use to assess an activity. And in fact a number of hotels and other hospitality points provide their customers with an evaluation form titled 'Did we meet your expectations?'.

Expectations often serve as a reference for people's level of demands. Some people might have high expectations of service and consequently demand that this be met.

People are becoming increasingly discerning as are their expectations with regard to the quality of experience they receive. This places pressure on industry to meet these increased expectations.

WHAT ARE THEIR NEEDS?

There is a degree of overlap between the motivations and needs of an audience. A need does not necessarily motivate someone; for example, the need for safety when attending a tour is not necessarily a motivator for that person. Some needs are implied, and are assumed to be catered for without request. For example, people would expect that their need for safety would be inherent in all tours. People might also expect that the tour would be of an acceptable standard and meet acceptable levels of service.

Within Australia there are over one million people with some form of disability, most of whom love to travel and be involved in group activities such as tours. This means that at some point in your Guide career you might well come across people with either a physical or intellectual disability and who will have special needs. With physical abilities you need to consider the length of time people will be walking and/or standing. Are there adequate rest stops? Are there any steep sections? Have you planned frequent breaks? If you are about to deliver a lengthy piece of commentary, it might be best to plan this delivery when people have the option to sit down.

Needs might also extend to culinary preferences whether by religious motivation, or for ethical or health reasons, for example vegetarians, vegans, lactose-intolerant, medical meals (for people with special medical requirements), kosher and kids' meals.

People also have differing needs as to how they interact with other people. Some people might be quite chatty, and enjoy talking even when you are presenting. Others might enjoy the opportunity to reflect, and while they might appear to be some distance away they could in fact be quite intent on what you are saying.

International people might also have special language needs and require the aid of an interpreter. Normally an interpreter accompanies such groups and doubles as the tour manager.

ACTIVITY: Identify five audience groups (e.g. elderly, backpackers) and list three needs specific to each group, assuming they are attending a one-day multisite tour. As a Guide how would you address these needs?

ACTIVITY: There has been a dramatic increase in people's use of the Internet as a primary source of information when planning their holidays. In this activity you need to imagine yourself as a tourist using the Internet to plan a visit around Victoria. Working with the AMOL website select two Art Trails from the following page http://www.amol.org.au/guide/guide_index.asp (alternatively go to the home page—www.amol.org.au—and from the menu select Guide to Museums, and on the subsequent page select Art Trails in Victoria). What would be your expectations of the attractions described on these trails? What would motivate you to visit these attractions? What factors could influence your holiday as you travel along the 'Art Trails' and visit the different attractions? Imagine you attend a tour at one of these attractions—how could the Guide satisfy your expectations and motivations? Is it necessary for these to be satisfied?

HOW DO YOU FIND OUT ABOUT YOUR AUDIENCE?

The degree to which you find out about your audience varies with how practical and relevant it is to your situation. For example, Jonathon Woods conducts tours of Kelly Hill Caves on Kangaroo Island, South Australia. He receives his tour briefing sheets through the main Kingscote Office on Kangaroo Island. Having worked at the caves for 18 months he knows 'pretty much who my audience is going to be', especially as his tours last for approximately one hour and are activity-specific. So his main concerns focus on how many people, where they are from and whether they have any special needs.

It is a similar situation with Dan Grieve who works at Cape Borda on Kangaroo Island. Cape Borda is a historic and remote lighthouse settlement located on the north-western coast of Kangaroo Island. The lighthouse commenced operations in 1858, and stands on a cliff 155 metres (510 feet) above the sea. The site features a small cannon which used to be fired to warn ships of danger, but is now fired once a day for the tourists. 'The firing of the cannon is always a blast with visitors. That and the stories I tell of the site. These remain reasonably consistent between tour groups but I always make sure I find out who is in my group and if necessary adjust my style to suit the particular group of visitors.'

Both Jonathon and Dan rely on their experience in how best to greet and then manage their visitors when they arrive at their site. But nevertheless they are always vigilant as to making sure the tour meets the needs of the audience.

Climb Leaders working at BridgeClimb know that the climbers who arrive to take the BridgeClimb experience will be screened by the booking system and promotional material. They know that people will be fit, above a certain age, and interested in soft adventure. Once they actually meet the group they make an assessment on:

- the length and type of commentary to deliver;
- anxiety levels of group members;
- the types of activities to include;
- cultural sensitivities—especially given the high number of international people they have on their climbs.

They make this assessment through chatting to individuals, and by watching their behaviour while running through the safety procedures.

SOME WAYS OF FINDING OUT ABOUT YOUR AUDIENCE

You could do the following:

- Phone the booking agent, tour operator, club secretary or other relevant group representative to find out further details.
- Conduct research through relevant tourism offices and liaise with other colleagues in the tourism industry.
- Put in place recording systems to capture this information at the time of booking.
- Create expectations which will attract corresponding interests through promotional material.
- Rely on experience and correlate responses with similar situations.

Perhaps one of the best and most accurate ways is to arrive early and meet people as they turn up for the activity.

An important quality of any guide is the ability to manage the diverse needs, expectations, motivations, interests and other characteristics of people who attend tours. It is important to research the variety of possible audience groups and their characteristics, to remain sensitive and attentive to individuals within your group, and to practise relevant group-management techniques. To assist you gain this knowledge and these skills join other tours, talk to a variety of people, and take an interest in a wide range of fields and subject areas.

Two valuable skills within this process are those of listening to your audience with an open mind, and being flexible enough to adapt to varying conditions and demands.

Knowing more about your audience prepares you. While you cannot know every person in every audience, the greater your experience and willingness to research, the greater your preparedness and opportunity to draw on this knowledge when you meet new audience groups. If possible attend other tours and learn from other Guides, talk to people attending these tours and get to know your visitors 'outside the role of a Guide'.

There are times, especially in the life of a freelance Guide, when you are called to lead a tour at very short notice. Being prepared will maximise your ability to deliver a positive experience for people within your tour group.

ACTIVITY: Research four audience groups using at least six different sources of information. These sources could include: attending a tour, talking to staff at a visitor information centre, liaising with tour operators and visiting a multicultural organisation.

BUILDING A RELATIONSHIP WITH YOUR AUDIENCE

A tour is a series of shared moments and part of a much longer relationship. Refer to our definition of Interpretation—'A learning experience which seeks to enrich the meaningful relationships we hold with our world, and to foster and build a set of values which supports these relationships'. These relationships are between the three components of the guiding environment—the Guide, the audience and the environment. They begin before the activity as you research your audience and the guiding environment, and through promotional activities, and they continue ad infinitum. The moments of your tour will always provide a reference point for memories, feelings, thoughts and reflections. These points of reference might be positive, negative or indifferent—as a Guide you are obviously striving for a positive relationship.

Why should you seek to build relationships with your audience? The simple answer is that without an audience you do not have a tourism industry. And without a tourism industry there is no tourism-related employment and you also miss out on the job satisfaction which comes from working as a Tourist Guide. It is important that every aspect of your operation promotes a professional service and product, and generates expectations which can be satisfied. The following lists are a few of the elements which you want to foster and build as part of any relationship. These all relate to the framework principle of an interpretive approach to guiding.

Some of the elements of this relationship which we want to build...

- cooperation;
- understanding;
- respect;
- friendship and friendliness;
- goodwill;
- honesty;
- professionalism;
- responsibility;
- courtesy;
- trustworthiness.

From an interpretive perspective Guides should ensure that they build, foster and strengthen the relationship between the audience and the environment. And Guides are not the only people who can work towards this aim, as there is a variety of people within the visitor experience chain who can provide interpretive experiences. Liaise and work with these people to ensure a great experience for your audience.

Within the tourism industry relationships are normally established between a particular sector and people from a particular market segment, for example between adventure travel companies and the backpacker market. These segments are a category of people with similar characteristics, needs, expectations and motivations and can include holiday makers, visiting friends and relatives, families, weekenders and backpackers.

Guides work across all market segments and therefore should always seek to enrich their behavioural flexibility, build their tool kit and never be complacent with knowing just one subject matter or one style of leading tours. This will boost their ability to facilitate a variety of tour experiences and ensure a positive experience for the greatest number of people.

ACTIVITY: Consider the following scenario. You are about to lead a short walk through the main street of your town or city. This is part of a new tour program intended to introduce people to the 'local' area in a friendly and personal way. How will you get to know your audience, and what relationships could be developed during this program?

PRINCIPLES FOR CONDUCTING A TOUR

In considering responses to the questions in the above activity you can develop a range of principles which need to be addressed when planning a tour. Most of these are commonsense as the characteristics of a tour which you enjoy and which would satisfy you would be similar to those of most other people. These principles can be considered as either universal principles or specific principles, and reflect the rights of both individuals and the group.

UNIVERSAL PRINCIPLES
Despite the diversity of people who might come along on your tours there are still a number of factors common to all individuals, and these should form the core or universal principles of how you relate to your audience. These principles are an essential criteria for all successful tours and include the following:

● The tour is conducted in a safe and secure manner for all participants.
● Participants are treated with care and respect.
● Guides have the adequate and appropriate skills and knowledge for leading the tour.
● Information is accurate and appropriate.

- The tour is fun/enjoyable/entertaining (exceptions might include tours through a significant place of respect such as a holocaust museum or indigenous sacred site).
- Guides display ethical behaviour, trust and honesty.
- The tour meets what was promised in promotional material.

SPECIFIC PRINCIPLES

Specific principles are relevant to particular groups, individuals and/or situations. They promote practices in which tours are conducted in a manner which respects the following:

- people with interests in specific subject areas;
- language considerations;
- age differences;
- socioeconomic factors;
- mobility and health—related to different physical needs;
- time constraints;
- religious beliefs;
- expectations of individuals;
- special needs of individuals;
- interests of the group;
- cultural values;
- opportunity to learn and gain knowledge.

Special Focus

Interpretation in galleries

An interview with *Jenny Manning*

Project Coordinator, Voluntary Guides
Education and Public Programs
National Gallery of Australia

What is the main challenge in providing interpretive experiences within the National Gallery and how do you manage this?
The National Gallery of Australia opened in 1982. Over the past 20 years many changes have taken place, both to the collections and to the building. The main challenge is that Art is a human product. Voluntary Guides are interpreting a painting of a tree rather than a tree and this becomes a complex interaction between the artist, the artwork, the interpreter and the visitor.

What type of tours do the voluntary Guides conduct at the gallery?
The National Gallery conducts a variety of tour-based services including:

- tours of the public collection, Australian art, International art and Aboriginal art;
- tours of visiting temporary exhibitions;
- tours for primary students of the permanent collection;
- special booked tours and VIP tours;
- after-hours tours;
- Outreach, whereby voluntary Guides travel to local institutions such as nursing homes and retirement villages to deliver slide talks.

How many volunteers do you have?
We have 135 Guides registered to deliver tours on the roster and a variety of other voluntary activities such as research, filing, social events and mentoring. There are 28 trainees undertaking a year's training in 2002.

What training programs do you offer your art gallery volunteer Guide staff?
Training falls into two main categories.

- Training for working Guides.
- Twice monthly in-services are delivered to the working Guides to keep them informed about rehangs, changes in house exhibitions and major temporary exhibitions.

This initial training for voluntary Guides lasts for one year, one day a week during school terms (that is, approximately 42 weeks). The course focuses on the following areas:

- visual analysis;
- communication skills, verbal and non-verbal (including school tour training);
- art history knowledge relevant to the collection.

What are the key outcomes volunteer Guides gain from this course?
The key outcomes include the opportunity for them to gain skills in:

- art appreciation and a background to artists in our collection;
- interpreting works of art using appropriate language for a wide variety of audiences.

What does 'Interpretation' mean to you?

- Focusing on the overlap of object, interpreter and viewer.
- It brings the object to life for the viewer in a way that is relevant to the viewer.

● You need to be relevant to your audience. As an example, I needed to prepare and deliver a talk to an audience within the gallery for a cocktail party. I presumed that the primary aim of these people was to socialise, have some fun and enjoy a light-hearted evening. In response, I prepared my talk so that it would highlight only key works, be quick and be delivered in a light-hearted, chatty and cheerful style with a touch of irreverence. By contrast a presentation delivered to a seminar would be more serious and would be based on a supported argument.

What are some of your principles in providing art-based interpretive experiences?

● Always begin with the image.
● Respect the magic of art. The interpreter is acting as an intermediary between the creator of the artwork and the viewer.
● An artwork is more like a poem than an article. Seek emotional response from viewers.
● Use language appropriate to the audience.
● Always be accurate with facts and figures.
● Always state when you are expressing a personal opinion.
● Respect the opinions and attitudes of the viewers.
● Empower the audience so they can interpret and respond to art in their own way.

What is the 'drop-in formula' you use?

A drop-in formula should be used sparingly as any formulaic interpretation becomes tedious after a while. However in emergencies when the work is unfamiliar to the Guide this formula is of use in that:

● It facilitates an emotive connection between the art piece and the audience.
● It encourages reflection on how the artist created this mood.
● It provides a brief background to the artist.

Facilitating an emotive connection. An interpreter has to allow for this; especially when working with abstract works. Some of the questions which you can use include:

● How is this work affecting you? What words does it evoke within you—for example, cold, brittle, warm, black

● How does the painting make you feel? For example, one person when interacting with a painting that featured red and black colours compared these colours to those of the Essendon Bombers Football Club in Melbourne, which for her was a happy association. The main emotional elements of a work of art are the scale in relation to the viewer and the colour and texture.

How an artist creates this mood. During this section emphasise the artist's decision-making process. By looking at the way the artwork is made, insights into the meaning behind the work are often revealed.

- How does the artist create this mood? Examples of responses can include strong contrasts of light and colour, the position and body language of the figures and the interrelationships between the shapes and the background of the painting.
- Does this painting reinforce your emotional response, and if so how?

It is important that in asking these questions, any response received by the audience is reinforced and validated.

The life of the artist. This last step provides some information on the significance of the artist. It is important, however, to relate biographical detail to the work on view.

Why do you work with themes within the National Gallery?
We find themes useful in that they do the following:

- They enable the interpreter to compare one work with another and to demonstrate how art changes over time.
- They demonstrate preparation.
- They make it easier to provide a take-home message and task. For example, on one tour with a group of schoolchildren I focused on the theme of colour. In one painting I concentrated on the variety of greens used by the artist. At the end of the tour I made the following comment, 'We looked at the colour green today; what I want you to do is to notice all the shades of green in the tree beside the bus when you leave the gallery.' The ability to discriminate colours which the children learnt in the gallery was thereby translated to experiences in real life.

What are some of the themes you work to within the gallery?
Some of the themes are:

- how the artist represents the human body;
- colour;
- the development of Abstraction;
- changing approaches to landscape in Australian art.

Special Focus

Reflections on managing a
Guide program from *Mirah Lambert*

Goulburn Regional Art Gallery

How did you recruit Guides for the Goulburn Regional Art Gallery?
Recruitment of Guides was undertaken through the Friends of Art Gallery and
a story in the local newspaper. The people who expressed an interest were also
guiding at the nearby cathedral, which meant they already had the necessary
skills and knowledge for guiding, such as group management and public
speaking, but just needed to build their art knowledge and appreciation.

What were the challenges in managing the Guide team?
One of the main challenges of managing a Guide team in a small gallery was
the inconsistencies associated with the level of crowds. We would have to ensure
that we had adequate numbers of Guides for big events and major exhibitions
(that is, the crowd pullers of regional galleries such as the Archibald Prize and
Art Express) but then there were lulls in between these periods where there was
little need for the same number of Guides, as the major group visitation was
school groups.

Other major issues with Guide training was to give them enough arts
training with a small staff (myself as Education Officer and the Director of the
Gallery) and occasionally exhibiting artists. Also, a high turnover of exhibitions
(approximately every four weeks) means constantly having to learn about a new
show, artist, story and so on. This was of particular concern for new Guides
who had not yet developed their confidence in their ability to deal with much
new information.

This meant we had to keep the motivation and morale within the group and
ensure they kept their skills and knowledge current.

Strategies practised by other galleries and which we considered at Goulburn
included the following:

- Monthly meetings provided opportunities to raise issues.
- Regular talks were linked in with the monthly meetings and were presented
  either by a curator, an artist or Guides. For Guides these talks were an opportunity to present and share their research and specialist knowledge with
  colleagues. These talks were recorded and incorporated into a Guide's library
  for future reference and research.

- Adequate communication channels between all staff working at the Goulburn Regional Art Gallery was ensured. In addition to our monthly meetings we also made sure all staff were able to view outgoing media releases, planning documents and any other information which outlined upcoming events and exhibitions. As with the tapes from the monthly talks these documents were also stored for future reference.

With small teams everyone gets involved in the variety of tasks associated with managing the gallery, which included working with a variety of audience types.

In what other ways did you provide training opportunities?
Travelling exhibitions are generally accompanied by an artist and/or curator who prepare and deliver public talks specific to the exhibition. We made it free but compulsory for Guides to attend these talks, which was a great way to ensure they had the necessary knowledge on the relevant works, but also an opportunity to meet people intimately associated with the exhibition.

Effective communication

What are the learning outcomes for this chapter?

By the end of this chapter you should be able to:

- Identify the main principles of effective communication.
- Enrich your communication skills.
- Identify non-verbal communication elements and demonstrate the appropriate use of non-verbal communication.
- Maintain effective communication with appropriate colleagues.
- Demonstrate effective communication skills when working with people from a broad range of backgrounds.
- Recognise cultural diversity and the characteristics of major inbound tourist groups.
- Identify techniques for speaking to people from a non-English-speaking background.
- Demonstrate listening-and-questioning skills for liaising with people to facilitate effective two-way communication.
- Apply communication techniques to build group cohesion.

THE COMMUNICATION PROCESS

Within any environment, an enormous wealth of information competes for your intellectual and emotional attention. In any one day you can be exposed to thousands of commercials, events and interpersonal and social experiences. Estimates vary, but your body receives anywhere between 40 000 and 10 000 000 impulses per second. You experience and process this mass of information in unique ways, and create associated meanings through your unique frames of reference.

These frames of reference have many labels including paradigms, mind-sets, perceptions and points of view—and regardless of their name they all ensure that you remain unique in how you interact with your environment. No two people will ever see a tree in the same way, hear the same sounds, or be touched in the same manner by a piece of music.

The aim of communication is to provide the opportunity for people to share the unique meanings they create of the world.

WHEN ARE COMMUNICATION SKILLS REQUIRED?
Guides require communication skills throughout all aspects of their tour operations. They liaise with the following industry colleagues:

● tour operators and other Guides;
● coach captains and bus drivers;
● tourist information officers;
● staff from relevant government organisations;
● hospitality staff working at cafés and restaurants;
● accommodation managers and employees;
● airport staff.

These liaison activities might be to:

● confirm operational and logistical details;
● ensure the promised level of service and product qualities;
● facilitate the management of any mishaps;
● receive any updated and/or local information not provided in the tour briefing.

Guides service their audience by:

● liaising with clients, visitors and customers;
● providing commentaries relevant to the tour.

FORMS OF COMMUNICATION
The main forms of communication are written, electronic and oral. Written communication includes:

● memos;
● briefing sheets;

- itineraries;
- procedure manuals;
- promotional material.

Electronic communication includes:

- email;
- Internet;
- text messages on mobile phones.

Oral communication includes:

- face to face
- over the phone.

Oral communication is the dominant form of communication undertaken by Guides, and provides the focus for the remainder of this chapter. One of the principles within an interpretive approach to guiding is to ensure you capture and engage your audience. This is achieved by ensuring your tour is interesting, relevant and enjoyable—all of which require effective communication skills.

Effective communication can be hard work but it can also be extremely rewarding. As a Guide, you are working in a people and service-based industry. And presumably you are working in this industry because you love to help people meet their needs, interests and expectations and to assist them to have a great time. Effective communication maximises the opportunities for you to assist people to achieve these goals.

FACTORS AFFECTING EFFECTIVE COMMUNICATION

Effective communication is not just the process of delivering a message, but rather the process of ensuring that the meaning attached to this message is shared by all concerned. This requires you to focus on the response you receive during your communication process, rather than just on the delivery of your message. It is by managing this response that you maximise the opportunity for effective communication.

In the same way, interpretation is about sharing meaning. For this to be effective interpretation needs to be based on the same principles and techniques associated with effective communication.

Effective communication occurs when there is a sharing of meaning.

The communication process requires a presenter (you, the Guide) and an audience (tourist, visitor, client or colleague). The presenter is the person delivering the message to an audience. The audience is the receiver of the message and might consist of one person or a crowd of thousands.

When you are leading tours and delivering presentations you are in both roles, because the moment you present you need to also be aware of your audience and their response to your presentation. This latter task places you in the role of 'audience' where you remain alert to feedback information.

This model of presenter and audience is illustrated in the following diagram:

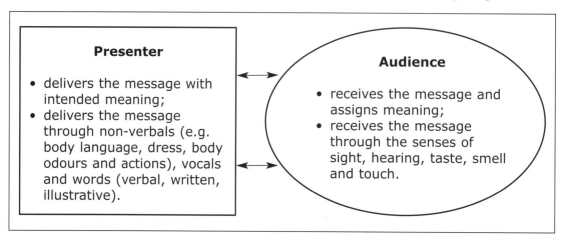

For communication to be effective there needs to be congruence between the intended meaning of the presenter and the meaning assigned by the audience—that is, a sharing of this meaning (overlap of the two circles in the following diagram). To ensure this occurs the presenter needs to focus on the response of the audience. Was it the intended response?

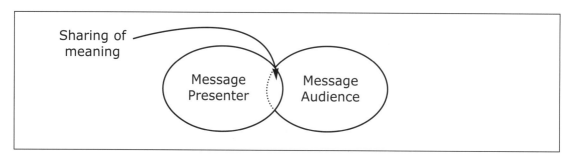

Your messages do not give meaning to your audience; rather your audience gives meaning to your message.

It's not what our message does to the listener, but what the listener does with our message that determines our success as communicators.
Mackay (1994)

BEING THE PRESENTER—DELIVERING THE MESSAGE

When delivering a presentation Guides rely on their non-verbals, voice and content (that is, words). Research indicates that the relative importance of these is 55 per cent non-verbals, 38 per cent vocals and 7 per cent content. This means that 93 per cent of your message is conveyed through the process of how you communicate (55 per cent non-verbals and 38 per cent vocals), while 7 per cent is conveyed through your content.

Being the presenter

So *how you communicate* is far more important than *what you communicate*—no great surprises in this statement. Within the guiding field there is a tremendous temptation to spend a disproportionate amount of time focusing on the *what* component—on researching facts and figures, and on getting the content perfect.

And ensuring that Guides have the correct facts and figures is an essential practice. But Guides also need to spend time on the *how* component of communication—on the process of communicating this content to their audience. To deliver interpretive tours you need to spend time practising your *how* communication skills. You need to develop skills in voice projection, anchoring, characterisation and working with your body, storytelling and improvisation. Conducting a tour will require you to get up and present to a group of people. In these situations you need to have at your disposal a collection of skills which have been refined with practice.

As the presenter you are always sending a message—whether it is in the clothes you wear, your mannerisms, your gestures or in your speech—and because of this you need to always remain alert to the messages you are sending. This begins with the first moment of contact you have with your tour group, even before you speak, during which your audience will form their 'first impressions' of you.

Non-verbal communication
Do not the most moving moments of our lives find us all without words.
Marcel Marceau

What you are speaks so loudly, I can't hear what you say.
Ralph Waldo Emerson

There are many forms of non-verbal communication.

Facial expressions
Our face is one of the most expressive parts of our body. It has been estimated that there are over 7000 facial gestures, and one of the most important when leading tours would be the good old smile. It is usually through the face that people pick up microexpressions, which are those subtle yet powerful messages that reveal inner

meanings, and which we focus on when listening to people. Microexpressions are also a critical element of your presentations.

Possible facial expressions may be:

- surprise, conveyed by:
  —raised eyebrows;
  —wide eyes;
  —a 'wow' expression of the mouth;
- happiness/joy, conveyed by:
  —corners of the mouth raised and turned up;
  —soft eyes and face.

When leading tours try, as much as possible, to be in a position that allows your audience to see your face—minimise the use of sunglasses (while ensuring relevant safety considerations for your eyes), be wary of hats which cover your face, and if you have facial hair keep it trim and neat.

The face is the image of the soul.
Cicero (Roman philosopher)

Eye contact

Eye contact is one of the most engaging aspects of non-verbal communication. Eye contact should be relaxed, friendly, soft and non-threatening—never use eye contact to stare down someone. Encourage yourself to look around at your entire audience. As discussed on page 63 it is through the visuals that people receive most of their environmental information.

Guides also need to remember that some cultures do not engage in eye contact; for example, indigenous Australians and some Asian cultures keep their eyes lowered to show respect. However, this does not mean that these people are not listening.

Movement, gestures and mannerisms

Your gestures and mannerisms are the non-verbal expressions of your body. They can enhance your messages or they can become painful distractions for your audience. You need to be aware of what gestures and mannerisms you are expressing and then assess whether or not they are appropriate to your situation. A few questions to ask yourself: How often do you move? Do you move in a repetitive rhythm or do you vary your movement patterns? How do you move and hold yourself; that is, what is your posture? Do you express an invigorating and inspiring energy or a lacklustre 'I'd rather be somewhere else energy'.

Your gestures and mannerisms are important anchors during moments of nervousness, such as when speaking to groups of people. During these times it is important to avoid distracting movements or, at the other extreme, becoming a statue. Rather your movements should be natural and relaxed, and consistent with the meaning of your presentation. You need to continually seek ways to incorporate movement so that it embellishes and enhances the message being presented, while not distracting from it (refer to pages 90–2 on anchors).

Positive non-verbal expressions include:

- facing the individual and group squarely;
- adopting a relaxed, attentive and open stance;
- having friendly mannerisms with a relaxed smile and expressive facial features;
- avoiding distractive and annoying habits.

Negative non-verbal expressions can include:

- tightly crossing arms;
- chewing gum or smoking;
- continually rubbing face, eyes, hair and other areas of the body;
- cracking knuckles
- looking repeatedly at your watch when talking with the group and/or individuals;
- shaking hands in a cold and weak manner;
- pacing back and forth;
- having hands on hips with legs placed spread-eagled;
- having hands in a fig-leaf position at crotch level with palms facing your body, or having hands in the reverse fig-leaf position in which hands are clasped behind your back;
- crossing your lower legs at the ankles;
- pointing with fingers.

(Refer to Table 4.2 which highlights the importance of context and premature speculation when working with expressions.)

 ACTIVITY: Stand in the following positions. What differences do you notice?

- Stand with a slumped posture, shuffling about with head bowed.
- Stand with your body weight over one hip and hands on hips.
- Stand erect, comfortable and well-balanced, with your shoulders and head up, and relaxed.

Describe your most common posture. Can you vary this with ease?

Clothes you wear
Clothes are one of the main ways in which people form their first impressions of you, even before you speak your first words.

Do a head-to-toe assessment:

- Are you wearing appropriate clothing?
- Does your clothing present a professional and proud image?
- What message are you conveying through your clothes? For example, if you are promoting safety, are you wearing the clothes to support your message?
- Do jewellery accessories such as necklaces, rings and bracelets complement your clothing and appearance?

Some tour companies provide their Guides with uniforms which can vary from a full uniform to part of a uniform, such as a shirt, skirt, blouse, scarf or just a hat. Often a name badge will also be provided—if not, make up your own. Ensure your uniform is neat, tidy and well-presented. Any part uniforms should be complemented by appropriate personal clothing.

Grooming

Good grooming includes:

- cleanliness and attention to personal hygiene;
- well-shaven or well-trimmed facial hair;
- clean and well-presented hair;
- neat and tidy clothing;
- frequent washing;
- appropriate use of deodorants or perfumes (that is, subtle but not overpowering);
- fresh breath and either neutral or pleasant body odours;
- clean and trim fingernails.

A note on body piercing

Body piercing is becoming an increasing focus of tour managers when setting customer-service standards. Should they allow presenters to have body piercings? This varies so much with the situation. From a stereotypical view, a group of young adventure seekers might respond quite well to body piercings whereas a group of retirees might find them offensive. Likewise, people from certain cultural backgrounds will have varying levels of tolerance to body piercings. If in doubt, take a conservative approach and remove visible body piercings.

Personal space

Although not quite a non-verbal characteristic, an awareness of personal space is extremely important, and non-verbal signals are the best way to manage personal space.

Personal space is a person's personal territory. It varies quite significantly between people depending on such factors as culture (Mediterranean cultures accept being up close whereas Asian and Anglo-Celtic cultures require a greater distance), environment, situation (e.g. personal space in a nightclub would be different from that on a walk in the desert), personality, self-confidence and self-esteem.

To respect other people's personal space you need to remain sensitive to other people's non-verbal cues as these will provide you with the best information as to whether or not they are comfortable or whether they feel their personal space is being threatened or violated. An obvious clue would be a person stepping away from you when you greet him or her at the start of the tour, or when you approach that person at any stage during the tour.

You need to remember that people are more sensitive to their personal space behind them, so do not approach people from behind but keep in sight.

BEING THE AUDIENCE—RECEIVING THE MESSAGE

During the communication process people receive messages through their sensory channels. The relative importance of these channels (for people without an impairment in one or more senses) are:

- eyes (visual channel—colours, shapes, brightness, movement and contrasts): 75 per cent;
- ears (auditory channel—tone, volume, pitch, modulation and emphasis): 12 per cent;
- other senses (taste, smell and touch): 13 per cent.

With a presentation situation most of the audience will receive information through the visual senses (the non-verbal communication channel of the presenter) and the auditory senses (the vocal communication channel of the presenter, which includes both vocal characteristics and the spoken words).

When leading tours you need to remain aware of the fact that the visuals are your dominant sense by:

Being the audience

- making sure everyone can see what you are talking about;
- drawing people's eyes towards an object—in the same way that a photographer will use light and a painter will use a vanishing point;
- challenging the visual by encouraging use of other senses.

In your role of presenter you also share the role of audience, because it is only by being in this role that you can 'listen' to and 'check-in' with your audience. You need to be alert to the subtle messages you receive in this 'audience' role and refine your ability to interpret these messages and assign meanings. Remember effective communication is a two-way process and you need to be able to travel in both directions.

ENSURING EFFECTIVE COMMUNICATION

MINIMISING THE EFFECT OF COMMUNICATION BARRIERS

Communication barriers are any elements which can interfere with effective communication. By remaining alert to the presence of possible barriers, and taking appropriate action, you can minimise their potentially adverse effects on your efforts to achieve effective communication.

These communication barriers include:

- cultural variations and personality differences;
- clash of perceptions and expectations;
- making rapid assumptions and misunderstandings (this is discussed later in the chapter in the section titled 'Avoiding premature speculation';
- technical glitches and breakdowns;
- time-related issues, for example people becoming increasingly anxious as the tour begins to run late;
- non-interest on the part of anyone within the communication process;
- making people feel threatened—either directly or by not ensuring their safety and security;
- environmental barriers, for example noise, smoke and distractions;
- inappropriate communication, for example commanding, criticising, judging and blaming people, and adopting threatening behaviour;
- use of inappropriate language, for example technical terms.

Most of these barriers can be addressed by maintaining a friendly, patient and professional attitude, and/or managing the environmental conditions to minimise any adverse impacts and effects.

 ACTIVITY: What is your perception of rapport? What is the need for rapport in the tourism industry? Why do you think it is important to work towards building and establishing rapport?

DISPELLING MYTHS

You can boost your effective communication by challenging some of the myths which surround the communication process (see Table 4.1).

BEING AWARE OF CULTURAL DIVERSITY

Guides work within one of the most front-line industries with regard to interacting with a wide variety of cultural groups. This cultural diversity includes not only visitors, tourists and their clients but also industry colleagues.

Table 4.1 Myths surrounding the communication process

Myth	Challenge—ensuring effective communication
You communicate only when you want to.	You are always communicating—it is an ongoing process.
Communication is achieved once you finish speaking.	Effective communication is a two-way process in which you need to focus on the response.
You communicate only with words.	Most communication is through the non-verbal aspects of communication.
If people appear confused, keep providing them with information.	More information does not necessarily lead to effective communication. People are confused for a variety of reasons, some of which have nothing to do with the information being provided. It might be that they cannot hear you and are experiencing language difficulties.
You communicate as if words have specific meanings.	Meanings are in people and not in words.
Your feelings play no part in the communication process.	Feelings are one of the most powerful aspects influencing communication.

Cultural diversity among industry colleagues

Australia is a society of incredible cultural variety. A culturally diverse workplace with people from a vast variety of cultures working together is part of the norm within Australian society rather than the exception. It is important that commonsense prevails, that cultural sensitivities are respected, and that people take the time to find out about each other and their individual needs. Listening and empathic communication skills are essential for Guides, along with patience, tolerance and understanding. They also need to remain sensitive to the break-up of traditional cultures as people assimilate within Australian society, because this can lead to some confusion. For example, what is generally considered normal behaviour for a traditional culture might be offensive for a first-generation person of that same culture.

The benefits of a multicultural Australia include:

● interesting place to live;
● great mix of languages;
● variety of perspectives on life;
● greater diversity in our work and social environment;
● immense culinary choice.

Respect the values and attitudes of individuals within your group...

Cultural diversity within your audience

In the same way that Guides need to respect cultural differences among colleagues, they also need to do the same with their audience. As a Guide, you might also need to be aware of the fact that people coming to Australia from another culture might experience varying degrees of cultural shock, with symptoms such as anxiety, frustration, embarrassment, confusion, discomfort and anger. Part of looking out for your audience is being aware of, and managing, these responses. You need to anticipate and prevent any potential misunderstandings, and have at the ready the skills necessary to manage these misunderstandings.

Language variations between cultures

Some cultures, for example Germanic cultures, focus almost solely on words to determine meaning without considering the context or other communication elements such as vocals and non-verbals. Other cultures such as Asian and Anglo-Celtic (e.g. Australian) cultures focus on the context of the message and take into consideration the non-verbals and vocals. These people do not just react to these considerations but develop an intuitive sense of possible meanings which they then listen to and decipher. Variations in how different cultures assign meaning can lead to misunderstandings.

The use of language also extends to the manner in which Guides refer to people by their names. This varies immensely between cultures, with some cultures preferring the first name last and last name first (e.g. Chinese cultures), whereas with other cultures the first name is spoken first (most Western cultures and Thailand). Ask the person to assist you, but better still research what would be the appropriate salutation for your audience.

When communicating with people from other cultures avoid using jargon, slang and complex words unless it is relevant to your situation, and you can somehow explain and simplify the words.

Some cultural characteristics of major inbound tourist groups

The following cultural characteristics are generalities. As mentioned, there is the opportunity for immense variety within cultural groups. Work with generalities but remain sensitive to the individual.

Japanese

The method of greeting Japanese people is normally with a bow, and it is unusual to greet them with a handshake. These people prefer to speak indirectly and allow for silences.

Japanese people are polite to each other, and do not readily express their feelings, being reserved in their mannerisms, gestures and eye contact. Generally their eyes are kept lowered, with extended eye contact being embarrassing (especially among women). They enjoy a degree of personal space and consider people standing or sitting too close to be disrespectful. If you need to point, use the entire hand rather than one finger. Japanese believe that saying 'No' is too abrupt and will express the negative in other ways.

Japanese dress to very neat and tidy standards and keep themselves very clean. They are accustomed to attentive service, are punctual and expect service to be efficient. Japanese people love shopping.

Germans

Germans can come across as being 'abrupt' and 'precise' when they communicate, which can be misunderstood for rudeness. However, it is their customary manner. Germans are orderly and well-groomed people, and place a great deal of importance on neat and tidy appearance.

Germans expect efficient and punctual service. At the same time Germans go on holiday to relax, and be free from the stresses of life back home. Germans enjoy packaged tours as they enjoy seeing the sights and making sure they see what there is to see. Australia is one of the most popular travel destinations for Germans after the United States.

Koreans

Eye contact and open communication styles are more acceptable between those of the same age and with younger Koreans. However, the same might be considered rude with a senior person, who commands a deal of respect in Korean society. Koreans generally limit any physical contact to a handshake.

Koreans are generally extremely courteous, and consider a 'Thank you' (with a bow of the head) to be extremely important.

Koreans like to visit popular places despite the crowds, and expect the opportunity to engage in a little shopping. They like to fit as much as possible into their travels.

Other elements to keep in mind are that within Korean society 4 is an unlucky number, that if you are writing a Korean a note never use red ink, and if you beckon someone do it with the palm down and with a fluttering of the fingers (avoid pointing or gesturing with one finger).

Indonesians

Indonesians are not a touching type culture (especially between strangers and women), although handshakes are an accepted form of greeting. They find loud voices offensive and maintain indirect eye contact. Prolonged eye contact might be seen as threatening or disrespectful. Smiling is an important part of Indonesian culture. However, as with other Asian cultures, facial expressions of Indonesians can be quite subtle and difficult to interpret for people from Western cultures.

Stance when talking with Indonesians is very important. Standing with hands on hips and/or in pockets, and/or with arms crossed over the chest are all considered to be disrespectful and rude, as is talking with sunglasses on, and pointing with your finger. Indonesians rarely disagree in public.

When sharing items with an Indonesian person, never hand over or receive any item with the left hand (handy to know if distributing maps, itineraries and other items). This is the same with all Muslim cultures and includes no eating of foods with the left hand.

North Americans—from the United States

North Americans are a culture with an extremely strong sense of patriotism. They expect a high level of service and friendliness, because this is the expected standard within the United States. People working in the hospitality industry within the United States need to supplement their wages with tips, and therefore provide the appropriate levels of service to promote tipping. Most Australians work for a wage and do not have this dependency, which can cause a greater variation in levels of service but also some confusion among Americans as to what is the accepted practice for tipping. If you receive a tip from an American, treat it as a compliment for the level of service you provided. If an American says 'Thank you' after receiving assistance and/or being provided with service, they appreciate having this gesture acknowledged with a 'You're welcome'.

Americans like to ask questions and can be quite vocal. They are generally informal, and love to laugh and have a good time.

Characteristics of other cultures

Some other cultural idiosyncrasies include the following:

- Not all cultures use 'please' or 'thank you'.
- It is impolite to whistle when among people from India.
- Within Arab cultures it is considered disrespectful to be laid back with hands in pockets, and adopting a slouching posture. At the same time they place high importance on eye contact, and men often greet in a manner similar to Mediterranean cultures (e.g. hug and a kiss), while touching women is frowned upon.
- There is no touching of women from a Muslim culture.
- Sniffing and spitting are acceptable in some cultures—these people might need to have it pointed out in a tactful and diplomatic manner that it is not acceptable in Australia.
- Many Asian people do not blow their noses in front of others.
- Younger people from Asian countries must show great respect for older people.
- Vietnamese people have a tendency to smile when a situation becomes too stressful. Thus an activity which we assume is going well might be the opposite for the Vietnamese visitor.
- With people from a Buddhist religion there is no touching on the head. This would

rule out the practice of patting children on the head as a form of greeting or encouragement.

- Many people from South-East Asian countries are not used to personalised service, but rather to a person servicing several people at once. This means they might well interrupt while you are talking with someone else.
- People from many of the Asian countries are sophisticated and experienced shoppers and like to know of appropriate shopping districts.

Speaking to people from a non-English-speaking background

- Pace your talk to ensure there is plenty of time for your audience to translate what you are saying into their own language—if you are working with a translator, be guided by that person. Keep in mind that translators do not always translate what you say—they might add information and leave out critical bits; check the response of your group to see if it is what you expect.
- Do not raise your voice (unless people can't hear you).
- Keep information in small, neat chunks and check that your audience understands— be clear in what you say and provide one message/idea at a time. It is the same with instructions—keep them simple and one at a time.
- When talking with people from cultures where it's impolite to say, 'No, I do not understand' but rather say 'Yes' or 'OK', ask them what they do understand. This should provide you with the necessary feedback.
- When giving instructions leave out double negatives, for example 'You can't go on this walk if you don't have the right shoes'. It would be clearer to say, 'You must have the right shoes to come on this walk'.
- Use simple, clear and direct English. Do not use broken English, for example 'You . . . stay here . . . wait . . . OK', or 'One o'clock . . . lunch . . . bus . . . leave . . . 2 o'clock'.
- Leave out jargon, slang and colloquialisms.
- Face people so they can see you, especially your facial expression and mouth. Speak to people rather than away from people and do not cover your mouth.
- If appropriate, exaggerate your body movements to emphasise relevant points.
- Do everything you can to preserve the dignity and self-esteem of your audience. Do not adopt a patronising or condescending attitude.
- Ensure the environment facilitates, and does not adversely affect, the communication process.
- When asking a question keep it simple. Ask one question at a time and avoid negative questions. For example, rather than ask the question 'You haven't been here before have you?' ask 'Have you been here before?'

AVOIDING PREMATURE SPECULATION

Whenever you rely on your assumptions within the communication process you need to be careful of a condition all people can suffer from called 'premature speculation'.

This condition occurs when people base their communication on first impressions and make assumptions, which are often stereotypic, as to the intended message of the other person. To avoid the consequence of this condition you need to extend your awareness to other elements within the communication context, as ultimately it is this context which gives meaning to our messages. Table 4.2 illustrates the range of meanings which can be associated with a particular gesture.

Table 4.2 Avoid premature speculation and check for alternative meanings

Gesture	Stereotypic meaning	Alternative meaning
Arms crossed	Disapproving, shut off	Cold 'Resting' arms Need to go to the toilet
Smile	Happy, fun, enjoyment	Sarcastic Concealing embarrassment in some cultures
Leaning head towards the speaker	Cannot hear the speaker	Cannot understand the words
Head nodding	Yes, agree	A polite 'no' in some cultures
Shuffling, becoming fidgety	Bored, not interested	Kinesthetic learner
Quick speech with high tone	Enthusiastic, quick talker	Nervous

ACTIVITY: List three other gestures, their stereotypic meanings and possible alternative meanings.

It is always best practice to interpret gestures in clusters rather than try to assign meaning just on the one gesture. Treat gestures as sentences rather than words and you will minimise the potential for misunderstanding. Do not make assumptions—seek clarification.

LISTENING—THE PATHWAY TO UNDERSTANDING

One of the most important and critical communication skills is effective listening. Listening and hearing are quite different. Hearing is the physiological process by which sound vibrates our auditory sensory organs, while listening is the process of seeking meaning within the communication process. Listening involves the whole body—tune into the expressions of a person who is actively listening and you will notice the high degree of engagement and focus towards the other person.

Effective listening requires that you remain alert and sensitive to all the elements taking place in the communication process. This includes both the 'tangible elements' such as body language, vocal tones and words being spoken, and 'non-tangible elements' such as the feelings, emotional state, attitudes and values of the other person. People bring all of these elements together to create their understanding of the message being communicated. As a Guide leading a tour group, you can do this whether you are listening to the message of one person or to the message being expressed by a group of people.

The idea is there, locked inside. All you have to do is remove the excess stone.
Michelangelo

Effective listening removes the excess stone to get to the 'guts of the matter'.

A man is not idle because he is absorbed in thought. There is a visible labour and there is an invisible labour.
Anon.

Effective listening focuses on both the visible and invisible.
Developing skills in effective listening is important for:

- ensuring clarity within the communication process;
- honouring what the other person is saying;
- obtaining more information on a particular issue;
- finding out about people on your tour;
- getting to core issues, especially when they involve emotionally charged people;
- identifying the needs, expectations and interests of people on your tour;
- promoting conversation;
- remaining focused, and if necessary obtaining more information on the issue at hand;
- remaining alert to the variety of 'offers' from another person and from the environment.

ACTIVITY: Consider the following questions and answer 'yes' or 'no'. List some of the principles of effective listening illustrated by these questions.

- When I am listening to another person my mind often wanders off the conversation.
- When I begin to disagree with the content of the conversation I become aggressive and start seeking an argument.
- I make sure we are talking about the same thing by letting the other person know my understanding of the situation.
- I start to become 'edgy' and anxious when I want to say something, and begin to ignore what the other person is saying.
- Most times I am able to listen to other people without drifting to other thoughts or wanting to interrupt before they finish speaking.
- I am usually able to focus when listening to another person despite surrounding distractions.
- I can't wait to get my point of view across and I like to make sure everyone knows about it.
- I find it hard to ignore my points of view and remain open-minded.
- When I am listening I usually prepare a response before the other person has finished speaking.
- I often ask questions to check in with the other person and to seek clarification.

THE PRINCIPLES OF EFFECTIVE LISTENING

Some of the principles of effective listening include the following:

- Listen without interrupting the other person (unless to clarify certain points).
- Remain focused on the other person and on what it is you are talking about—avoid going off on tangents during the conversation.
- Engage your non-verbals to demonstrate encouragement, sincerity and interest—face the person, adopt a non-threatening posture with open gestures, be attentive and listen with your whole body.
- Respect personal space and other cultural considerations (e.g. while eye contact is an essential component of some cultures, lack of eye contact is expected by some indigenous and Asian cultures).
- Listen with focus and empathy—picking the fluff from your clothes while listening to someone does not demonstrate empathy and focus.
- Avoid distracting mannerisms and gestures, for example flicking your hair, cleaning your nails, looking at other people and answering your mobile phone.
- Allow silences (if relevant and appropriate).

- Encourage the other person by asking open-ended questions which can promote conversation, and by providing vocal utterances (ahh-ahh, hmmm) and encouraging phrases such as 'That's amazing', 'Your're kidding me' and 'You did what?'.
- When appropriate check in with the other person to make sure you are both on the same track of conversation.
- Make sure the environment is conducive to effective listening with minimal distractions including noise.
- Listen to behaviour as this is where the real meaning is: 'Listen more to what I do and less to what I say' and 'Behaviour provides more of a truthful insight'.

Whenever you are talking, listen for cues that the other person would like to speak, for example inhaling of breath, becoming tense and restless when previously being relaxed, raising hands and shoulders, and generally becoming more attentive. Noticing these cues keeps you alert to the needs and interests of your group, and provides opportunities to receive their perspective of a situation.

WORKING WITH QUESTIONS

The process of listening often involves questions. Questions are a great tool you can use to build empathy with your audience and to understand both the stated and implied (unstated) needs of your audience.

WHY ASK QUESTIONS?
We ask questions:

- to motivate people by gaining their attention and interest;
- to find out more information about a particular person, situation or event;
- to get people thinking about a particular topic;
- to bring focus to a conversation and/or presentation, especially when people are talking in generalities;
- to clarify and verify different perspectives;
- to ensure we comprehend a situation.

For example, imagine a visitor walks into a visitor centre seeking a map. One possible scenario is as follows:

Visitor: Would you have a map of Australiana National Park, please?
Staff member hands over the map with a smile.

Another possible scenario is as follows:

Visitor: Would you have a map of Australiana National Park, please?
Staff member: (handing over the map) Any special interests you have in mind during your trip?
Visitor: Yes, I would like to get to the flat rock area.

Staff member:	Would you like me to show you where that is? It's a great area.
Visitor:	Yes, I heard it is a great place to see lyrebirds.
Staff member:	Lyrebirds! If you like I could show you some other locations which have lyrebirds. I could also give you a brochure on that particular bird.

ACTIVITY: What differences do you notice about the two scenarios? How do the techniques used by the staff member differ between the two scenarios?

CLOSED AND OPEN QUESTIONS
Closed questions

Closed questions are restrictive within a conversation. They typically promote one-word or two-word answers, which are usually a 'yes' or 'no', or a specific piece of information, for example:

- Is this your first trip?
- Do you find it hot here?
- What is the capital city of your country?
- Do you think this is one of the most beautiful places you have ever visited?

Closed questions are useful when you need to:

- check information, for example 'Is this your wallet?' 'Yes!'
- clarify meanings, for example 'Have you been here before?' 'Yes!'
- gain quick bits of information, for example 'Is this your daughter?' 'Yes!'

Some people might be compulsive talkers and demand attention. If necessary in these situations you can effectively use closed questions to narrow down, and bring greater focus to, your conversation.

Open questions

Open questions require an extended response, for example:

- What did you enjoy about this trip?
- Why are you travelling to Australia?
- What are your thoughts on the trip so far?
- How did that happen?
- How do you get your hair to sit so still on such a windy day?

Open questions are useful for:

- promoting conversation, for example 'What did you enjoy about your last trip to Australia?'
- exploring reasons and individual viewpoints, for example 'Why did you decide to buy that item?'
- determining the causes of problems, for example 'How did this happen?'
- exploring motivations of people, for example 'Why do you travel around Australia every two years?'
- demonstrating genuine empathy towards other people, for example 'It seems you're on a high today. What happened?'
- getting people to think, for example 'Why do you think they built the house in this particular way?' and 'What do you think the artist was attempting to convey?'
- seeking the meaning within an abstract passage of speech, for example, 'Exactly what are you getting at?'

 ACTIVITY: Rewrite the following as open questions.
1. Is this visit part of a packaged tour?
2. Are you a regular traveller?
3. Did you enjoy your tour?
4. Do you like this landscape?

WHEN ASKING QUESTIONS

Questions should be carefully worded. They should be:

- simple and direct—avoid any ambiguous, trick, obscure or complex questions (multiple questions within the one question) or at least break them down so they become simple and clear;
- asked one at a time;
- well-defined—especially when dealing with diverse cultural groups, avoid ambiguity;
- reasonable and respectful;
- relevant to the situation;
- shared with the rest of the group, but only if relevant and appropriate.

When you ask a question allow a reasonable period of time for a response. Be comfortable with silence. Resist the temptation to answer the question yourself.

Special Focus

Interpretation in botanic gardens

Thoughts and ideas from a coffee-table chat with *Peter Lehmann* and *Jo Pillinger*

Education Officers,
the Australian National Botanic Gardens

What is the background of the National Botanic Gardens?

The National Botanic Gardens, located in Canberra, is one of the largest botanic gardens in Australia. It is 90 hectares, of which 40 hectares have been developed.

In addition to decorative plantings, the Gardens' plant displays are organised into taxonomic or ecological groups. Taxonomic displays feature related plants, such as wattles (*Acacia* species); and ecological displays contain plants which grow in similar environments, such as rainforests.

This has required extensive work to modify the environmental conditions to ensure plants can grow, for example water reticulation systems within the rainforest gully through to extensive rock placements. These rock placements absorb the heat during summer and slowly release the same heat during winter—thus minimising the effect of the hundred or so frosts which occur each year, and allowing the cultivation of frost-sensitive plants.

What type of public tours do you run in the Gardens?

- Scheduled guided walks are provided for the visiting public so anyone can join in. With these tours, Guides need to remain flexible as they often do not know who their audience is until the tour starts.
- Sometimes there are special requests for coach and group tours, which allow the Gardens to plan for these, often special-interest, tours.
- Self-guided and facilitated activities for school groups.

What is your definition of 'Interpretation'?

It is about getting people to focus, and when focused to pose a question and provide enough of a clue to get people thinking and vocalising and sharing their thoughts. It is about facilitating audience participation and not just giving information. The best interpretive experience is when people want more.

Extended thoughts on the characteristics of an interpretive approach include:

- It provides greater freedom in the styles of leading tours.
- It caters for greater skill level.

- It provides a range of questions and answers from the simple through to the sophisticated.
- You are less bound by the need for formal evaluation of student performance.
- There is greater focus on meeting the needs and characteristics of the audience.
- It draws on the life experience of your audience.
- It gets people to think.
- It is more challenging and pushes the bounds.
- It aims to create a desire to have people come back.
- It promotes the philosophy that 'The lesson goes on'.

Interpretation is different from education in that education:

- is learning that needs to be achieved and with two connations—that there needs to be an answer and that this answer needs to be correct;
- concludes with the statement 'I've learnt my lesson';
- is more formal and disciplined.

How do you involve members of your audience?

Some of the ways we seek to involve our audience include:

- ensure that there is a diversity of scenarios and approaches within the tour;
- ask open-ended questions, listen to responses and build on these responses;
- constantly seek to interact with our audience;
- invoke the senses—touch, smell, listen.

How do you encourage interaction?
With the environment

A very simple example might be: at a tea-tree we would encourage people to rub the leaf and sniff its fragrance. Then we would ask: 'What do you think indigenous people used these leaves for?' Then working with the responses we would say, 'The fragrance you can smell is the tea-tree oil produced by the tree, and it is used by Europeans for the same purposes as indigenous people'. We normally start off with tea-trees because the name is one which most people can associate with; that is, everyone has heard of tea-tree oil. We then go off to other plants and look at how and when they are used. Thus we work from most familiar to least familiar.

To encourage interaction from people from other nationalities we ask them to show us the plants most like those from their country. This often generates interesting discussions about cultivation of plants, similarities of distant plants and the origins of plants.

Working with questions

Questions are great for focusing people. We ask questions such as:

- What else can we see?
- What other characteristics do you think are unique to this plant?
- How do you think that was made?
- Why do you think the plant grows in this particular way?

When asking questions we make it seem as though we are genuinely wondering; that is, that we do not know the answer.

We also do not necessarily provide the answer but rather leave people in suspense and with some clues as to how they can answer the question themselves. We believe that sprinkling this suspense throughout the tour leaves people with a whet appetite, a desire to find out more and a sense of wonder.

Use of props

Props could include:

- plant samples collected by Botanic Gardens staff although with some plants we would pick a flower or leaf for the group to share;
- light meter—to demonstrate changes in light between different forests and how this relates to the particular flora type, intensity of green colour and level of chlorophyll in the leaves (chlorophyll being what a plant needs to absorb light, so the greener the leaf, the more chlorophyll—thus where light intensity is low, leaves are greener);
- temperature/humidity meter.

Using props ensures variety in our presentations and audience participation. Props allow people to get involved and to stimulate their other senses. Props are also great when needing to manage people who are noisy, disruptive and sometimes a nuisance. Props provide another opportunity to connect with these people. For example, with disruptive kids we encourage them to be responsible for looking after certain props, and this responsibility usually engages them in the tour. Once you become confident in the use of props, they also serve as great anchors if ever you become nervous or lose your composure. We make sure that everyone who uses props knows how to use them.

Metaphors

We work with metaphors quite a bit to make it easier for people to grasp and understand some of the concepts we are promoting. For example, when talking about ways in which indigenous people used paperbark to cook food we compare it to cooking the good old potato. We would say something like:

'Do you like your spuds thrown straight into the fire? Most people do not, so what do we do? We normally wrap them in alfoil. The same with traditionally living Aboriginal people—some wrap their food in paperbark.' Generally people then extend on this concept by asking questions such as: Why doesn't bark burn? How do Aboriginal people get the bark? How does it work?

What do you hope people will gain from tours at the Gardens?
We hope people will appreciate:

- the importance of native flora to indigenous people and other current-day Australians;
- the ambience—landscape—feel, sounds, smells, quiet, sounds of birds;
- the variety/diversity of adaptations of native flora that is in these Gardens;
- the importance of these Botanic Gardens;
- the importance of this place and will want to come back.

What are some of the unique conditions in providing interpretive experiences within the Australian National Botanic Gardens?
Some of these conditions include:

- The Gardens are unique in their design and layout and immense diversity of plants—we have 7000 species of Australian native plants.
- We are working outside, which means we are dependent on the weather and need to manage the usual challenges of outdoor activities—variations in weather from hot to cold, rainy to sunny, and windy to calm.
- The Gardens are a 'living' environment. This provides opportunities to bring in concepts such as life cycles. For example, there are a few trees dying from a fungal disease, which links to the concept that all the plants within the Gardens will one day be dead, yet in that process they pollinate and produce seedlings to continue the life cycle.
- We are managing hazards—which can also be opportunities—such as snakes, creepy crawlies and overhanging branches.
- We are dealing with change—different flowers, smells, textures, colours and birds flying in. We have natural change but also change because it is a modified environment—for example, some areas closed for maintenance.
- The Gardens are landscaped according to ecological, nomenclature (classifications) and habitats (rainforests, mallee) and there are streams within the Gardens. Landscaping works within the Gardens provide us with the opportunity to talk about modified environments—landscape features— rocks to absorb heat through summer and then slowly release that same heat during winter which reduces the effects of frost; planting warmer and desert

plants nearer the buildings to receive greater radiation; use of environment to grow plants not from that environment; and adding moisture to create rainforest.

● We need to manage groups along narrow paths—logistics with group sizes— so one way to reduce the logistics is to reduce the number of people on tours. (This is one way of dealing with groups on narrow paths. What are some other ways?)

The Gardens attract a diversity of people from all around the world. This, coupled with the variety of situations which we encounter in our everyday activities, means we need to remain flexible with our tours and maintain this flexibility right to the end. We promote the approach that our style of leading a group of people depends on the characteristics of that group, and not as much on what we are keen to promote.

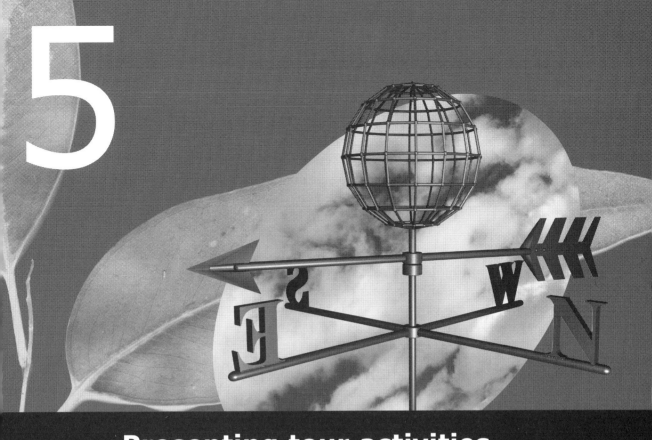

Presenting tour activities

What are the learning outcomes for this chapter?

By the end of this chapter you should be able to:
● Demonstrate effective presentation skills.
● Use interpretive and presentation techniques to create an enriching, informative and entertaining experience for your audience.
● Present commentaries and other information to tour groups.
● Demonstrate the effective use of interpretive and presentation techniques when delivering tours.
● Demonstrate the effective use of microphones.
● Manage nerves when delivering a presentation.
● Add strength and colour to your voice.

EFFECTIVE PRESENTATION TECHNIQUES

As a Guide you will spend a considerable amount of your time delivering presentations to a wide variety of audiences. This will generally be for the purpose of delivering your commentary but it can also include providing relevant orientation and logistical information. Sometimes Guides are involved in giving talks and speeches to special-interest groups, or in delivering promotional talks. Whatever the reason, the need to deliver presentations will require you to develop and hone your skills in public speaking, which is the focus for this chapter (and, in particular, for the purpose of leading tour groups).

When delivering presentations you are doing more than just sharing ideas and thoughts with an audience. You are providing a reflection of yourself and your attributes, your credibility, your product, the company/organisation you might be representing, and the value you are placing on that situation. All of these elements have an effect on your audience and on the way they receive your presentation. Additionally, they might also be affected by:

● the environment—the situation, other people, the level of noise and the temperature;
● what is going on within themselves—whether they are feeling warm, comfortable, distracted and so on.

The more you can manage and align these elements so that they complement each other, the easier it will be for your audience to focus on the message and intent of your presentation, which in turn works towards addressing the interpretive principles of guiding.

Whatever the presentation, it needs to be relevant to your audience and to the situation. If it lacks this relevance, it will be difficult for your audience to maintain interest no matter how well you deliver your presentation. To ensure your presentation is relevant find out as much as possible about your audience and their needs before your tour (refer to Chapter 3).

You can motivate your audience by letting them know how the tour will be relevant to them. This can include referring to affective elements and promoting a tour that will be fun, enjoyable and exciting, and to cognitive elements such as 'hot off the press' information, and the prospect of hearing about fascinating anecdotes. You can also motivate your audience by sharing your emotional enthusiasm. Interpretation is not just about presenting facts and information; it's also about feelings and affecting people in a manner that excites them to develop a positive appreciation of your chosen message.

An important principle when delivering a presentation is to talk to, and not at, your audience. Establish your credibility early on and seek to build rapport and establish a sense of partnership, rather than a one-sided delivery. Use a conversational style sprinkled with personal nouns and pronouns such as 'you', 'your', 'we' and 'us' to instil a sense of group unity. Face and talk to your whole group, and avoid talking to just a few people.

It's also important to develop a sense of self-awareness and the ability to check in with how well you believe you are presenting, in particular to ensure that you are relaxed when you are presenting as being relaxed helps put your audience at ease, improves your voice projection and clarity, and allows for smooth and clear body movements. One way to do this is to be aware of your body centre when presenting. Your body centre is that point in your body which leads your movements.

 ACTIVITY: Try to find your body centre. Now place your body centre in other parts of your body; move about and feel the difference. For example, if your body centre is in your stomach, place it in your chest, in your head or in your feet. Experiment with different body centres and their effect on how you present. Which body centre feels more relaxed when presenting? Does this change with different presentations?

The following are a few tips and ideas to provide a quick reference summary of possible effective presentation techniques. They focus particularly on delivering commentaries.

PRESENTATION TECHNIQUES WITH A FOCUS ON YOUR AUDIENCE

- At the start of your tour is a great opportunity to:
  —fine-tune your presentation to the situation;
  —find out additional information about your audience and whether there are any knowledgeable people who might be able to provide information from their area of expertise.
- If people question and/or challenge you, involve them; ask whether they have something to contribute. While leading an activity remember that people have a right to talk but that the group also has a right not to be disturbed. Your responsibility is to balance the rights of individuals with the rights of the group.

PRESENTATION TECHNIQUES WITH A FOCUS ON YOURSELF

- Boost your confidence by taking the time to prepare, plan, organise and rehearse your commentary and other speaking elements of your tour. Feel confident in your level of knowledge by doing extensive research. Be confident—aim to manage your nerves rather than attempt to control and overcome them. Practise deep breathing to assist you manage nervous situations.
- Smile—it's contagious and helps to put people at ease, and it's a greeting accepted by most

Smile – it's contagious and helps to put people at ease

cultures. Keep in mind that in some cultures smiles are sometimes used to mask embarrassment and/or conceal ill feelings.

A smile is so much richer when it is shared, and a laugh so much louder.
John Pastorelli

- Whenever possible do not read from notes. Remember the old presentation adage—'Familarise, do not memorise. Talk, do not read.' Like the storyteller, the story is much more alive when it is told rather than read as you can focus more energy on your expression, rather than on what you are trying to read. There are occasions when you need to present on an unfamiliar topic or object, and then reading from notes may be a necessity. During such times try to sprinkle information which does not require the notes, for example personal stories, anecdotes, thoughts and ideas. Can you become a character who is reading the notes as part of a story? For example, if the notes are from a historical journal can you become a character who is narrating this event in history?
- Engage in friendly and non-threatening eye contact, although remain sensitive to the fact that a number of cultures consider direct eye contact to be a sign of disrespect. There are also many people who become extremely uncomfortable when a presenter 'stares them down'. The best practice is to remain sensitive to the individual and to individual situations—take your lead from them by 'listening' to their behaviour.
- Ensure your voice and non-verbal mannerisms are clear and easy to understand—use your voice to dramatise, capture attention, illustrate and emphasise.
- Demonstrate positive, friendly and open non-verbal expressions—be aware of your body language when presenting and ensure it remains appropriate to your situation. Your gestures and mannerisms are your visual narrative which should complement your spoken narrative.
- Share the meaning an object or place has for you. Include within your tour an indication of what the environment means to you. If it is a quiet rock pool within a stand of majestic scribbly gums, what do you as a Guide feel about it? Do you enjoy the changing light of day? Do you enjoy the smells of the area? If it is a historic site, do you enjoy the locals and their stories? Do you have a deep-felt respect for the strength and tenacity of workers who constructed its buildings? This takes the commentary away from just a listing of facts and objective information and provides a subjective insight (within the appropriate context this can enrich your commentary). It also allows you to incorporate

Use your **VOICE** to dramatise, capture attention, illustrate, **EMPHASISE!**

emotions into the time you spend with your audience. Be enthusiastic, demonstrate the same principles you are discussing, and be immersed and 'present' in the experience.

● If using a microphone, make sure you know how to use it. It is best practice to arrive early and check on microphone equipment.

● If you do not know the answer to a question, admit it and offer to find out the answer, or see whether anyone in your group knows the answer. Whenever you have to say, 'I'm sorry, I do not know' you are being provided with a learning opportunity.

PRESENTATION TECHNIQUES WITH A FOCUS ON ENVIRONMENTAL CONDITIONS

● Work with environmental conditions to embellish your presentation and enrich your commentary; for example, the late afternoon light is often ideal for visiting indigenous sites, historic buildings (especially if the light arrives at an angle to the building) and lookouts. If possible, plan for and utilise such moments (while remaining sensitive to its inherent magic).

● Attempt to use the environmental conditions as a means of reflection. If it's a cold day, encourage people to reflect on how indigenous people kept warm. Encourage your audience to think about what it would have been like to be an explorer in times of extended rain periods or to live in a tent as a convict or gold prospector, and what shelters were used by bushrangers and people growing up on the streets during the Depression years.

● Manage any environmental distractions and potentially adverse conditions by moving to a different area, engaging appropriate presentation techniques (raising voice and exaggerated gestures) and appropriate group management techniques (huddling people, speaking from a point where everyone can hear and see you), and/or working with the environmental conditions (e.g. speaking upwind of your

Be aware of environmental noise when leading activities

What are the challenges and hazards being faced by this Guide?

audience so the wind carries your voice). Environmental distractions can include the following:

—traffic;

—sea noise—surf and wind;

—the sun (when presenting ensure people in the group are positioned so the sun is not in their eyes, and that you position yourself so that people can easily focus on you in the given light; Guides who are working outdoors need to take adequate precautions to protect their skin and their eyes from extended periods of exposure to the sun and environmental elements);

—strong and gusty wind;

—cold or heat (if it's a cold day, seek opportunities to get warm, which might include making sure everyone has adequate and appropriate clothing at the start of the tour; likewise, if it is a hot day, stop and seek locations which are cooler such as shade areas);

—crowds of nearby people (e.g. near a meeting area within a museum);

—elements within your group including chatty people, kids in 'play mode' and dominating people who love to interrupt.

● Allow silence to develop. Plan for the use of silence in your activity. Everything needs space to live and breathe. It is the same with your activity. Encourage 'environmental listening'. Provide opportunities for features and events within the landscape to speak for themselves.

I enjoy the silence in a church before the service more than any sermon.
Ralph Waldo Emerson

The notes I handle no better than any other pianist. But the pauses between the notes—ah, that is where the art resides.
Artur Schnabel

How can I interpret the feelings within me when I cannot find the words? I will never pretend to interpret what I cannot describe or fully understand. I do not know the names of the colours of the dawns, nor can I describe the feeling aroused by the morning scents.
Harold Senior, one of the first rangers with the NSW National Parks and Wildlife Service, based at Royal National Park

Allow silence to develop...

A few points to keep in mind

- For every action there is a reaction—ensure it is the reaction you intend to happen and which is favourable within the context of your activity.
- Actions speak louder than words—ensure your actions support and complement the message you wish to convey. The same applies with your manner of dress.
- You cannot withdraw any statement you make, even if made incorrectly; so leave out information that may offend such as bad-taste jokes, racial comments and sexual innuendos. Maintain commonsense when communicating with your audience. If you use humour, be sure that it follows the ATT rule—appropriate, tasteful and timely.
- Leave your negative personal baggage out of the moment when working with your audience. An audience is generally not interested in your problems and concerns and whether you are having a bad day. They are only interested in those things which might create a positive experience for them. If you have an attitude oriented toward high quality customer service, the spin-off for you is that in creating a positive experience for the customer you also gain a positive experience.

ACTIVITY: Think about the following questions. What is the difference between a Guide leading a group and a group leading themselves on a self-guided activity (e.g. following signs along a track)? Guides are more expensive than signs so why have Guides? What characteristics and qualities do Guides bring? Make a list of the advantages of having a Guide lead a group.

Leave your personal baggage out of the moment when leading tours

WORKING WITH MICROPHONES

At some point in your guiding career you will be required to use a microphone. For some Guides, such as those leading coach tours, using a microphone is a daily practice whereas for other Guides working in remote areas or leading walking tours it might be as infrequent as once every few years.

Microphones are part of a PA (public address) system. They can be one of a number of types including hand-held units, lapel units, headset units, megaphones and bracket-mounted units.

Lapel microphones are fixed to some part of your clothing, usually around chest height. Lapel microphones are normally quite sensitive, so you need to be careful that they are located away from areas which could receive excessive rubbing and which could cause irritating sounds. Lapel microphones are also normally connected to a transmitter unit which is attached to a belt and which then has a wireless feed to a nearby power unit.

Headset microphones are like lapel units in that they are hands-free. Headset microphones are normally fixed to the head like a set of headphones, with a movable bracket for positioning the microphone in front of the mouth. Such a microphone set-up, connected to a two-way radio, is used by climb leaders (Guides) leading climbs (tours) over the Sydney Harbour Bridge. As climbers (audience) are also connected to this system via a two-way radio and ear-piece climb leaders can choose to speak to their group while stationary or while on the move, and without needing to strain their voices to project above the high levels of ambient noise.

Bracket-mounted microphones are quite restrictive, and are generally used by Driver-Guides who provide commentaries and other verbal information as part of their tour management activities.

Hand-held microphones are the most common type of microphone used by Guides. They can be connected to either a portable or fixed amplification unit. Portable units include those carried around by hand and which are used by Guides when managing large groups, and/or when managing groups in loud areas, or when the Guide does not have a strong voice. Fixed amplification units are those attached by lead to a socket which leads to an amplification unit. This includes those units in coaches which enable the person to stand facing the group when the coach is stationary and also to be seated and provide a 'running commentary' while the coach is moving.

Guides are also involved in delivering presentations with the aid of microphones attached to lecterns or other stage structures.

TIPS FOR WORKING WITH MICROPHONES
When working with a microphone be sure that it is switched on, that the PA system is projecting the correct volume, and that all leads and associated equipment are in working order.

Your voice is the principal means by which you communicate when working with microphones. This is particularly relevant when you are working with coaches and might be sitting in the front seat while your passengers are looking out the windows. You need to ensure that you speak with a clear, well-enunciated and well-paced voice, and use short and simple words and phrases.

You might notice 'popping sounds' when speaking into a microphone. These are generally caused by the 'plosive' sounds of your voice, for example 'p' and 'b'. One way to avoid the popping sound is to speak 'over' the microphone rather than into it. Different microphones are also more sensitive to these sounds, so if possible work with another type of microphone.

When working with hand-held microphones you also need to ensure that the microphone follows your mouth. For example, if delivering a commentary while on a coach your face turns as you glance from one side of the coach to the other, but the microphone remains in the same position. The result is that your voice fades in and out as it passes over the microphone. One technique to manage this situation is to place the microphone gently on your chin and ensure that where your chin goes your microphone surely follows.

MANAGING THE NERVOUS TWITCH

During a presentation situation many people find themselves becoming uncomfortable and nervous, and experiencing a heightened state of energy. This is particularly relevant for people presenting for the first time.

The following are a few signs which might alert you to being in a nervous state:

Do you get nervous when delivering presentations?

- sweaty palms;
- a quick pulse;
- repeating yourself;
- speeding up your rate of speech;
- clenching your jaw;
- tightness in the chest;
- fidgety movements, pacing and shifting weight from foot to foot;
- avoiding eye contact;
- difficulty in listening to people;
- difficulty with silence and pauses when speaking;
- a general feeling of tension in the body.

ANCHORS FOR MANAGING NERVOUS TENSION

The body often responds to a nervous state by anchoring its behaviour in some way. For example, people might cross their arms, they might fidget or they might lean on an object. Watch people presenting to a large group and notice any repetitive mannerisms such as swaying back and forth, crossing arms, holding onto a prop or stepping between two spots on the ground. People might also rely on verbal

Anchors for managing nervous tension

anchors indicated by expressions such as repetitive use of 'ah', 'um' and 'eeeh', and also abrasive comments (which they often regret later).

Watch people as they enter a crowded space and notice the anchors they use; for example, people entering a crowded bar or party might respond to the situation by getting the drinks, finding a seat, putting hands in pockets or some other grounding activity.

There are no right or wrong anchors as the body is simply attempting to look after itself. However, there are appropriate and inappropriate anchors. The following are suggested anchors to assist you manage the nervous twitch—whether these are appropriate or not depends on your situation.

- A great anchor is to deliver your presentation on a familiar subject, that is, a subject which you believe you know well. This can also be extended to include familiar surrounds.
- Memorise the first two to three minutes of your presentation. Sprinkle specialist knowledge throughout your presentation as anchor points. Be careful with memorising too much, because the body has a tendency to forget at exactly the time you need it to remember—Murphy's Law. It is much better to rehearse a series of ideas and concepts and build from these during your presentation.
- If you reach an extreme state of nervousness, pause for a few seconds while you take a deep, diaphragmatic breath (discussed later in this chapter). Steady and ground yourself and then continue. Deep breathing is one of the best ways to ground and steady yourself when in a state of nervous energy. Remember—*pause, deep breath and think 'relax'*.
- Maintain a positive attitude—challenge your fears. Remember the audience wants you to succeed. Think 'I'm having a conversation with my audience' rather than 'I have to give a perfect presentation'. Maintain enthusiasm.
- Focus on positive outcomes. Ask yourself how you would like to feel after the presentation and then work out how you will achieve this. What would you like to hear, see and feel? (Ensure these are expressed in positive terms.)
- Focus outward. Who has the smiling face, the cute face or the friendly face? What colours are people wearing? Anyone sleeping? Anyone laughing? Speak to the friendly faces. What promotes nervousness is an inward focus on negative thoughts—what if I make a bad mistake? What if the people think I'm stupid? I can't do this? A degree of inward focus is necessary for 'checking-in' and making sure things are going along smoothly; for example, am I speaking too fast? Can everyone see me? Beyond this constructive use, an inward focus can become self-fulfilling, obsessive and destructive.
- If you go blank, remember you're the only one who has forgotten what you were about to say; rather than stress out, relax, breathe, take a drink of water, ask questions or summarise what you just said.
- Develop physical anchor points within your body. As an example, some people

crunch their toes while others push forefinger and thumb together. Work one out for yourself, making sure it is not distracting to your audience.

● Be prepared—rehearse, practise and rehearse some more. Anticipate what questions your audience might ask.

● Do a mental and verbal run beforehand. Do a visualisation run; that is, before the presentation find yourself a quiet area and visualise yourself delivering the presentation (if possible practise aloud). It is best practice to undertake a dry run of your tour whenever possible. Obviously this might be difficult for lengthy tours, but whenever practical seek out opportunities to go over and rehearse your materials while travelling between sites.

● Meet and get to know your audience before your tour starts. In that way, you increase the chance that you are talking with 'friends'.

The following, if used for extended periods, could become inappropriate anchors:

● crossing lower legs while standing;
● leaning on objects (e.g. post, wall or tree);
● crossing arms, fidgeting with objects or placing hands in pockets (so that you can fidget some more);
● slapping hands together or slapping hands on thighs and other parts of the anatomy;
● using 'oh', 'um' and 'you know' excessively in your speech;
● using crude remarks and offensive jokes is never appropriate (these are subtle anchors but they are quite destructive; some people rely on such material when delivering a presentation in the hope it generates a laugh or favourable reaction, which in turn is an anchor).

A FEW NOTES ON BEING NERVOUS

If you experience nerves when delivering a presentation you're not alone. It's a natural and normal reaction experienced by actors, performers and professional speakers. It actually provides you with an edge when presenting and ensures that you're in a heightened and alert state. However, like all things, it needs to remain in balance and too much nervous energy can become detrimental to your presentation and to your health. If you feel your nerves are on the excessive side consider the following ideas.

Challenge your perceptions. Often you fuel your nerves by becoming worried and fearful that your audience knows you are nervous. Ask a colleague, friend or other person to watch how you come across when delivering a presentation. You might well be surprised when you find out that you do not appear to be nervous but really quite relaxed. And even if you do appear nervous most members of an audience will be quite supportive of you, providing it is not excessive and overly distracting.

You can also ask yourself 'What am I nervous about', and then find the cause and manage it with appropriate dialogue and self-talk. Questions which might assist you in this quest include:

- Is it fear of rejection? Who is rejecting you? How do you know?
- Is it fear of failure? Who said you have failed? Accept your positive moments and attempts.
- Is it fear of forgetting? Practise, rehearse and take some resource material and reference cards.
- Is it the expectations you place on yourself? Ease up, have fun, be professional but also light-hearted and enjoy the time you spend with your group in the same way you would enjoy conversations with friends.
- Is it fear that you only have one chance? If you are true to the situation and give it your best, then that is the best you could do. Learn from it.

BUILDING YOUR SELF-CONFIDENCE

How well you manage your nerves and deliver an effective presentation has a great deal to do with your level of self-confidence. Some of the ways you can increase your self-confidence include the following:

- Be kind to yourself.
- Praise yourself. We seem to be good at imaging and creating negative thoughts about ourselves and our situations; so shift the energy to create positive thoughts and images.
- Encourage yourself.
- Be fair with yourself. Do not put pressure on yourself with unrealistic burdens.
- Take responsibility when things do not go to plan by reviewing your procedures leading up to the event. What other planning activities might have prevented such a situation? Blaming someone or something does not promote the necessary skills and knowledge to ensure a similar situation does not reoccur.
- Join a public speaking course or club (refer to your local telephone directory for possible contacts). And seek out opportunities to deliver short presentations, for example introducing a guest speaker, leading small groups around a visitor centre or local area, and greeting people when they arrive in an area before referring them to another person or area.
- Engage in the Japanese 'Kaizen' philosophy of 'improvements with small and incremental steps'.

ADDING STRENGTH AND COLOUR TO YOUR VOICE

The devil hath not in all his quivers' choice
An arrow for the heart like a sweet voice.
Lord Byron

VOCALS AND BREATH

Vocal sounds and breath are inseparable. It is breath which vibrates the vocal cords, and it is the vocal cords which constitute the basis of vocal sounds. Ensuring a vibrant and efficient control of these sounds requires effective control of your breathing.

The preferred breathing for enriching your vocal sounds is deep breathing, which involves the diaphragm, intercostal muscles and abdominal muscles (the intercostal muscles are those muscles between the ribs). Deep breathing provides the following benefits:

- The lungs are able to receive greater volumes of air.
- The lungs are flushed of any 'dead air'.
- The internal organs are massaged by the movement of the diaphragm and abdominal muscles.
- There is potential for greater control of both the inhalation and the exhalation processes—the exhalation process is used in effective voice production.
- It makes the voice stronger with richer tones.
- It enables people to 'ground and centre' themselves when needing to manage nervous energy.

Despite these benefits most people breathe high in the chest (shallow or clavicular breathing). This is typically a reflection of your upbringing as the majority of people have never been taught about deep breathing, apart from those involved with yoga, meditation and Eastern religious practices.

When breath is high in the chest the resulting volume of air is reduced, together with your ability to effectively control the exhalation process. Shallow breathing restricts how you manage your voice. It also restricts how you manage your breath during stressful periods. In these situations your body requires more oxygen to compensate for the increased usage being generated through nervous energy. Shallow breathing causes people to pant as they strive for more air, and every so often to pause for a deep sigh (which more often than not is still shallow breathing as evidenced by a significant rise of the shoulders). These situations cause people to remain tight in the chest and become tense around the throat, shoulders, face and jaws. A common consequence of this tension is a 'shaky' voice.

When working with vocals the general rule is that shallow breathing is not considered to be acceptable, as it restricts the potential you have for effectively managing your vocal sounds.

Increasing your deep breathing

Take a deep breath while watching yourself in the mirror. Do your shoulders rise? If so, you are most likely practising shallow or clavicular breathing. Try to take a big lung full of air while shallow breathing. You should feel the breath being restricted by the rib cage which does not provide for any significant degrees of expansion; this is why your shoulders rise. This causes tension in the throat and neck muscles. The reason shallow breathing is sometimes referred to as 'clavicular breathing' is that it involves the clavicular or collarbone areas of the shoulders, which is why shallow breathing can lead to tension and muscle soreness around the shoulder and neck areas.

Developing a feel for deep breathing

One way to develop a feel for deep breathing is to face a wall and push against it as if pushing it down. Angle yourself into the wall, relax your shoulders and take a deep breath. You should feel the breath pushing into your lower ribs, almost as if the breath is trying to travel down into your buttock area. Now stand as if speaking to a group of people, take a deep breath and capture this same sensation of the breath travelling deep into your torso area towards the abdomen.

Another way to check deep breathing is to place your hands across your lower ribs, just below the breast area of your chest. Have your fingers touching just below the sternum. As you take a deep breath you should see your fingers come apart as your chest expands and your lower ribs come apart.

Look in the mirror again, and this time take a deep breath. You should see more of your abdomen area expand and minimal movement of your shoulders. With deep breathing you might well experience some movement in the shoulders but it should be slight. Another way to practise deep breathing is to take a deep and full breath and pant (like a dog on a hot day or after a quick run); you should feel movement only in the abdominal and diaphragm area.

Another thing to notice with deep breathing is your pulse rate. This should slow down during any periods of deep breathing, which is why this is a great method for controlling nervous energy when your pulse rate is racing.

Breathing—exhaling

People's normal breathing pattern, when not involved in speech or stressful situations, is one of a gentle and slow intake of air followed by a quicker outflow before a pause. To maximise the effectiveness of your breath and its role in assisting your vocals you need to reverse this cycle so that your out-breath is slow and controlled.

Practise being aware of your breath and notice your rate of in-breath and rate of out-breath. Practise taking deep breaths and then counting on the out-breath. Without straining and running out of breath what number did you get to? Now try to increase this number as part of a daily practice routine. For example, take a deep in-breath and slowly count to 10 on the out-breath. Next try for progressively longer out-breaths; for example, perhaps count to 15. Remember not to strain the voice in trying for higher numbers. Become aware of when you are running low on breath and finish speaking while you still have strength in your voice. In speaking aloud these numbers, aim for consistency in your sound and avoid any quivering sounds or any sense of straining your breath or sound.

Remember to breathe

It might sound silly but a number of people during bouts of nervousness literally forget to breathe. Getting into deep breathing as a habit allows your body to receive much more oxygen, to minimise any potential for experiencing periods of oxygen depletion, and to relax and get on with the task at hand.

ARTICULATION

Developing your ear is an important element to improving your voice and your articulation—critically listen to your voice and its projection. Also listen to actors, professional voice-over people and narrators, and to television and radio presenters. Raise your level of voice consciousness. Tape your voice and listen while speaking different pieces of writing, recalling a story from memory or describing an object—and listen to the differences.

Articulation of your voice is undertaken by your tongue, teeth, lips, and soft and hard palates, and the array of muscles, ligaments and cartilage in your facial area. Improving your articulation requires regular exercise of these parts of your body, and a vocal warm-up before you begin to lead your tour.

Your organs of articulation (speech organs)

Lips

Sound the following consonants: 'p' and 'b'. Notice that 'pressure' tends to build up behind the lips and is then released. This is why these are called plosive sounds. They are particularly noticeable when speaking into a microphone and result in a popping sound over the speakers. This can be avoided by speaking 'over' the microphone.

Teeth

Your teeth play an important role in the articulation of sound, whether they are involved directly such as when sounding the consonants 'g' and 's', or indirectly when they are used in conjunction with the tongue as in the sounding of 'l'.

As a point of interest 's' requires the finest coordination of your articulation organs. That is why it is the first sound to suffer from excessive alcohol consumption.

Soft palate

Sound the consonant 'k'. Feel where your tongue is touching the roof of your mouth—this is your soft palate area. The soft palate area adjoins and forms part of the air passage between the nose and throat.

Hard palate

Sound the consonants 'd' and 't'. Feel where your tongue is touching the roof of your mouth. This should be further forward in the mouth than when sounding the letter 'k', and this is your hard palate area.

Nasal sounds

Sound the consonant 'm'. You should notice that it produces a nasal sound, which involves the lips. Now sound the consonant 'n'. You should notice a nasal sound involving the hard palate and tongue (the tongue should feel as though it is touching an area slightly back from that when making a 'd' and 't' sound).

Practice

ACTIVITY: Sound the following words and notice which speech organs are in use:
Daily—loo—hall—boo—many—plum—butter—picked a peck of pickled pepper

Practise articulating a variety of vocal sounds each day. It is better to practise for short intervals on a regular basis than to practise for a long stretch on an infrequent basis, for example 20 minutes a day is better than one hour a week.

Select a passage and practise speaking it with the voices of different characters in various situations, for example:

● a person who is the centre of attention at a party;
● a senior executive presenting to major shareholders in a boardroom;
● a politician;
● someone sitting in a church;
● a spruiker selling goods on a busy street.

Tongue twisters are a great way to practise. Try the following:

● Peter Piper picked a peck of pickled pepper.
● Bibby Bobby bought a bat. Bibby Bobby bought a ball. With that bat he banged the ball.
● Sue sells seashells by the seashore. She saw a sea monster; she don't go there no more.
● Fresh fried fish, fish fresh fried, fried fish fresh, fish fried fresh.
● Sister Susie sews silk socks, seated serenely on the satin sofa.

VOCAL PROJECTION

When attempting to project your voice, avoid tension in your throat area which often happens as a natural consequence of trying to speak loudly. Remember to keep your throat open. One way to practise this and develop a feel for the sensation of an open throat is to go through the motion of a big yawn. Inhale a deep breath as you would for a yawn and when you exhale incorporate sound with your breath—any sound will do. Another way to assist your projection is to talk to an imaginary person beyond the last member of the audience—this ensures that everyone will be able to hear you.

You can also ensure adequate and effective vocal projection by facing your audience, and not looking at the ground or away from your audience (that is, with a twisted neck), and by ensuring your body is in a relaxed state (see opposite).

Looking after your voice

The working environment of Guides is perhaps one of the most challenging for the human voice, particularly when you are working outdoors and you have to contend with heat, dry winds, noise, gusty conditions and dust.

One of the most important considerations when looking after your voice is to remain alert to signals being provided by your body. These might include soreness in the throat and face, dryness of the mouth and throat, tightness of muscles around the neck and facial areas, and/or hoarseness of breath. If these symptoms appear, it is recommended that you take a period of rest from excessive vocal activity. Seek appropriate medical attention if you have any concerns about your voice. **It is strongly recommended that all Guides undertake appropriate vocal skills training.**

The following are a few tips to assist you in looking after your voice:

- Whenever possible avoid straining the voice on dry, windy and/or hot days. In periods of high wind remain alert to the possibilities of speaking to your group on the leeside of windbreaks such as buildings and coaches, or gather your group in close. Also avoid straining your vocal cords through screaming; volume can be achieved without screaming.
- The mouth and tongue are mostly lubricated with saliva while the pharynx and nasal passages are lubricated by mucus. These keep the vocal cords and resonators well-lubricated. You need to complement and assist this work of the body by taking regular sips of water (and, if appropriate, saliva-producing lollies such as lozenges—ask at a chemist). Soft drinks are not a substitute for water as they tend to dehydrate the body. Water is always the best option.
- Develop deep and controlled breathing using the diaphragm and abdominal muscles.
- Stay relaxed. Whenever you are presenting you should try to be in a relaxed state—relaxed in your face, jaws, shoulders, legs, spine and trunk. Depending on the presentation situation you should try to keep your knees unlocked whenever possible and adopt a relaxed stance. A physical warm-up to go with your vocal warm-up is strongly recommended. A relaxed body is a pleasure to be in.

- Warm up your vocal cords, lips, cheeks, tongue, jaw muscle, shoulders and spine (discussed on pages 99 and 104).
- Avoid milky substances before leading your tour group and/or making other presentations. These tend to line the throat and vocal organs, restricting their effectiveness.
- Ensure you have effective articulation, especially when you require volume, to minimise the restriction of vocal sounds and thereby reduce workload on the vocal cords and breath.

Relaxing for vocal projection

Tension in any part of the body can have a detrimental effect on the voice, usually restricting the range of vocal quality by constricting breath, tensing jaws and throat, and encouraging shallow or clavicular breathing. What you are after is a state of relaxed readiness from which you can speak with ease and project with confidence. A good/effective/powerful voice also comes in a strong, healthy posture.

The following checklist can be used to find and release areas of tension. Remember: *key word = relax*.

- *Neck and head*. Tension in the neck area can restrict the voice and breathing. You require a relaxed neck resting comfortably on your spine, and your throat needs to be open (try yawning to release muscular tension in the throat area).
- *Jaw*. This is a common area for tension. The jaw is important for breath and for the articulation of sounds and needs to remain relaxed. Try a gentle massage in the area where the jaw hinges with the skull and vocal warm-up exercises.
- *Shoulders*. These should be relaxed and able to hang freely without slumping. They should not be pulled back as if being called to attention. A pair of relaxed shoulders assists greatly with deep breathing; shoulders along with the jaw are a common area for stress.
- *Spine*. Avoid a slumped or bolt-upright position. Keep the spine relaxed. The spine not only influences breath and voice but also affects how you present yourself to an audience.
- *Upper chest*. Breathing should be able to flow 'through' the upper chest area; the area should be relaxed and not 'pulled up' as in the command 'stomach in, chest out'. Be aware of tightening in the chest when breathing (indicates upper chest breathing or tension in the upper chest area).
- *Stomach and abdominal areas*. Keep these areas relaxed, and avoid sucking in your stomach to 'mask' stomach flabbiness.
- *Legs*. Keep your legs relaxed with knees unlocked.
- *Feet and positioning*. Feet should be 'relaxed', evenly spaced and approximately shoulder width apart. You should feel balanced and in a state of alertness.

VOCAL CHARACTERISTICS/QUALITIES

Your voice is composed of a variety of qualities, all of which can be used to enrich and enhance your vocal sounds. These qualities include volume, pitch, emphasis, tone (soft, loud, rich and warm), intonation, volume (soft/hard) and enunciation.

Volume

Volume is the relative loudness or softness of your speech, sometimes related to strength of voice.

A loud voice can be useful for:

● gathering a group together;
● speaking to large groups;
● speaking over noise;
● speaking into strong winds.

Changes in volume can be useful in the following situations:

● You can focus attention. Changes in volume often attract focus from the group as it is a break from the normal volume. A soft voice used with control and confidence can be just as commanding as a loud and thunderous voice.
● You can enrich the moods you wish to convey. For example, by using a soft and light voice you can add mystique and suspense, and by using a loud voice you can add a sense of command.

When trying to speak loudly you need to be careful not to scream, as it is often not a controlled use of the voice and can result in damage to the vocal cords. A loud voice is one which utilises deep breathing, relaxed vocal cords, and an open and relaxed throat.

One way to maximise the relaxation within the throat area is to make a 'ha' sound and yawn. With the 'ha' sound feel the openness it creates; do it with a relaxed jaw and an open mouth, letting the sound pass out of the mouth on a gentle breath. You can also work with the 'ha' sound to check breathiness of your voice.

ACTIVITY: The following is one way to experience the difference. Find yourself a soundproof room or somewhere you can speak with reasonable volume. Try to speak at a loud volume, and notice if there is any tension in your throat area and if so where. Now yawn a few times—deep and breathful yawns. Capture the 'open throat' sensation generated by a yawn. With your throat relaxed and in this open state project your voice. Can you notice a difference? Does it sound different? Hopefully you will find that projecting your voice with a relaxed and open throat created minimal tension in your throat. You should also have noticed a change in the pitch and tone of your voice.

Working with your breath and keeping your throat open and relaxed will ensure you have a voice that carries.

During any loud voice work the demand on your vocal cords is high with an increased potential to cause them damage. One of the first signs of straining the vocal cords is a sore throat, which should be your cue to relax and seek other ways to convey your message. Repeated and lengthy periods of loud volume work should be avoided, especially in stressful environmental conditions—dry days, windy and dusty conditions, high traffic volumes and high smog days.

If you are unsure about whether or not your voice is carrying you can increase the range of your vocal projection by imagining your group as being further away by about half as much as they are and project to that imaginary line. For example, if the last person in your group is 5 metres away, imagine that person to be 7–8 metres away and project to that distance. When speaking at great volume, be careful that your voice is not so loud that your audience finds it hard to hear the words. Remember that your aim is to project your voice and not to scream or shout.

Pace

Pace is the speed at which you speak your words, with the average rate of speech being approximately 110 to 130 words per minute. This can vary depending on:

- your natural rate of speech;
- nervous energy—nerves usually increase your rate of speech;
- your intentions and any deliberate measures you take to evoke a particular response in your audience.

Pace can be altered by the:

- length of pauses you use;
- duration of these pauses;
- actual speed in which you articulate sounds.

We can work with pace for the following effects:

- to express different emotions, for example fast pace = excitement; slow pace = boredom, sadness and reflection;
- to describe a slow-moving activity, for example 'Now that you have heard the story you might well imagine how life would have ambled along for people living in this particular area'.
- to describe a fast-moving activity, for example 'With stealth and precision the soldier ants jumped to the defence of their nest!'

Ways to explore and develop a 'feel' for pace

Practise reading a set speech within different time periods. For example, write or select a piece of writing of approximately 100 words, and practise reading this passage within 45 seconds, 60 seconds, 30 seconds and 90 seconds. Play with these time variations and develop a feel for variations in rate of speech.

What do you notice about the different time periods? With each speed incorporate other vocal techniques. For example, for the slower rate of speech sprinkle some pausing and low tones.

Select different dramatic pieces and ascribe a particular emotion and feeling to each text. Next complement this feeling with varying rates of speech.

Pauses

Pauses are breaks in your speech. There are several types of pauses relating to how they are used and include:

- phrasing pause, which coincides with punctuation;
- breathing pause, which coincides with renewing breath;
- emotional pause, to enhance emotional effect;
- emphatic pause, to enhance the effect of a word or phrase.

An example of the use of pausing is: 'In this corner . . . (*pause*) . . . on this very bed . . . (*pause*) . . . she wrote out the last page of her diary.'

Pauses are used a great deal in poetry, along with emphasis. They can also be used when encouraging members of the audience to think and/or reflect, and to gather attention from the group. For example, if you are telling a group of people some important logistical information and a few people begin to speak out of turn in a disruptive manner, a short pause will often direct the group's attention to them and assist you to regain group focus.

Inflexion

Inflexion is the stress or kick or flick you give a particular word or phrase. It is similar to stressing examples below.

Pitch

Pitch relates to the frequency of vibration of the vocal cords; the highs, middles and lows of your voice; and the musical note. A lower pitch can be used to express sadness, remorse or respect while higher pitches generally reflect excitement or happiness. For example, 'You could hear the old lady shuffling her feet as she wandered the house searching for . . .' If you wanted to reflect a sense of sadness, this statement would be spoken in a lower pitch. The same applies to mystique, although to induce an element of suspense a higher pitch could be used.

Stressing

Stressing is related to intonation in that you stress certain words based on the meaning you wish to convey.

An example of working with 'stressing' can be seen in the following simple sentence: 'The *dog* sat in front of the fireplace.' The word 'dog' is stressed to indicate that it was the dog which sat in front of the fireplace and nothing else. It could indicate a sense of frustration that the dog had the cheek to place itself in front of the fireplace. But if you stressed the word 'fireplace' as in 'The dog sat in front of the *fireplace*', you would be indicating *where* the dog had sat.

You can also play with stressing by asking questions. For example, consider the following sentence: 'This artwork took 15 years to paint.' The meaning is changed when different questions are asked.

- Which artwork? *This* artwork took 15 years to paint.
- How long did it take? This artwork took *15 years* to paint.
- What medium was used? This artwork took 15 years to *paint*.

Intonation

Intonation is the rise and fall of pitch during speech, and is generally of two types—the rising tune and the falling tune:

- Example of falling tune: 'I want him taken over there at *once*' (spoken in a commanding voice the 'once' would be in a lower tone).
- Example of rising tune: 'Will you be joining *us*?' (said as a question seeking a 'yes' or 'no' response, the 'us' would be of a higher pitch).

Working with tone is an effective way to avoid a monotonous and dull voice. It is through tone of voice that you can express a great deal of meaning. For example:

- high tone—enthusiasm;
- rising tone—surprise;
- high tone spoken with slow pace—disbelief or questioning.

The tone of your voice relates to how the sound produced by your breath and vocal cords is modified by the body's resonators. These include your pharynx, mouth, sinuses and nasal areas, and to a lesser extent your chest. It is these resonators which provide volume, richness and tone to your voice.

Rhythm

Rhythm is related to pauses and to how you arrange vocal characteristics such as pitch, volume and pace. For example: '(*quick pace, mid-tone to high tone, mid-volume*) Sailing through fierce storms, with winds and waves lashing the boat, testing the tempers of each and every sailor . . . (*pause, next sentence with a drop in volume, pace and pitch*) it was at that moment that . . .'

Enunciation

Enunciation is the articulation and pronunciation of your words to ensure clarity, distinction and precision in your vocal sounds. Enunciation is used throughout your speech.

WARM-UP EXERCISES

It is highly recommended that you warm up your vocals, especially when working in extreme conditions; for example, on a windy, hot and dusty day; when leading a city sights walking tour with plenty of traffic; or a coastal walk with pounding surf and strong winds.

Some warm-up exercises include the following:

- Exercise your lips by blowing bubbles.
- Purse your lips and rotate them in an exaggerated movement to warm up your lips and cheeks.
- To exercise your cheeks, place your tongue behind your top teeth and speak; do the same with your tongue behind your lower teeth.
- Gently place your teeth together and speak with the teeth together.
- Open your mouth wide and stick out your tongue without it touching any part of your lips. You should feel a stretch of those tongue muscles within your throat.
- Yawning is an excellent warm-up. Also, the feeling you receive of an open throat is what you are after. You might have been told to open your mouth when you speak to people, which is great advice but it usually focuses on the front of the mouth (that is, around the lips) and you need to also open the rear of your mouth.
- Play with vocal sounds. Practise making various sounds, for example a steam whistle, choo choo train, plane flying overhead and animal noises such as bird calls.

Try to exaggerate the movements of your speech organs, being careful of undue strain. You should notice that these organs will become a little sore, which means you are exercising them in new ways. That is a good thing for their endurance and articulation prowess.

Special Focus

Interpretation at Taronga Zoo, Sydney

**An interview with *Steve McAuley* and *Genelle Sharrock*
with assistance from *Francis diLeva***

What is the background of Taronga Zoo?
Taronga Zoo and Western Plains Zoo are both managed by the Zoological Parks Board of New South Wales.

Taronga Zoo was first opened in 1916 after a number of animals were moved from a previous zoo site in Centennial Park. It is an area of approximately 33 hectares situated on the northern shores of Sydney Harbour at Mosman. Taronga Zoo is responsible for the care of over 2000 species of animals and another 400 species/subspecies—a number of which are classified as rare and/or endangered. Approximately 1.4 million people visit Taronga Zoo each year, some of whom take part in the variety of tour programs on offer. These include ZooRise Breakfast tours, VIP Aussie Gold Tours, Australian Walkabout Tours, and educational and special-interest tours by appointment.

Western Plains Zoo was opened in 1977 and is located in central western New South Wales, near Dubbo (approximately 500 kilometres northwest of Sydney). It is located on an area of approximately 300 hectares with a collection of over 1400 species and 130 species/subspecies. Approximately 300 000 people visit the zoo each year. Apart from self-guided activities, visitors can attend keeper talks, animal-feeding sessions, early morning walks and behind-the-scenes tours.

What does 'Interpretation' mean to you?

Interpretation is helping people to see what they're looking at. And in saying this, it is not restricted to the visual domain but rather it uses sensory cues to draw attention to a particular situation and to generate focus. Interpretation is knowledge plus observation; using these together helps in the communication process. It is also about ensuring that your tour programs are relevant to the situation.

An interpretive approach involves the above elements but brought together into a coherent story. That is, the tour flows.

What types of tours do you run at Taronga Zoo?

Taronga Zoo conducts a variety of tours including:

- tours of Australian animals;
- behind-the-scenes tours;
- general zoo tours as requested—which in most cases focus on Australian animals as well as animals from other parts of the world.

In running these tours do you have a prescribed route you follow?

No. We have a sequence of precincts we follow which depends on audience requests, but we adapt our specific tour route depending on animal activity and environmental conditions.

Who leads interpretive tours at Taronga Zoo?
Tours are led by:

- Zoo Friends volunteers (who number close to 400 people between Taronga Zoo and Western Plains Zoo);
- zoo keepers;
- education staff.

Tours are also led by ourselves (Steve and Genelle) and we are involved in developing and supervising the design and delivery of these tours.

What training programs are provided to staff who lead tours?
There are the two main training programs:

- Zoo Friends volunteer training program;
- Life Sciences Function Work Training program for the zoo keepers.

The volunteers go through an eight-week training program in tour-guiding techniques. Steve manages this program and believes that, apart from learning skills and knowledge, the program is extremely effective in building the self-esteem and confidence of all trainees. There are many instances where volunteers begin the training as frightened individuals, yet become quite confident public speakers and Guides.

A team approach is promoted throughout the training with trainees encouraged to learn from each other, and to extend their learning beyond the formalised training environment into the workplace.

We have predetermined messages which we provide during the training but we do not promote scripted commentaries. Such an approach makes it difficult for the tour to be truly interpretive as the zoo environment is so changeable.

This extends to the choice of theme for a tour which is generally determined by:

- request of audience;
- physical nature of the environment, for example if it is raining we might shift to a nocturnal animals tour and take advantage of the nocturnal houses which are undercover;
- level of activity of the animals.

We prefer people to identify and connect with their own styles, and then to build and foster this uniqueness as they develop their guiding skills.

The subject areas included in the training are:

- where to find information;
- encouraging people to learn from each other;

- working with silence;
- public speaking skills;
- combining observational skills with knowledge.

Once they complete their initial training and assessment both volunteers and keepers are provided with opportunities to extend their training into other areas; that is, they can undertake extension training. This involves intensive one-on-one training with the supervisor and training staff. This 'specialist training' generally focuses on getting close to animals so Guides need to be trained in animal-handling techniques.

Which major groups of people attend tours?
The major groups are:

- general visitors, which includes both Australian residents and overseas tourists;
- VIP tours;
- tours for people with special needs;
- corporate functions.

What do you hope people will gain from coming on your tours?
We would hope that people gain the following:

- sense of wonder;
- appreciation of the place of animals in the world;
- the beauty of animal adaptation and how this allows them to fit into this place;
- awareness of the importance of conservation.

If these are achieved, we believe it is because people are moved by the sheer presence of an animal, and by experiencing the smells, sights, sounds and in some cases touch of that animal. This experience is then enriched and made meaningful through the Guides and their use of stories which include personal anecdotes, facts, informed and focused observation skills, and interpretive skills.

How do you involve people on your tours?
- We relate to things they're familiar with.
- We encourage directed observations; for example, we might encourage people to 'look at the ears of the elephants'.
- We engage the senses. For example, at the Binturong Exhibit we stop the group and ask people, 'What can you smell?'—this is basically a stand-and-sniff activity. We then discuss people's responses and describe the smell which

is like fresh popcorn. We discuss how this smell is a special scent which dribbles from the anal gland and then stays among the vegetation to indicate where these animals have been and that they are ready to mate.

- If talking and working with kids, we crouch to their level.
- We also get people involved physically. For example, our animal presentations will sometimes include the opportunity for people to touch the animals. In these situations we ask people to put up one finger—people are then allowed to stroke the animal using one finger. Such an activity often brings an element of fun into the presentation while promoting respect for the animal.

What are some of the challenges you face when leading tours within the zoo environment?

Challenges include the following:

- *Working with animals*. Animals are living and respond to their own motivations. This means they might be out of view when we arrive with a group, or they could be asleep, or they could be awake but inactive. To manage these situations Guides need to be adaptable, flexible and able to think on their feet.
- *Turning non-communicators into communicators*. Potential Guides have the knowledge and enthusiasm, but to start with they do not necessarily have the communication skills.
- *The hilly terrain of Taronga Zoo*. People do not want to walk up and down hills so we have to plan tours accordingly. At Western Plains Zoo, tours are restricted to mornings and late afternoons during hot weather.
- *At Western Plains Zoo the tour is busbound*. People are picked up in a minibus and driven behind the scenes in the same bus. Guides need to manage the logistics of people being constantly moved on and off the bus. Sometimes people might get on the bus, only to travel for 50 metres before getting off again. Guides need to be quick to adapt when, after such situations, the animals are then out of view.

Who are the Three Interpreters?

There is a rumour that Taronga Zoo has a group of zoo keepers calling themselves the Three Interpreters. This rumour was confirmed by Steve and Genelle and the following was provided by Adam Battaglia who is one of these three interpreters.

We are three zoo keepers who expressed an interest in improving our guiding skills, after which we were selected to attend the first training course provided by the zoo's Life Sciences Function Work Training Program.

Until we attended this training course we were leading tours based on the odd skills and knowledge we picked up on the job—some of which were effective while others were less so. What we were keen to do was to improve and build the effective aspects of our tours.

And that's what the course provided. It provided us with the skills to manage those situations when we were stuck, when we 'knew' that the tour wasn't going quite right, and when we had to think on our feet and adapt in a hurry, and how to make a tour relevant and engaging for our participants. It also gave us a huge boost of self-confidence for delivering presentations, and provided us with the tools to build structure into our tour.

This structure means we now incorporate a planning aspect into our tours so that we know when we need props, what we are going to say and what themes we might follow, which exhibits we'll visit, and that a tour has a beginning and a middle and an end. I used to just let tours die at the end but now I feel I end with a solid wrap-up and with positive messages.

So why the name the Three Interpreters?

'The name started up after a party we all went to. I guess you had to be there!'

6

Planning and developing tour activities

What are the learning outcomes for this chapter?

By the end of this chapter you should be able to:
● Plan, research and develop a structure for tours.
● Establish the interpretive and commercial objectives of the activity.
● Plan and develop a tour to address the specific needs of an audience.
● Identify and demonstrate the planning, management and evaluation activities required for tours.
● Identify the need for the activity.
● Develop resources to support the activity.
● Identify and describe the stages of a tour.
● Identify strategies for implementing risk management and occupational health and safety procedures when planning and implementing tours.
● Incorporate learning styles when planning and delivering tours.
● Incorporate the concept of perception layering when planning and delivering tours.
● Incorporate creative thinking into the planning and delivery of tours.

TOUR STRUCTURES AND TOUR STAGES

Tours are extremely varied in their structure, purpose, audience group and the locales in which they take place. One of the consequences of this diversity is that there is no standard way of delivering a tour. They will be influenced by the characteristics of the components within the extremely dynamic guiding environment.

The following model is one approach for structuring tours which can be modified and adapted to suit most tour types. It follows the same structure as any good story; that is, the tour has a beginning, a middle and an end. And like the building of any good story it also includes a planning and preparation phase, and an evaluation phase.

Appendix 5 provides Tour Planning Sheets used by the Department of Conservation and Land Management WA.

Tour stages	When this occurs	Activities include
Planning and designing the tour	Prior to the scheduled activity	This stage includes all activities associated with the planning and preparation of the tour such as: ● Assess a tour brief. ● Develop tour objectives. ● Research. ● Design the tour—build the commentary, decide on the theme and message of your tour and develop tour objectives. ● Assess the tour itinerary, route and activities. ● Prepare logistical elements (e.g. obtain coach signs and meeting signs, check weather and other environmental considerations, and decide on contingency plans). ● Liaise with operators and other relevant people to gather as much information on your audience as is possible and appropriate including collecting passenger lists when relevant.

Tour stages	When this occurs	Activities include
Conducting the tour	Beginning stage	The beginning stage commences the moment you set out to your activity meeting point and leads into the middle stage of the tour. The beginning of the tour includes the following periods:
	Precontact	● Precontact period is for vocal and body warm-ups, and final checks of equipment (can occur before or at the activity starting point).
	Meet-and-greet	● This is the meet-and-greet and staging of your group for the start of the activity (occurs at the starting point).
	Welcome	● The welcome is the start of the activity, in which you outline the tour and provide relevant information and activities which frame the logistical aspects of the tour (occurs at the starting point).
	Middle stage	Occurs away from the starting point (that is, the site for beginning your tour). The middle stage of the tour has three parts—the introduction, body and conclusion.
	Introduction	● The introduction is when you begin to deliver your commentary and frame the significance of this particular tour.
	Body	● The body of the tour involves delivering the commentary and conducting activities which

Tour stages	When this occurs		Activities include
		Conclusion	support the theme of the tour; that is, it focuses on those elements which highlight the significance of this particular tour. ● The conclusion brings the commentary to a close, and wraps up any points of significance, especially the theme and messages. If possible, it is best conducted away from where you plan to end your tour.
	End stage	Farewell and goodbyes	This occurs either back at the starting point or some other activity exit point. The end stage is the logistical wrap and final closure of the tour and includes your farewells, the opportunity to promote other activities, and assisting people with forward arrangements.
Evaluating the tour	Upon completion of your tour		The evaluation stage is when you spend time reflecting on how the tour went. You ask questions which focus on both the positive and negative elements of your tour. What worked well? What did not work so well? What could be improved and how?

PLANNING AND DESIGNING THE TOUR

This phase of constructing your interpretive activity includes the following:
● Review the tour brief.
● Develop tour objectives. Why are you running this tour? What is the purpose of the tour?

- Research the needs of the people who will make up your audience and the stories you could tell, and liaise with operators and other relevant people to gather information about the planned tour.
- Build the commentary of your tour. Decide on the theme and message of your tour—what is it going to be about?
- Research and check the route and activity-sequence options.
- Develop and assess your tour itinerary. Decide on relevant activities for the tour. What resources might you require?

Planning

- Prepare logistical elements (e.g. obtain coach signs and meeting signs, check weather and other environmental considerations, and decide on contingency plans).

REVIEWING THE TOUR BRIEF

Tour briefs can be provided in a face-to-face meeting, over the phone or in written form such as faxes and electronic copies. The main purpose of a tour brief is to provide Guides with the relevant information to plan and deliver their tour. This information can include:

- procedures, itineraries and operational logistics of your tour, which might include information on attractions to visit, optional tours, accommodation, necessary and relevant documents, and modes of transport;
- background and characteristics of the tour group including number of people, origin of travel, whether they are travelling as part of a group, their socioeconomic and cultural background, language and interests, and whether there are any special needs and expectations;
- any special requirements for that particular tour;
- details of other people who might be involved in the tour;
- contact details for emergencies and procedures for the same.

After conducting the tour you might also be required to attend a debriefing session to assist with evaluating the tour. This might require you to complete a report which can be filled out at the end of your tour or more frequently on extended tours (especially with respect to reporting incidents which occur while the tour is in progress). These reports can document:

- compliments, complaints and/or any other feedback received by the Guide;
- mishaps or incidents;
- deviations to scheduled itinerary and why these occurred;
- suggestions for improving the operation of the tour.

Reports can also serve as a focus for any debriefing activities which take place after a tour.

WHAT ARE THE OBJECTIVES OF YOUR TOUR?

Tours are conducted for a variety of reasons, and knowing what these reasons are provides essential information when planning activities. To focus your planning efforts answer the following questions:

- Why are you running this tour?
- What is the aim of this tour?
- What do you want to achieve?
- How would you like your audience to be thinking, feeling and behaving?
- What would you like your audience to take away from your tour?

The responses to these questions help establish your objectives. The benefits of working with objectives include the following:

- Objectives provide a focus and direction for your tour planning and delivery efforts, on what it is you want to say, and on what you expect your audience to gain from the tour.
- They provide a benchmark for evaluating the tour.
- They ensure you are developing the most effective theme and tour activities for the needs of your tour.
- You are forced to work out what it is you are trying to achieve.
- They help you clarify what you plan as the desired state of your audience.
- They help you establish what level and depth of detail is required.
- They provide a focus for the practical, logistical and operational perspectives of your tour.

Objectives can be considered from both an operational and audience perspective. The following provide some thoughts and questions which you can ask yourself when developing objectives.

Objectives with reference to the operational aspects of the tour

The following objectives are relevant to the management operations of your tour. In thinking about these objectives you might ask yourself:

- How will you determine the pricing structure for your tour?
- What promotional material will your audience have read?
- How are you going to run the tour?
- What activities will you include?
- How will you ensure that environmental impacts are minimised?

These operational objectives might need to be aligned with relevant policies and external management frameworks. For example, the *Great Barrier Reef Marine Park*

Tourism Operators Handbook (December 2000) introduces and promotes the concept of best environmental practices for activities (such as guidelines for fish feeding, turtle watching, and waste and sewage disposal) conducted within the marine park (not just while in or on the water, but including the associated coral cays and continental islands). As a tour operator working from this handbook the principles associated with this concept would need to be incorporated within your tour.

Objectives with direct reference to the audience
Knowledge (cognitive) objectives
These objectives relate to what knowledge you would like your audience to learn from your activity. In thinking about knowledge objectives you could ask yourself:

- What knowledge do you want to share with your audience?
- What anecdotal information can you provide your audience?
- What would be important orientation information to assist their visit?
- What ideas do you want your audience to consider about the event and/or place you are visiting?

Behavioural (skill) objectives
These objectives relate to how you want your audience to behave, both during your tour and after your tour, and what skills you want your audience to gain. In thinking about behavioural objectives you could ask yourself:

- How are you going to get your audience involved?
- How will you facilitate their learning of skills; for example, how will they be able to identify birds, recognise architectural styles or appreciate a particular work of art?
- What respectful behaviour will you expect from your audience?
- What behavioural ground rules will you put in place?

Emotional (affective) objectives
What emotions and feelings do you hope your audience will experience both during and after the tour? In thinking about emotional objectives you could ask yourself:

- How will you ensure they enjoy themselves and are left with feelings of contentment?
- How will you generate excitement?
- How are you going to facilitate a positive experience for the visitor?
- How will you evoke relevant feelings, for example suspense, curiosity, respect or wonder?
- How will you ensure people appreciate the sites visited during the tour?
- How will you generate a willingness to find out more about the messages you share with your audience?

Writing objective statements

For your objectives to be effective you need to express them using statements that show the objectives to be:

● measurable;

(*Note*: It is sometimes difficult to write affective objectives which are measurable and observable, as the affect of the tour might not be evident until after the tour finishes.)

● observable;
● written with verbs which are clear and specific;
● realistic;
● written using positive statements, for example 'will be able to' and 'to encourage'.

Consider the following two objectives related to the same tour:

● Objective A: People will have fun on my tour.
● Objective B: I will provide a variety of humorous stories, games and interactive, light-hearted activities.

The first objective (A) is weak. While you could observe 'fun on your tour' the objective is difficult to measure, it lacks clarity and it is not specific. However, the second objective (B) addresses the criteria of an effective objective outlined above, and is a much stronger and workable objective.

Effective objective statements include words such as:

● *Identify* the different periods in history.
● *Explain* the difference between a wet forest and dry forest.
● *Describe* the process of pollination.
● *Illustrate* what life was like during the early period of European settlement.

Examples of objectives

Here are some examples of the different types of objectives:

● knowledge objectives:
   —to explain the periods of occupation of a historic building;
   —to describe the different habitats of a particular national park,
● behavioural objectives:
   —to ensure participants will observe the ground rules of the tour;
   —to give people the skills to be able to identify the features of a building and their associated architectural style;
● emotional objectives:
   —to foster within people support for the goals of your organisation;
   —to encourage people to value the unique and significant characteristics of the site;
● operational objectives:
   —to utilise effective communication skills to build relationships and foster rapport with your audience;
   —to operate in a manner which is consistent with minimal impact practices.

Deciding on a list of objectives

The idea with objectives is not to create a long 'wish list' but to create a tight 'must-do list'—activities which you consider to be essential to running your tour in an efficient, effective and professional manner.

Once objectives are set they should not be considered as the end point of a process. Instead, they need to be revisited, rewritten, deleted, assessed and evaluated as appropriate.

ACTIVITY: Select a site suitable for a tour, for example a national park, historic house or city landscape. You are about to design a two-hour tour of this site. Write a set of objectives for this tour.

DESIGNING THE TOUR

Finding out about your audience

Information on your audience might arrive through a briefing sheet or booking sheet, or it might involve quite extensive research (refer to pages 45–6). Whatever the degree of effort, you have to make sure that you find out as much as possible about the needs, expectations, motivations and interests of people within your audience. Your audience is an extremely varied group of people, and the more time you spend finding out about these people, the more chance you have of building a tour which will be relevant and enjoyable to each individual.

Building the commentary

This stage involves developing the commentary element of the tour which occurs during the middle stage of your tour. An outline of the process involved in building a tour commentary is given on pages 168–81.

A commentary works in closely with your tour objectives and itinerary, and incorporates the variety of activities you plan for your audience. Considerations when developing your commentary include the following:

● Have you developed a theme for your activity—a single statement that encapsulates what the tour is about? Have you prepared a skeleton for your commentary which builds on this theme and which includes your key ideas and messages? Have you fleshed out these main points? Have you broken the information into digestible chunks? One technique to achieve the latter is to work with the headline-and-point technique.

● Why you are saying what you are saying? Is it to make a point? Is it just to fill in time? Is it connected to the other parts of your commentary and tour? Will it be of benefit to your audience and to the environment?

- Do you need to research any particular areas to improve your knowledge? Even if you answer 'no' to this question, always seek to improve your knowledge. Spend time researching and learning new facts and figures. Search out relevant journals, organisations, councils and other government organisations, the Internet and libraries. Develop a database of fascinating trivia, points and anecdotes.
- Will you be interspersing facts and statistics with stories, anecdotes and activities?
- What resources and/or equipment and/or props and/or reference material can you bring along on the tour? What sites will you be visiting?
- What guiding techniques will you employ?
- How will you be involving the group and encouraging interaction and participation? Have you researched the needs, motivations and possible expectations of your audience? Do you know who will be in your audience? (Refer to Chapter 3, 'Your audience'.)

RESEARCHING AND CHECKING THE ACTIVITY ROUTE

This is when you are working with the environment and making sure the site is suitable for conducting your activity. It is the time you spend finding out about the area you will be working in, and exploring it from a variety of perspectives and aspects. This might involve liaising with relevant organisations responsible for managing the area(s) relevant to your tour route.

Some of the questions you can ask include:

- What is the route for the activity?
- What are some of the significant features and characteristics of the site? Is there anything of interest? What are some of the highlights of the route?
- What sites will you be visiting and are they interesting, adequate and relevant?
- Is it suitable for the characteristics of your audience (their needs, expectations, interests, and for the number of people)?
- What is the accessibility like—is there provision for people with special needs?
- What comforts are there—plenty of shade if a summer activity, and plenty of rest stops if leading a group of seniors or people with physical disabilities?
- What services are there? Especially if the tour will go for quite a while it may be best to meet where there are services.
- What safety concerns are there? Have you conducted a risk audit? For example, if you are conducting a bushwalk and there have recently been extremely strong winds, there might be the potential for hanging tree limbs and dangerous tree limbs. What arrangements have you made in case of emergencies? (Refer to the section titled 'Occupational health and safety, risk management and liabilities' later in this chapter.)

Can you use any special features and characteristics of the site to captivate your audience? For example, Guy Patching conducts tours of the Quarantine Station in Sydney. His first stop is at a point in the station where he can take advantage of the views west over the Quarantine Station headland, across the harbour and towards the city of Sydney. At this stop he asks his visitors the following questions: How long did it take you to get here and how did you travel here? He then compares these times and means of transport with those of the period when the Quarantine Station was constructed. He asks people to look out over the landscape and begins his commentary with the following: 'As we look out over the harbour we get a feel for how far away we are, and it was this isolation which led to this site being chosen as the Quarantine Station. I invite you to come with me as we explore the history of the Quarantine Station.'

Be sensitive to your environment; listen to the opportunities it provides and which you can incorporate into your tour.

Creative imagination defined: I put the first brush stroke on the canvas. After that, it is up to the canvas to do at least half the work.
James Brooks—painter

THE TOUR ITINERARY—INCORPORATING ACTIVITIES INTO YOUR TOUR

Itineraries are your tour 'blueprint'. They provide the logistical and operational framework for your tour and include details such as timings, dates, routes, stops and length of stops, and information on the types of attractions and accommodation establishments. Ensure that all these details are correct, practical and relevant to your tour. The types of activities which you include in your itinerary should support your theme and tour objectives, and work in with your timings. Ask yourself:

- What activities have you planned? Where will the stops take place? Can you mix up your transport options by including public transport with walking, or arranging for coaches to pick up at different destinations?
- What are some of the points of interest and highlights of the tour?
- What resources and/or equipment and/or props and/or reference material can you bring along on the tour?
- Are the timings strict or do you have some flexibility to take advantage of spontaneous moments?
- Do you provide for moments of tension and release? Do you provide active periods as well as passive periods? Do you provide variations in the style of activities?

PREPARING AND CHECKING LOGISTICAL COMPONENTS/ELEMENTS

If you receive a tour brief then you should check that you understand all the information provided. You should also check that the information in the brief corresponds with that provided in any promotional materials, and that it is accurate and relevant to your tour (e.g. check the itinerary against that being provided to the visitor).

You might also need to do the following:

- Reconfirm details of your tour.
- Finalise some aspects of the tour.
- Familiarise yourself with any optional tours.
- Ensure you have relevant contact details and sources of assistance in case of emergencies.
- Prepare contingency plans for the unexpected and spontaneous, and allow enough flexibility in your approach to incorporate such moments.
- Check any equipment and props—not just that they are working but that you know how to use them. Props can include spotlights for evening walks, reference books, old/new photos, anecdotes, poems/stories, magnifying glasses and artefacts.
- Check the weather map, or make provision for checking it before the activity starts.

Liaising with other industry colleagues

Find out who else will be involved in this tour and undertake the proper liaison (e.g. coach captains, retail store owners, tour operators, attraction staff and other Guides).

Most tours will require you to collect a passenger list, booking sheet or other record of people attending your tour. When working with prepackaged tours you might also be provided with an itinerary.

In working with inbound markets check whether there are any specific conditions that need to be investigated, for example Approved Destination Status from the People's Republic of China. As a point of interest Australia was the first Western country to be awarded Approved Destination Status, which allows leisure tourists from China to visit Australia via a special visa arrangement.

Rehearsing and practice run

Do a practice run of the activity and rehearse your presentation skills.

 ACTIVITY: Working with the Australian Museums and Galleries Online website select a heritage-based attraction (from the home-page menu select 'Guide to Museums', select the website URL's option and then select an attraction). Choose an attraction outside your home state, and from a subject area outside your normal field of interest. For example, you might be interested in the cultural heritage of Victorian towns yet choose the 'Age of Fishes Museum in NSW'. Using the information provided (including contact details for obtaining additional information) develop a 60-minute tour of your chosen attraction. The tour needs to include a topic, a theme and an outline of the information presented as a series of 'must knows' using the 'headline and point' format.

What are some of the limitations of conducting research when there is no opportunity to visit an attraction and/or site? How can you manage these limitations? When would you need to conduct such research 'from a distance'?

CONDUCTING THE TOUR

Running the tour

BEGINNING STAGE
This stage of your tour includes the following periods:

- precontact period (can occur at or away from the activity starting point);
- meet-and-greet and staging (occurs at the activity starting point);
- welcome and the start of the activity (occurs at the activity starting point).

Precontact period
This is the time spent before your audience arrives. It provides you with an opportunity to warm up your vocals, check your appearance, check your equipment and generally get yourself into a relaxed state.

Whenever possible arrive at your activity site at least 20 minutes before the scheduled meeting time. Even more time is needed if you have to organise any logistical activities such as checking and gathering equipment. Ideally, equipment should be checked at the end of previous activities just in case something needs repairing.

If there is more than one leader, decide who will be undertaking what part of the tour and how you will be working together. The same applies if you are working with a coach—you should liaise with the coach captain as to the proposed route and timing of the tour, making sure your respective itineraries correspond. Coach captains are also a great source of anecdotes and other interesting information which can be incorporated into a coach-based tour. (*Note:* Coach captain is used as a generic term and not all drivers go by this name—other names include Driver-Guides, bus driver and driver. Liaise with your coach captain as to his or her preferred title.)

Meet-and-greet and staging

This period begins at the first moment of contact with any member of your audience and continues as you gather the group for the start of the tour (this latter activity is often referred to as the staging of your group). During this period you get to know your audience, check your research and validate your thoughts and planning efforts, and (based on your assessment) readjust the tour to suit the current situation.

At the same time your audience will be getting to know you, and assessing your capabilities, attitudes and personality. Use the time to establish your credibility, to create a warm and friendly atmosphere, to put people at ease, and to set the scene for an enjoyable time.

It is during this period that your audience begins to interface with the environment.

Greet people as they arrive at the activity site. During this period you might check people against a passenger or booking sheet to ensure that all people who have booked are present. You might also need to follow up on any missing persons.

You should also check the following: Are people on the right tour? Have they undertaken all the necessary requirements? Do they know that they are leaving and not returning for a few hours . . . or several hours? Have they made the necessary arrangements and toilet stops? Are they wearing the appropriate clothing? Are they carrying the appropriate gear? Are there any alarm bells with regard to medical conditions? What about potentially challenging individuals who were dragged along

Meet-and-greet

to the activity by their parents or by their spouse? Is anyone in the group beginning to express concerns, special interests or challenging expectations?

Find out whether there are knowledgeable people within the group who might be able to share their expertise at relevant points during the tour.

It is also an opportunity to listen to the 'language' of your group, and their level of understanding of the concepts and ideas you will be exploring and discussing. Bring a couple of terms into your conversation and assess people's responses—do they already know the terms? Do they ask you for an explanation? What is their topic of conversation?

It might be at this point that you need to speak to people if they are not suitably attired. For example, if you are leading a hiking trip through a remote area and someone turns up wearing sandals then it would be advisable to talk to that person and assess whether he or she has other footwear. Any personal issues involving individuals, such as inappropriate footwear, is best undertaken on a one-to-one basis. And if you do refuse someone from a tour, give your reason.

Encourage people to meet each other. For lengthy tours you might introduce a few ice-breaker activities to encourage a degree of social interaction before the tour gets under way, or on a coach for extended tours.

It is an opportunity for both yourself and the audience to confirm necessary logistical information about the tour, and to consider the capabilities of your group.

Welcome and start of activity

The welcome presentation component of your tour begins at the staging area. It is here that you gather people together and welcome them as a group. It is important that you start on time, even if you are still waiting for latecomers or if there has been a hitch in operations.

Let people know what's going on. For example, 'Hi everyone, it's 9 am which is the start time for our activity. We are still waiting on a few people, so I hope you will be okay if we wait another five minutes before getting under way.' This way, you have at least acknowledged those people who did arrive on time.

The practice of timeliness is even more important with extended tours as you need to establish the habit early that being on time means being on time, and when you say be back at the coach by 2 pm that you mean 2 pm. If you are lax with your times, people will develop a corresponding habit of being lax as well.

As part of the welcome presentation, mention your name and also that of any other persons who might be working with you on the tour (e.g. coach captains, other Guides and on-site staff). While you might have discussed the above information with individuals it is best to confirm with the whole group. With extended tours or multisite tours you might have to cover again selected elements of the above at each site. You may include the following information (as relevant and appropriate):

- Give a very brief background of yourself, for example 'I've been working in this museum for five years and over that time have worked with quite a lot of the displays. Today I will be taking you to what I believe to be some of the unique and more fascinating displays'.
- State your location. For example: 'Welcome to Billymort's Cottage, home to five generations of gold miners'; 'Welcome to today's walking tour of The Rocks' or 'Welcome to our little town of Reddyduster. I've heard that you've been on that bus for three hours to get here today, so I'm going to make sure you have one of the best tours you've ever experienced, and give you a few tales to talk about on the return trip'.
- Provide orientation details such as services and facilities. Some meeting points might have several tours departing at the same time, so it is best to check that people are on the right tour.
- Outline the tour and any points of interest worth mentioning about the significance of the site.
- Outline how long the activity will take and when you are due back. If appropriate and practical use a map to indicate the route of the tour and adjoining areas, so that people gain an idea of where they are going. Explain the route they will be taking and any difficult sections, and make sure they have the necessary gear and equipment.
- If it is a car-based activity remind people to check that their cars are locked and valuables are left out of sight.
- Identify any ground rules people might need to observe; try as much as possible to stay in the positive by telling people what you want them to do rather than not to do. For example, if you do not want people to pick wildflowers then think of a positive alternative you want them to do; perhaps it is to encourage people to smell the flowers, observe the florets, look at the variety of flower shapes and types, notice the insects which frequent the flowers, and to leave the flowers as they found them.
- If you are working on a site (e.g. mine site or waste transfer station) with specific ground rules, these will need to be provided to your audience.

This period of your tour is primarily concerned with welcoming people and providing the relevant logistical information. It is about bringing individuals together as a

group, grounding them so they are ready for the activity, and setting the mood and tone of the tour.

You should also do a head count, especially for adventure-based activities such as snorkelling, canoeing and hiking. And keep doing your head counts throughout the tour.

It's also important to continue putting people at ease and building rapport between yourself and individuals, between yourself and the audience as a group, and among the individuals within the audience. There are various ways to get people to feel at ease including the following:

- Display a friendly, encouraging and engaging attitude.
- Ask questions related to where people are from and whether anyone has visited the area previously, or if it is an early morning walk ask what time people woke up to be there that morning.
- Use humour, for example for a city walking tour you could say, 'I would like the group to stay together. As we will be going past several pubs I would like to know how many people I might expect to finish the tour, as those pubs might just create the temptation for this tour to become a self-guided tour'.
- Incorporate activities, for example if you've managed to establish a positive and friendly feel among the group then, after you finish your introductions and before you lead people in the activity you could say, 'If you all could rub your hands together and say after me—"Gee I'm looking forward to this tour"'. BridgeClimb gather people and have them introduce themselves by name and suburb. Climb leaders are trained to remember names so they can refer to people by name throughout the climb which enriches the personalised experience.
- Use personal words such as 'you' and 'everyone' or refer to people's names.

MIDDLE STAGE

The middle stage of your tour is when you focus on the significance of this particular tour. It includes three periods—the introduction, body and conclusion. In this way it differs very little from any presentation.

Introduction

This is the point of your tour when you begin to deliver your commentary and focus on the theme of the tour (discussed on pages 170–9).

For example, if conducting an activity with a habitat theme, this would be where you start introducing the concept of habitats.

> As I mentioned before, Scribbly Waters National Park is a special reserve because it still has areas of vegetation which are largely intact and relatively undisturbed. It is within these areas, or remnants, that we can find an amazing variety of habitats— places where animals can find food, shy away from predators and build a home. For people a habitat might be a suburb which provides shops, open fields and houses. Each species of animal has a liking for a certain habitat. During this creepy walk we will be spying out those little critters which have a liking for living in the microhabitat end of town.

Whenever possible begin the tour away from, but still within site of, the staging area in case there are latecomers, and attempt to stop where there is an interesting and relevant object to share with the group.

Body

This period of the tour can provide some of the most challenging yet rewarding moments.

During the body of the tour you promote the theme of your tour and deliver your key ideas and messages. You flesh out the tour with anecdotes and other stories, activities and relevant information.

You should also seek to involve and engage people by asking questions such as:

● What did you notice about the change in the environment over the last 100 metres?
● What do you think caused this change?
● What do you think caused this erosion in the landscape?

- How might people have spent their time?
- How do you feel about this area?

Interrelate experiences. For example, imagine you are leading a tour in south-eastern Queensland which is focusing on habitats. You have already talked about the western mountain slopes being drier than the eastern and southern mountain slopes, and have highlighted the differences in vegetation types between the different slopes. You could then stop the group, and ask them to work out which direction the slope faces by using the information just provided.

People do not just receive information from you. They are receiving a continual stream of information from the environment during the periods between scheduled stops, so encourage environmental listening. Give people ideas and activities to try between stops such as comparisons between areas, which can then be discussed at the next stop. Information which has already been presented could then be applied to the next period of the activity. Encourage people to become aware of relationships between areas visited during the activity and also stimulate them to engage their senses. Also provide opportunities for people to be alone with their own experiences.

Utilise the unexpected and spontaneous. If possible weave them into the theme and story of your activity. Complement the content of your tour with appropriate vocal variations and non-verbal expressions such as those discussed in Chapters 4 and 5. Use descriptive verbs together with expressive and active phrasing (discussed in Chapter 7).

Be aware of opportunities to present information on the same subject but from differing spaces. For example, in Towlers Bay within Ku-ring-gai Chase National Park there are two concrete slabs which represent the remains of two houses from the Depression era. One approach which works at this site is to present the objective, factual information at the first slab. This sets the historic context for the site. The second slab is then used for reflective activities and for encouraging people to imagine life in the area.

Mix up the activities and content being delivered within the commentary. Work with stories, bring along props, tell anecdotes and share stories.

Conclusion

Highlight key concepts made during the tour with a series of points. Bring the tour to a close. Wrap up with a conclusive statement which encapsulates the theme and messages you were trying to promote. Thank people for attending the activity. Provide initial closure for the activity.

129

END STAGE

This occurs at the activity exit point and provides the final closure. It is an opportunity to promote other activities and tours, answer questions, and thank people again for attending. Ask whether people enjoyed your activity and if so what specific elements they liked.

Once the tour is completed you might need to complete any tour report forms, check and store equipment, and undertake other logistical procedures. Information on the quality of the tour should be forwarded to relevant people as soon as possible, for example any minor accidents, any complaints, potential hazards which were noted during the tour, suggestions for improvements and any unusual incidents.

EVALUATING THE TOUR

This occurs as soon as practical after the tour has finished. It is an extremely important period of any tour however short or long. Spend some time reviewing the activity. How did it go? What worked and why? What didn't work and why not? Could it have been improved? Did the tour achieve what you wanted it to achieve? Check your written objectives. Start a reflective diary that is yours and yours alone— so you can be as truthful as you like!

REASONS FOR EVALUATION

Evaluation is useful for a range of reasons including:

- brings about improvements;
- assesses the worth and value of a particular activity;
- provides a means of comparison;
- provides ongoing information as environmental and operational elements change;
- provides feedback;
- helps maintain quality control;

- enables you to constantly monitor and improve tour components;
- improves consistency of the level of service;
- enhances the level of service above customer expectations;
- enables you to measure your tour against your objectives (are you achieving your objectives and are your objectives achievable, or do they need to be revised?).

AREAS TO EVALUATE

There are a number of areas which can be evaluated including:

- logistics surrounding the tour including bookings, liaison with audience and liaison with colleagues;
- audience response and impression of the tour;
- Guide's response and impression of the tour;
- how effectively the tour was conducted;
- how useful was the equipment;
- assessment of resources and equipment (any defects or breakdowns, mishaps or positive experiences?).

When conducting a more formal evaluation you need to ask yourself: What is it I want to know and why do I want to know it and what is the best way to obtain it? With the latter you could undertake:

- questionnaires;
- interviews;
- checklists;
- group feedback and discussion;
- observation of audience behaviour;
- logs and itinerary checks;
- surveys.

If your audience are to be involved in any formal evaluation try to do this as soon as possible after the tour.

One approach is to construct an evaluation checklist matrix such as the one given on page 132.

Activity	Very good	OK	Needs improvement	Comments
Appropriate dress of Guide				
Starting and ending on time				
Welcoming people and putting them at ease				
Keeping audience interested				
Presented in a positive and enthusiastic manner				
Clarity of messages and ideas				

Others items which you could include in such a matrix are:
- appropriate activity stops and sites;
- planning for and managing diversity within your audience;
- respect for the sites and people visited;
- safety and security of your group;
- involvement of people in your presentation;
- vocal variety in your presentation;
- clear tour structure—beginning, middle and end;
- people challenged to look at things in new ways—'imagine if' and 'what if' rather than just giving a description of something;
- revealing the significance of the tour;
- use of props, specimens, artefacts, photos and drawings to illustrate concepts, facts and other aspects of the commentary;
- a flexible attitude to handling contingencies as they came up.

You could also ask yourself the following questions to promote an extended response:

- How do you feel the tour went?
- Was the audience what you expected? If not, how could you have planned differently and prepared differently? How else could you have found out about your audience?
- What do you feel were the positive moments of the tour?
- What do you feel people gained from the tour?
- What would you do differently next time?

ACTIVITY: Think about the evaluation checklist matrix and list what a Guide would need to do to achieve a ranking of 'Very good', 'OK' or 'Needs improvement' in each category.

ACTIVITY: Try the following quiz.
● What are tour objectives?
● Why would you incorporate objectives into your tour?
● What are the key points of a tour objective?
● What is the role of a theme?
● Why would you work with themes?
● What's the difference between a theme and a topic?

OCCUPATIONAL HEALTH AND SAFETY, RISK MANAGEMENT AND LIABILITIES

It is not the role of this book to provide an in-depth coverage of legal and insurance-based issues. Rather it is recommended that you seek professional legal advice by contacting one of the professional Tourist Guide bodies (details in Bibliography) that should be able to recommend a legal profession specialising in guiding and other tourism activities.

In essence a tour is a contract between two or more parties—a tour provider (tour operator/tour guide/tour leader), the relevant audience (client/visitor/customer) and/or an attraction, site or other organisation. This contract can be written or verbal, and consists of a variety of both implied and stated obligations to ensure the following:

● The safety and well-being of all parties is protected.
● The tour delivers what it promises to deliver.
● The tour is conducted within a legal and ethical framework.
● All tour conditions which are stated in any operational and/or legal documents are adhered to.
● All people involved with the tour behave responsibly—it is important for your audience to realise that they also have an obligation to themselves, to others and to you and your respective organisation.

The obligations of the tour provider include the following:

● Manage occupational health and safety issues.

- Liaise with relevant organisations to obtain appropriate approvals and operating frameworks.
- Implement a duty of care which includes adopting risk-management procedures.
- Manage liabilities which includes:
  —make audience aware of terms and conditions;
  —ensure there are no hidden extras;
  —fulfill expectations;
  —manage any unexpected incidents within the stated terms and conditions.

Special Focus
Managing occupational health and safety issues

Kerrie-Anne McPhee
International tour manager and professional Tour Guide

In the basket of skills and talents possessed by the Tour Guide should be an awareness of occupational health and safety (OHS). This means Guides should consider health and safety aspects in the working environment which pertain to themselves and their customers.

In previous times, the term 'commonsense' has been used to suggest that through the home environment, education and life experiences, an individual would develop the knowledge and skills necessary for living, working and socialising. This was often presumed to include most, if not all, mental and physical ability required to exist and operate effectively and safely in a local or known environment, according to the particular stage in the individual's life. This presumption often disallowed for different cultural, social and environmental influences. In today's multicultural society and ever-changing world, we are becoming increasingly aware that the 'common' part of this term may be much more diverse than previously thought. The result is a need to clearly communicate information as it relates to particular situations and circumstances.

Communicating information to groups or individuals regarding health, well-being, safety and hazards is becoming an increasing responsibility within the role of the Guide or tour manager. The inclusion of a statement in the small-print section of a brochure or flyer is less frequently being regarded as sufficient explanation to cover the aspects that may be encountered on tour. Guides and tour operators are diligently striving to provide positive and memorable experiences for their customers, and this may include venturing into areas infrequently accessed by the public and void of facilities. These points, coupled with the further development of Australian Industrial Law, and the resulting update of corporate and individual responsibilities, have contributed to the growing need for all parties to clearly comprehend and operate within consequent operating procedures developed to support and comply with legal and industrial regulations and obligations. For Guides this means—learn about where you are touring and keep your people appropriately briefed!

Is it time for the Tour Guide or tour manager to shake in their shoes at the thought of becoming an 'OHS expert'? Not quite. Positions do exist in government and industry for officers and specialists in this field. For Guides, however, the vital requirement is to achieve an awareness of OHS and how it applies to their particular role.

Anyone who has worked or travelled on an aircraft or cruise vessel will be familiar with printed material and safety briefings provided on equipment and evacuation procedures. This approach is sometimes (but not as uniformly) adopted for touring coaches and motor vehicles. To a lesser extent information is available on vehicles such as trains, buses and trams—there is often a sign or printed instruction indicating emergency exits, or equipment such as fire extinguishers and brake activators. This latter approach is also applied at locations such as sites, attractions, accommodation and transport terminals, where emergency exits and equipment are identified by signs or instructions. Therefore, we have regular access to relevant OHS information without necessarily realising it, and it's part of the role of Guides to highlight important points to their customers.

Consider this scenario. If a Guide was to assume that everyone will experience the tour in a healthy and safe manner because all customers readily understand and notice OHS information, and because the group is only visiting one site, for example a historic building, what happens when the Guide leads the group across a road from the coach stop to the building and the last two members of the group—American tourists who have managed to straggle behind everyone else—look in the wrong direction to check traffic (which at home in the United States is the correct direction)? How safe is everyone now at this one site?

In between leaving OHS knowledge and understanding to your customers and mentioning where to place every step at each site is the role of the Guide in developing awareness and managing OHS issues, similar to aircrew—it is part of the service delivery.

So what does the Guide need to be aware of in regard to OHS? The Guide needs to be aware of the following:

- requirement to operate in a manner appropriate for OHS;
- operating procedures for OHS;
- first-aid requirements;
- risk management;
- information updates.

REQUIREMENT TO OPERATE IN A MANNER APPROPRIATE FOR OHS

Occupational health and safety legislation has been developed in Australia with the aim of preventing work-related injuries, and identifying rights and obligations of relevant parties. Guides need to be aware of the requirements to operate in a manner that is safe for themselves and their customers.

So what tools do you need in your kit to integrate OHS into your tour? You need the following:

- general knowledge of requirements for the site, local area and country;
- knowledge of the industry and company requirements;
- ability to operate in a reasonable and responsible manner appropriate to the guiding role;
- skill in effectively communicating briefing information, and addressing situations as they occur;
- awareness of where and how to seek assistance when required;
- understanding of related documentation and processing procedures.

Some organisations provide scripted OHS briefing information to Guides for communicating to customers prior to, or within the early commencement of, the tour. If this is not available, it is recommended that the Guide cover key OHS information at this time; additional details can be added as they become relevant.

It is essential that this briefing be delivered in a responsible way; to make light of it may undermine the importance and to overemphasise it may cause unease. The information is intended to assist your customers in preparing for their experience, and the objective is for everyone to have a positive and memorable tour—in a safe and healthy manner. Briefings should be constructed in a positive manner and integrated into the commentary. It should be delivered as an important component, rather than as the dominant element that overshadows the theme and subject content.

ACTIVITY: Consider the following two examples. Identify what key points are included in both briefings, and then decide which briefing you prefer and why.

Guide A

Our walk today commences here at the Visitor Information Centre. It will take us along the marked pathway through the Botanical Gardens, and we will cross a pedestrian footbridge to reach our final destination—the garden café. The tour duration will be 45 minutes, the pathway is flat and shaded, and your support is requested in protecting this significant area by keeping yourself and all items within the designated pathway. Please stay with me throughout the walk, and should you need to leave the tour before the end please let me know. Refreshment, toilet and first-aid facilities are available in both the Visitor Information Centre and the café. If you have any questions during the tour, please ask me. Welcome to our walk and I hope you enjoy it.

Guide B

We are about to start the walk. By the way I have to tell you these points:

● Don't leave the path.
● Don't touch the plants or animals.
● Don't drop anything in the gardens.
● Don't trip when you walk.
● Stay out of the sun to avoid sunstroke.
● Don't stray from the group.
● Don't cross the road; use the footbridge.
● There are no refreshment, toilet or first-aid facilities in the gardens; if you need them they are in the Visitor Information Centre or the café.

We'll be finished in 45 minutes, and we will have fun!

OPERATING PROCEDURES FOR OHS

Guides need to be aware of the relevant industry or organisational operating procedures related to OHS. The written or verbal instructions regarding how to carry out tasks are often referred to as 'operating procedures'. These are usually developed to assist people involved in a task to understand what is required, and they are often helpful in comprehending how things work.

Here is an example. A Guide is about to start a half-day walking tour. The tour operator has instructed that the Guide must check all the full names of the customers against the passenger list and then telephone the office to report whether the actual number of customers is more, less or the same, and whether there are any changes in names. This is the operating procedure for that operator. The next day, the Guide is booked to do a similar tour with another operator, and the Guide receives another set of instructions. This time the Guide is required to collect a voucher from each customer, do a head count and then reconfirm the total customer number and hand the vouchers to the operator representative, who is also present. The operating procedure is different, because this operator allocates the name check to the representative instead of the Guide, and the Guide's role in this instance is to reconfirm the total customer number and collect vouchers. So how does this relate to OHS? If there is no record of how many people are in the tour group, and there is an emergency evacuation at a site, how does anybody know how many people should be accounted for?

When it comes to OHS operating procedures Guides need to identify and clarify the information and procedures pertaining to their guiding role for the particular organisations and areas they are working with. These may include:

● reporting verbally to company representatives;
● completing documentation;
● diarising any OHS incidents or potential problems;
● promoting and recording information updates.

Remember, the aim of OHS is to prevent work-related injury, and operating procedures can vary across the tourism industry. It is not necessarily correct to assume 'one procedure applies to all'.

FIRST-AID REQUIREMENTS

In some areas of the guiding industry it is a requirement to hold a current first-aid certificate; in other areas it is not. In some of the Australian training courses it is a mandatory component of study and in others it is not.

It is, however, becoming more common for employers to request that Guides are familiar with and/or trained in first aid. Be aware that there is a range of certificate levels available. First-Aid Certificate—Level II is frequently requested, and those guiding in a variety of situations and/or remote areas may be asked about skills and certification at higher levels, and/or in remote emergency care.

For example, active membership of the Institute of Australian Tourist Guides requires a current first-aid certificate.

If you are requested to obtain certification, you will need to complete it to the specified certificate level, and when applicable update the qualification. Currently this type of certification has a specified duration, and requires renewal and updating after several years.

In the situation where the Guide is not required to hold first-aid certification, there is likely to be an induction provided regarding relevant operating procedures. For example, a Guide may lead a group around a museum and the Guide may not be required to be trained in first-aid; however, the operating procedures may instruct that 'in the case of first aid or an emergency the Guide is to seek assistance from the first-aid officer located in a particular area of the museum'.

It is recommended that the Guide ask about these requirements, if they have been overlooked. In addition, it is suggested that the Guide identify the local phone number for emergency assistance in case the identified support system fails. It is worth noting that currently in Australia the telephone number for emergency assistance is 000 (not to be mistaken with 911 as publicised on American television programs).

RISK MANAGEMENT

What is risk management and how does it relate to OHS? Consider this concept. Initially, there needs to be an OHS awareness and understanding developed; this assists in developing practices which support the aim of achieving good health and safety in the work environment. Risk management provides the opportunity to identify and analyse potential risks, and then develop an appropriate strategy for management purposes.

Currently, models of risk-management documents are available from a range of industry representatives; for example, the Victorian Tour Operators Association (VTOA) provides a model relevant to the Better Business Tourism Accreditation Program.

Again there are specialists who hold positions in this field. So for the Guide—consider the OHS issues in your work environment, ask whether a risk-management plan is in place, and inquire about the operating procedures applicable to you.

The subject of risk management will be discussed in the following section by Rosie Williams from the NSW National Parks and Wildlife Service.

INFORMATION UPDATES

By now you are aware that it is part of the overall Guide's role to identify, collate and interpret information, but it is not enough to do this once and rest on your achievements—there is a need to maintain a level of currency. This means ongoing updates in commentary topics, industry and general knowledge, as well as operating procedures—and OHS can fall into all three categories. There is a broad range of material available, with a considerable amount of relevant and succinct information on offer.

Information can be accessed through:

- *Government departments and agencies.* Internet sites and booklets (some free of charge or at low cost) are available through relevant government departments and agencies in each state and territory.
- *Literature, videos and the media.* Books, magazines, journals, newsletters, videos, media and the Internet are available through retail outlets, libraries and communication channels.

- *Association memberships and subscriptions.* A number of associations hold meetings to discuss issues raised by tour operators and Guides regarding situations and circumstances they encounter. Some associations distribute newsletters or bulletins which include articles regarding industry changes and updates.
- *Professional development.* Conferences, seminars and workshops are periodically offered by industry representatives, associations or education providers.
- *Training.* A number of tour-guiding courses are available, and the Australian National Training Packages currently offer a range of OHS-related units, including one from the Tourism Training Package titled 'Follow Health, Safety and Security Procedures'.

It is essential to contact information sources for regular OHS updates to keep abreast of changes and developments.

Conclusion

As tours continue to develop and reach into more challenging sites and environments, and travellers seek more diversified, exploratory and sophisticated experiences, the variety of information that will need to be provided in differing circumstances will increase.

The information provided in this section is based on current Australian operations and requirements, and is intended to introduce individuals to some of the OHS considerations and issues relevant to tour guiding.

ACTIVITY: Identify the name and contact details of the government department and/or agency in your state or territory that distribute information regarding OHS to the public. Locate where a model of a risk management strategy can be accessed in your state or territory.

Special Focus

Risk management

Rosie Williams, NSW Coordinator
National Parks Discovery—Walks, Talks and Tours,
NSW National Parks and Wildlife Service

What is risk management?
Risk management is the process of planning, organising, directing and controlling resources and activities in order to minimise the adverse effects of

accidental losses on that organisation in the most cost-effective way. It is used widely to minimise exposure to risk of injury, accident, delay, breakdown, physical damage or financial loss.

The concept of risk can be considered from two perspectives:

- the likelihood of something happening;
- the consequences if it happens.

Risk represents an interaction between:

- a *hazard* that has the potential to do some damage;
- the *people* who may be damaged;
- an *environment* that may make the hazard more (or less) serious.

In managing risk associated with occupational health and safety a rule of thumb is the health and safety of staff and customers. New South Wales has adopted new occupational health and safety legislation: *Occupational Health and Safety Act 2000* and the Occupational Health and Safety Regulations 2001.

The new OHS Act and Regulations took effect on 1 September 2001. There is a transitional period of 12 months for all businesses to implement any new requirements within the Regulations. Small employers (with no more than 20 employees) have a two-year period to implement the risk-management requirements of the Regulations.

The risk-management plan

Development of a **risk-management plan** is an essential part of the interpretive tour planning process. It ensures that:

- you minimise risk to people on tour, to yourself and/or colleagues;
- you comply with legislative requirements related to OHS;
- the likelihood of prosecution of your company and/or individual staff members is reduced;
- the possibility of economic or financial, physical damage, injury or delay is reduced.

National Parks Discovery—Walks, Talks and Tours

The NSW National Parks and Wildlife Service (NPWS) manage conservation of natural and cultural heritage in NSW, including national parks and reserves. As part of their National Parks Discovery—Walks, Talks and Tours community education program the NPWS conduct a range of guided activities throughout NSW. Procedures have been developed to support a systematic way of identifying and managing risk relating to all Discovery program activities.

Considerations that have formed part of these new procedures include the ability to:

- identify possible hazards relating to all Discovery activities;
- assess and rate the risks involved in relation to hazards identified;
- identify appropriate safety and risk minimisation measures that will control and/or eliminate the potential risks (this might involve site maintenance, changing tour arrangements, postponing the tour to a more suitable time or deciding not to proceed if the risks are perceived to be too great);
- identify who is responsible/accountable for implementing measures to control/minimise risks;
- continuously monitor and evaluate effectiveness of measures used to control/minimise risks;
- ensure a balanced Discovery program risk-management consultation process;
- continuously provide advice and assistance on OHS management to Discovery staff.

Discovery program risk-management strategy

Each NPWS region must develop a Discovery risk-management strategy that outlines locations to be used for Discovery activities, details of the types of activities that will be involved, precautions and equipment to minimise risks, and actions to be taken in the event of an emergency.

The following Discovery program risk-management process is based on the Australian Standard 4360:99:

- *Establish the context* in which visitors and staff will be undertaking Discovery program activities; this involves the preparation of a 'Proposal for an Interpretive Activity' form and a 'Identification of Possible Hazards' form.
- *Analyse the risk.* Identify issues and make deductions about the nature/ degree of the risk. Details are recorded on a 'Job Safety Analysis' form which provides a record to demonstrate compliance with the *Occupational Health and Safety Act 2000.*
- *Treat the risk.* Establish strategies to deal with risks and measures for implementation of such information, training and procedures, to be built into the program.
- *Risk Briefing.* A Risk Briefing to tour participants must be developed based on the risk identified and actions to be taken, and delivered to participants by the Discovery ranger at start of tour. A record of Risk Briefing to tour participants must be maintained as part of the program management.

Some examples of areas of risk management for Discovery activities:

- Geographically isolated sites
- Use of equipment
- Age/ability of customers
- Sites close to cliffs or water
- Broken/picked vegetation
- Feeding native wildlife
- Litter
- Flash photography
- Noise
- Handling of money

- Safety equipment
- Communication equipment
- Physical exertion
- Potentially dangerous wildlife
- Soil erosion/compression
- Handling animals
- Fire
- Playing taped animal and bird calls
- Incompatible activities

Identification of possible hazards

Should the proposed activity be adopted a Job Safety Analysis will be conducted. Completion of the following section will assist with the identification of possible hazards/risks that need to be considered.

Possible hazards for the public

Element (example)	Hazard (example)	Corrective action (example)	Who will ensure this happens? (example)
Cliffs	• Unprotected edges • Tour numbers • Unaccompanied children	• Warning at start of tour • Close monitoring when passing cliffs • Set maximum attendance figures • Brochure details relating to unaccompanied children	• Discovery ranger • Discovery ranger • Manager/booking officer/Discovery ranger

Possible hazards for Discovery ranger (Tourist Guide)

Element (example)	Hazard (example)	Corrective action (example)	Who will ensure this happens? (example)
No bookings required	Too many people arrive	• Ensure booking details are promoted well internally and externally • Split into small groups • Offer another time	• Tour manager/ promotional material • Discovery ranger • Discovery ranger

Possible hazards for the environment

Element (example)	Hazard (example)	Corrective action (example)	Who will ensure this happens? (example)
Lots of people visiting the same place	• Soil erosion • Soil compaction • Damage to flora/fauna	• Ensure that tour sites are rotated on a regular basis	• Tour manager

Possible cultural risk/impact

Element (example)	Hazard (example)	Corrective action (example)	Who will ensure this happens? (example)
Aboriginal rock engraving	• Ensure visit is permitted • Damage	• Permission from local community to visit • Identify appropriate educational information to be shared with customers • Develop guidelines for appropriate visitation • Develop measures to physically protect site • Brief customers before visiting site	• Tour manager • Tour manager/Discovery ranger • Site manager/local community/tour manager • Discovery ranger

The above provides an overview of how the NPSW are planning to manage risk for their tour programs.

 ACTIVITY: Obtain promotional information on a tour (as suggestions contact a travel agent, local land management agency or tour operator). Identify the elements, hazards and risks associated with the activity. How could these risks be controlled/minimised? Who would be responsible for developing and implementing a risk-management plan? What organisations do you need to contact to obtain relevant information on managing risk?

AN OVERVIEW OF LIABILITIES RELEVANT TO GUIDES AND OPERATORS

Organisations can become liable when they fail to fulfill certain obligations. To avoid these situations tour providers need to ensure that they:

- provide what was promised in any promotional material—and to the level which was promised;
- conduct activities in a manner which ensures nil or the least amount of risk to tour participants;
- ensure the safety of all participants at all stages of a tour;
- ensure the comfort of all participants;
- remain within the accepted framework of the tour which can include:
  —not organising optional tours outside of what was planned/promised;
  —avoiding unplanned and unscheduled activities and/or deviating from what was planned and promoted;
  —adhering to conditions imposed by relevant organisations.

Failure to meet these obligations can cause organisations to become liable for:

- loss of enjoyment;
- injury;
- breach of contract;
- breach of conditions.

Tour organisations also have an obligation to ensure all parties are aware of the terms and conditions associated with a nominated tour. These terms and conditions can include:

- cancellation policies and conditions and fees;
- payment and other considerations;
- forfeiting of deposits;
- unforseen changes in prices;
- what is and is not included in the tour fees and prices;
- responsibilities of the tour operator and/or Guide in times of unforseen circumstances.

 ACTIVITY: Collect several tour brochures from a travel agent. Identify the obligations of the tour operator. As a Guide leading this tour how would you ensure these obligations were met?

Contingency plans

Tour operators have an obligation to deliver what they promise to deliver and Guides play a significant role in meeting this obligation.

However, despite the best and most admirable efforts things can go astray. In such times Guides are in one of the most challenging positions as they often need to manage the situation in situ and while thinking on their feet. An invaluable resource during such times is a contingency plan.

Such plans can include the following details:

- who to contact in case of emergency;
- emergency procedures relevant to the locale you will be operating in;
- outline of operating procedures for different areas.

To prepare and/or review a contingency plan, consider everything which could possibly go wrong. Next, develop a list of strategies for how you would deal with these events. And now what resources do you require to undertake these strategies?

ACTIVITY: Plan a full-day coach tour which will visit a variety of sites. As part of this plan prepare a contingency plan which you would take with you.

TOURS AS A LEARNING EXPERIENCE

Within this book Interpretation is defined as 'A learning experience which seeks to enrich the meaningful relationships we hold with our world, and to foster and build a set of values which supports these relationships'.

Learning is generally considered to occur within the following three domains—cognitive, psychomotor and affective (sometimes referred to as the head, the hands and the heart respectively):

- Cognitive learning is concerned with the development of knowledge such as learning new facts and figures about a local area, a museum or a bird species.
- Psychomotor learning is concerned with developing skills such as learning a new trade, or finding out how to identify a bird or particular style of architecture, or how to navigate in the bush. This involves making relationships between various pieces of information and sorting out contexts.
- Affective learning is concerned with influencing the affective domain of the emotions, feelings and values.

If you were to prioritise these domains from an interpretive perspective you would seek to influence the affective domain before the others, as it is in this domain that motivations are generated. A positive learning experience encourages people to learn, to develop a positive attitude, to value the focus and process of their learning, and to act as loyal ambassadors of the learning providers. The psychomotor and cognitive learning domains have a lesser influence on the motivations of an individual, yet are still critical to a learning experience.

Think about a great tour or Guide-based experience. What made it great? Was it the amount of information which was provided? Or was it the manner in which the Guide provided this information? Was it the way in which the Guide managed the events? In the majority of situations an audience will remember and associate more of the content of a tour when it has been presented in an engaging, entertaining and enlivening manner.

This focus on how it was presented could be as simple as spending time socialising with people during the tour and talking about their pet interests or as detailed as researching the needs of the group and ensuring that the tour would satisfy these needs. Focusing on the 'how' means making sure that people are relaxed and comfortable, that they do not feel threatened, that they are having fun and are being stimulated, and that their needs are being met.

In the end if people leave with nothing but one fact yet a positive experience, you will have at least increased the chances that they will become ambassadors to your cause—that they will have the motivation to find out more at a later date.

LEARNING STYLES

Individual cultures have their unique characteristics. People often display their individual tastes for clothes, fashion and foods. The same with learning styles. As individuals we all learn in unique and individual ways. Learning styles provides us with an opportunity to develop a greater understanding of the preferences people have for learning.

Together with an awareness of individual learning styles you can also assist learning by:

- ensuring you apply effective communication principles which includes minimising any barriers and distortions;
- acknowledging and respecting the unique attributes and viewpoints of individuals;
- ensuring you have the attention of your audience;
- incorporating opportunities for social interaction;
- creating exciting, enthusiastic and inspiring environments.

Why explore learning styles? It is worthwhile exploring learning styles:

- to develop an awareness of how you learn, and once you have this awareness to challenge yourself by operating in other styles;
- to highlight your uniqueness;
- to promote empathy and the concept of valuing differences.

Two learning models are presented here which can be used when planning activities to maximise the learning opportunity for people: the VAK learning model and the 4Mat® learning model.

In working with learning styles you need to remember that it's obviously a general representation of what is an extremely difficult activity. To group the amazing uniqueness of humans into categories can only be a guide to how people learn and communicate. Yet it's still useful to challenge how you normally present and how else you could present. To how you learn and how else you could learn. To how others learn and how you could encourage learning among the maximum number of people.

VAK learning model

The VAK model refers to the three modes of sensory stimulation: visual, auditory and kinaesthetic.

Visual

Preferred characteristics of visual learners are as follows:

- They look and see, and enjoy visual stimulations such as colour and perspectives.
- They base their first impressions on appearance.
- They think in pictures.
- They talk quickly and like to maintain eye contact.
- They like to be complimented on the way they look and tend to take time with grooming and appearance.
- They are organised people, they love being taken to new places and they enjoy shopping.
- They use visual language such as 'see', 'watch', 'point of view', 'it appears to be' and 'illustrate the point'.

To satisfy visual learners when planning and conducting tours:

- Incorporate opportunities for people to see and connect with visual items.
- Use visual-based language.
- Point to things using your arm or an object to direct the eyes of your audience.

Auditory

Preferred characteristics of auditory learners are as follows:

- They react according to the sounds and words they hear.
- They love conversation and listen intently, appearing to pay attention to detail.
- They are very good on the phone.
- They enjoy auditory language such as 'sounds great', 'hear what you are saying' and 'that has a ring to it'.
- They think in words and enjoy poetry and metered text.
- They like and want to hear encouragement.
- They love music and rhythm.
- They learn things by listening.

To satisfy auditory learners when planning and conducting tours:

- Vary the vocal delivery of your commentary.
- Incorporate poetry and metered text within your commentary.
- Encourage people to listen to surrounding sounds.
- Provide opportunities for people to reflect in silence.

Kinaesthetic

Preferred characteristics of kinaesthetic learners are as follows:

- They experience life through their feelings.
- They are highly tactile, sensitive and prone to moodiness.
- They like to be around others and enjoy plenty of affection.
- They like things which arouse a sense of smell, taste and touch.
- They use their hands when they talk, like to move and are physical in the body.
- They enjoy kinaesthetic-based language and like to speak in feelings such as 'I feel', 'I can handle', 'hold on' and 'get in touch'.
- When needing to make a point they tend to focus on emotions and feelings.

To satisfy kinaesthetic learners when planning and conducting tours:

- Provide opportunities for people to handle objects, to 'get their hands dirty', to move and to be physical.
- Incorporate kinaesthetic based language such as 'this smooth surface', 'the rough sandstone of these walls' or 'what it must have felt like'.

4Mat® learning model

The following model is based on the Kolb model of learning styles and was developed by Bernice McCarthy. It is based on a vertical and horizontal axis continuum which creates four quadrants.

The *vertical axis* relates to how people interact with an event/stimulus. The top of the axis represents those people who prefer a concrete experience, that is, they sense

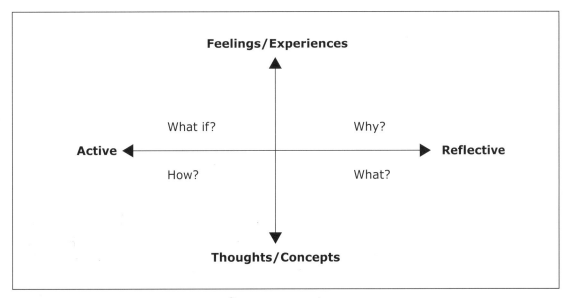

Source: Based on Bernice McCarthy's 4Mat® model at www.aboutlearning.com.

it and feel it (which can be emotive feeling as well as sensory feeling); while the bottom of the axis represents those people who like to conceptualise, make models and are more abstract in their initial relationship to the event.

The *horizontal axis* relates to how people process this interaction with an event/stimulus. At the left are the doers, those who get in there and want to make it happen; and on the right are those who like to reflect, 'stand back' and ponder.

Characteristics within the 4Mat® system

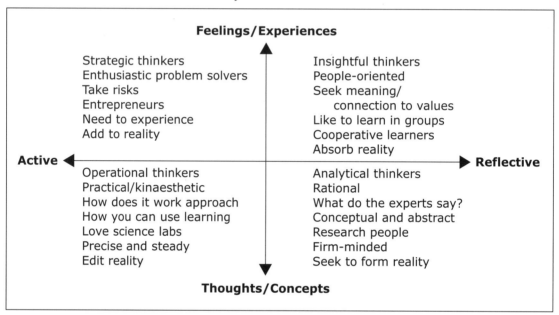

	Feelings/Experiences	
Strategic thinkers		Insightful thinkers
Enthusiastic problem solvers		People-oriented
Take risks		Seek meaning/
Entrepreneurs		connection to values
Need to experience		Like to learn in groups
Add to reality		Cooperative learners
		Absorb reality

Active ← → Reflective

Operational thinkers		Analytical thinkers
Practical/kinaesthetic		Rational
How does it work approach		What do the experts say?
How you can use learning		Conceptual and abstract
Love science labs		Research people
Precise and steady		Firm-minded
Edit reality		Seek to form reality

Thoughts/Concepts

Source: Based on Bernice McCarthy's model at www.aboutlearning.com.

4Mat® learning quadrants in greater detail
Why? quadrant (top right)
People with a preference towards this quadrant:

- are good listeners because they can relate to the emotive element (that is, they feel) and yet do not jump in and talk over the top because they like to reflect on the event;
- enjoy feelings of excitement and experience;
- respect others and enjoy social learning opportunities such as group involvement, chatting to people and being interactive with other people;
- trust their insights;
- enjoy reflection time;
- think relevance is important—to values, worth to people and society;
- like to personalise an event and relate this to their own experience.

When planning tours for people with a *Why?* preference provide:

- an overview of the tour so they can gain an idea of context;
- opportunities to find relevance/meaning to them and society as they are values-based people who like to feel/sense and yet reflect and connect with the significance;
- opportunities to discuss personal stories;
- opportunities to 'think' and reflect in between stops;
- opportunities for reflection;
- reasons for doing what you are doing; this is where the research of your audience is extremely important.

What? quadrant (bottom right)
People with a preference towards the *What?* quadrant:

- like detail, trivia and credible information based on research or presented by an expert;
- enjoy concepts and abstracts;
- identify with specific examples.

Ideas to incorporate into planning your activity so as to satisfy people with a *What?* preference:

- facts, figures and statistics—perhaps refer to a facts sheet which is read out to demonstrate its authenticity;
- quotes from famous people and research evidence;
- clear information and interesting details;
- scientific information;
- dates for events and people.

How? quadrant (bottom left)
People with a preference towards the *How?* quadrant are generally those people who want to make things happen, who like to get hold of concepts and then do something with them—the engineers of this world. They like to know how things work and to experiment with concepts. These people enjoy:

- process;
- demonstrations;
- explanation of basic concepts;
- finding out how such and such was formed, and how things work;
- abstract concepts to help explain how something works;
- finding out about the function of an object;
- activities which are hands on.

When planning tours for people with a *How?* preference provide:

- process-based activities—show how things work, and demonstrate links between concepts and ideas and 'information clusters';

- opportunities to get involved in the activity so as to experience;
- working with props and how to do something (e.g. how to look for koalas);
- how something works—concept in nature that can be applied to something practical, something they can put into practice.

What if? quadrant (top left)
People with a preference towards the *What if?* quadrant are your entrepreneur types—challenging what they experience, trying out new things and imaging new scenarios. These people enjoy:

- different ways of seeing things;
- options—lots of them;
- being involved and engaging their sensations;
- different views;
- the future—and imagining—future scenarios.

When planning tours for people with a *What if?* preference provide:

- *What if?* scenarios, for example if the world didn't have trees, what do you think would happen? Imagine travelling the world at the speed of light;
- opportunities to explore several perspectives, for example 'Let's explore this museum piece from several perspectives. Firstly . . .'
- opportunities to fill in the gaps, for example, 'what's missing from this scenario?'

WORKING WITH THE 4MAT® NATURAL LEARNING CYCLE WHEN PLANNING ACTIVITIES

The 4Mat® Natural Cycle also provides a great checklist for ensuring diversity within any activity and can be used as a bit of a checklist whenever planning for activities. For example:

- If planning for an activity you focus on the *Why?* quadrant which encourages you to consider how your activity will be relevant to a particular audience. Why are you doing what you are doing? Why are you running this particular tour?
- The *What?* quadrant encourages you to research and find out some in-depth material about the activity.
- The *How?* quadrant encourages you to consider how you're going to run the tour and also the processes involved.
- The *What if?* quadrant helps in planning issues such as what if you experience an accident, and are you prepared for any unlikely event? Also in the commentary, you could encourage people to think of what things might have been like.

 ACTIVITY: Think about the following questions and, if possible, discuss your answers with a friend.

- Do you prefer the VAK or 4Mat® learning model? Why?
- Do you have a preferred or dominant style for learning? Which style is this?
- Do you know other people with different learning styles from your own? What are the characteristics of their learning styles?

PERCEPTION LAYERING

To see a World in a grain of sand
And a Heaven in a wild flower
Hold Infinity in the palm of your hand
And Eternity in an hour.
William Blake

WHAT IS PERCEPTION LAYERING?

Perception layering is a concept and technique which encourages you to explore the multitude of stories contained within each and every feature of your landscape. It promotes the idea that any point in space has a multitude of dimensions—it just depends on your perception.

For example, if you were standing on the edge of a freeway you might choose to survey and discuss the historical periods in the development of that freeway, what materials were used, what impact it had on the surrounding landscape, how this impact was managed, how the freeway has impacted on the flow of traffic and people through surrounding communities, whether the freeway replaced a historical road, whether the freeway follows an indigenous or early settler transport route, how it is managed and maintained, the stories of people who use the freeway for holiday travel or who commute on the freeway each day, and how the traffic is managed.

Even the local suburban street changes between weekdays and weekends, with a difference in the number of children playing, the number of people tending to lawns and gardens, movement of traffic, sounds of sport and other weekend leisure activities, and even in the fact that more houses would appear open and occupied.

When you interact with your environment you can focus on any one of a multitude of perspectives. These perspectives are all layers within the environment which you can select for use in your tour. Even the simplest of objects has a multitude of stories which are intertwined and ready for the interpretive picking. To evoke these perspectives you can ask a variety of questions focusing on who, what, where, how, when, why and what if. For example:

- What are its main physical features?
- What material is it made of?
- How was it made?

- How was it designed?
- How is it used and by whom?
- What is its history?
- Who was involved in this object?
- What features are used in its classification and identification?

Take the example of a small tree found on a track within a bushland area. If you were to deliver a presentation you could focus on any of the following:

- *Type of tree and its characteristics.* What are its distinguishing features such as the type and pattern of bark and types of seeds?
- *Human uses of this tree.* Was the tree used by indigenous people? Did European settlers have any use for this type of tree?
- *Shapes and colours.* What is unique about its shape? How did it form its particular shape? What causes the various colours?
- *Habitat.* What habitat does it provide, and for what species of flora and fauna?

If you take a smaller feature, such as the brick from a historic house, your presentation could focus on the following:

- *Its history.* When was it fired? Who fired it? Why was it fired in that particular style and with those materials? What was used before this type of brick? What is the origin of the materials used? Where were they quarried?
- *Characters.* What stories are there of people who designed the brick, who quarried the materials and who worked the furnaces?
- *Architecture.* How does this particular brick contribute to the building's architecture?

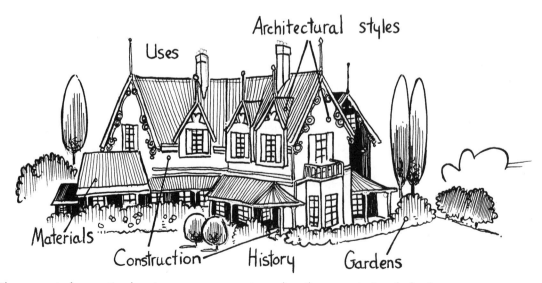

The concept of perception layering encourages you to explore the many stories of a landscape

- *Its physical characteristics.* What are its identification and classification features? What materials were used in the firing of the brick? Why is it that particular colour? How was it made? Are there any maker marks?
- *Uses.* How is it used and how was it used (past and present). Did it have any unusual uses?
- *Habitats.* Once the bricks form walls, do they provide habitats for any animals?
- *Associations.* What do the bricks reveal about social status, wealth, economic conditions, lifestyles, artistic and design tastes, and social conditions of the building? What does the object reveal about the skills and resources involved in its creation and use?

Perception layering can also be used to reflect on how a landscape and its associated meanings have changed over time. For example, a few years ago Balmain Power Station within the inner Sydney suburb of Balmain was demolished to make way for a housing estate. What was once a site boasting a building of historical significance has become a site that children deem significant as a playground, that parents consider to be a safe zone for their children, and that people can consider to be their home and neighbourhood.

If you were to conduct a tour of the site from a historical perspective you could focus on the old power station, how it was constructed, its role in providing power to Sydney and perhaps why it was located where it was. Whereas, if you were conducting a tour focusing on the current landscape, you could include the encroachment of high-density housing estates within Sydney, the characteristics of these estates, the attributes of people who live there, how these estates plan for playgrounds, and the recreational opportunities available for children. Or you could build and link both perspectives into your tour.

What often dominates your perceptions within the environment are the obvious features: the large buildings, the historically rich areas, the large trees, the bright flowers and the main features within a museum diorama. As Tourist Guides, the concept of perception layering encourages you to challenge these dominant perceptions and explore the many stories contained within the landscape's fabric. And then to explore the myriad of interrelationships between these same stories.

When we try to pick up anything by itself we find the universe attached to it.
John Muir

PERCEPTION LAYERING AND DEVELOPING THEMES
Perception layering becomes very useful when working with themes (see pages 170–178). The theme provides your tour with a focus and is the unifying thread on which you base your activities and commentaries. For themes to be effective the activities and information within your commentaries must remain consistent with the chosen theme.

For example, if your topic is history and your theme is exploring the historical periods of a 200-year-old cottage, then your focus would remain within these parameters. You would not start talking about the bird colony 100 kilometres away unless it was somehow relevant to your cottage.

Your tour would focus on that layer within the landscape or event which is relevant to the theme. By being able to explore the environment in terms of multiple layers you can select that layer which is most relevant to your theme. And the more layers you can create through the process of perception layering, the greater your choice of which layer to use within your commentaries.

To demonstrate let us take an object such as a tree and three tours.

- Tour A is a historical sites tour, and is focused on a historic theme. When this tour arrives at the tree the information being presented could include historic use of this and surrounding trees, early settlers and the use of trees in housing.
- Tour B is a microhabitat tour with a theme focused on the same topic. When this tour arrives at the same tree the information being presented could include microhabitats of the bark, microhabitats of the surrounding leaf litter, and the macrohabitats versus the microhabitats of the tree.
- Tour C is an environmental education activity focusing on ecological relationships within the landscape. When this tour arrives at the tree the information being provided could include the type of tree and why it is located where it is, its relationship to other trees and reproduction strategies.

Same tree—three tours—three themes—three different perspectives.

The effectiveness of perception layering is greatly increased with the use of creative thinking techniques.

CREATIVE THINKING
PEOPLE AND THEIR UNIQUE SELVES

People interact with the environment based on their constructed frames of reference. Some people refer to these as their personal paradigms, mind-sets and points of view. These frames of reference are based on experiences, attitudes, thoughts, feelings, emotions, values, memories and other intrinsic human elements.

Repetitive use of these frames of reference will often form a distinct pattern which you recognise as habits, addictions, tendencies and mannerisms—your *modus operandi*. These learnt patterns together with genetic patterns are the mechanism through which you filter the infinite array of environmental information received by your sensory system and focus on what is relevant and meaningful.

These frames of reference are what influence behaviour and not the objective information you receive from your environment—that is, you react based on your perceptions of what is going on around you. And it is these frames of reference you carry with you when you go on tour, travel, work, visit friends and interact with your environment.

We each take our unique perceptions from a presentation

Take the scenario of a busload of people who pull up at a beachside carpark. From the bus emerge a group of surfers, several sunbathers, a few parents and their teenage children.

● The surfers become aware of the right-hand break, the rip near the south point and possible channels for paddling out the back.
● The sunbathers become aware of the spot which will maximise exposure of their bronzed and well-toned bodies to passing crowds.
● Parents look for the safest place for their children to swim and frolic on the beach.
● Teenage children seek the best places to distance themselves from their parents.

Each surveyed the same landscape but focused only on those aspects which were relevant and meaningful for their recreational pursuits.

When you communicate with other people and seek to share meanings you cannot simply transfer meanings between people. Rather, you express your meaning through the process of communication. And by its very nature this expression is not the meaning but a representation of it.

CREATIVE THINKING—AN INTRODUCTION
Creative thinking challenges your dominant frames of reference, mind-sets, patterns and routines. Changing established patterns and unlearning what you have learnt can be one of the most challenging processes of creative thinking.

A great deal of creativity is just as much about making new connections between existing items/elements as it is about creating new ones.

We do not have to change what we see, only the way we see it.
Anon.

Within the guiding field creative thinking can be used to generate ideas for:

- expanding on your points of view which leads you into the perception layering domain discussed earlier;
- developing content and style of commentaries;
- having fun;
- implementing a marketing and advertising strategy;
- building a repertoire of guiding and presentation techniques;
- developing itineraries;
- negotiating situations, which always benefit from being able to generate and consider more than one point of view;
- challenging clichés and offering a fresh approach;
- developing themes and story-lines.

PRINCIPLES OF CREATIVE THINKING
Creative thinking is a deliberate process concerned with generating alternatives rather than with finding the right answer. In the domain of creative thinking there is no right answer.

Creative thinking relies on the following:

- momentum;
- a desire to seek alternatives;
- removing the context of right and wrong;
- removing the concept of failure;
- accepting that some techniques might appear foolish;
- challenging your belief that you are not creative, by realising creative thinking is a deliberate process that can be learnt rather than a process which relies on natural talent.

CREATIVE THINKING TECHNIQUES
The following are several creative thinking techniques which can be useful for various aspects of guiding:

- 60-second plunge;
- why?
- advance and extend;
- random word associations;
- brainstorm tree.

60-second plunge

Choose your focus (e.g. ideas for a tour) and then do the following:

- In 60 seconds write down as many one-word associations as you can (if needed you can write more than one word to capture a thought but attempt to keep it to one word).
- It is important that once the timer starts you keep going, even if you have to repeat a word several times. Momentum is one of the critical elements of this technique.
- Leave editing until after the 60-seconds is finished.

After the 60 seconds you would have a variety of words which you can use on their own or you can start to link certain words and focus on any apparent lines of thinking or themes.

Why?

With the 'why' technique you keep asking questions starting with 'why?'. This technique is useful for extracting meaning from a situation, problem or behaviour.

'Why?' is a useful way to start a question when planning activities. Why exactly are you conducting this activity? Why do you want to undertake a certain activity? Why are people coming along on this tour? Why do you feel this site is special and significant?

Advance and extend

This technique encourages you to provide both movement and description when developing and delivering a commentary. The movement is the 'advance' and the description is the 'extend'.

For example, the second paragraph of the following story (once the people have sat down) begins with an 'extend' in that they receive a description of Old Milly.

> Well folks here we are. In the last room of the house. The room where they say it all happened. Sit down and let me share with you just some of the tales spoken from these walls. I'll ask you to listen in . . . get close . . . that's it.
>
> Dear Old Milly called her children here on her birthday. A day of celebration it was. Sitting there on the old rocking chair, shawl wrapped round her neck. Little round glasses resting gently on her nose.

'Advance and extend' can also be used as a check-in mechanism for the progress of your tour. For example, if you stopped at a particular feature (e.g. a historic statue) you would begin to describe this feature. This is the 'extend' part of your tour—how long do you feel your audience would like to hear about the statue before wanting to move on, that is, before an 'advance' is called for? The same applies to your commentary—how much description should you provide about a certain object before providing additional perspectives?

Random word associations

This is sometimes referred to as the Da Vinci method. Select your topic and then select a number of elements within this topic.

Take as an example the topic 'Designing some new activities'. Elements related to this topic could be activity types, activity venues, possible audience types, time considerations and methods of running the activities. These elements provide the title for their respective columns, within which we list a pre-determined number of associated words. For example, the following table lists five words for each element.

Types	Venues	Audience	Time	Methods
birdwalk	bushland	children	summer	hand lens
nocturnal	library	adults	night	walk
snorkelling	council	generation X	dawn	puppets
micro-hop	school	retirees	4 hours	stories
artistic	Heathcote National Park	families	day	slides

Now combine word(s) from each of the five columns. An example of an activity might be nocturnal activity in a local library conducted for children in the evening using puppets and stories. Extending on this idea you could decide to conduct the nocturnal activity about animals of the night. You run the activity at the local library because of access to young children and their parents, and create ambience by using minimal overhead lighting and introducing floor lighting.

Brainstorm tree

Start with a central concept and then choose a number between 4 and 8. For this central concept you write the same number of associations as the number you chose. For example, if as your central concept you chose 'Subject ideas to include in a commentary on a building', and then chose the number 5, you would record 'building' as the central concept and write five associations. These might be:

historic, architecture, composition, uses, spatial relationship

You now treat each of these as a central concept and record another five associations. You now have 25 ideas related to your initial concept. For example:

- *historic*—period, materials, characters, style, uses;
- *architecture*—style, windows, materials, spatial context, personalities;
- *composition*—materials, origins, colours, textures, crystal composition;
- *spatial relationships*—context to other buildings, height, planning controls, foundation support, engineering;
- *uses*—uniqueness of tenants, lease arrangements, habitats for wildlife, reference point, aerial and telecommunication devices.

Special Focus

A 'novel' approach to museum Interpretation

Bernie Cavanagh, Senior Education Officer
Historic Houses Trust of New South Wales

This article suggests a fresh way of looking at historic house museums, and recommends a particular approach to historic house Interpretation. It proposes an an analogy, comparing the nature of historic house museums to that of literature (which I hope explains my clever pun in the title). It's not a very sophisticated analogy, and is based on the simple idea that both historic houses and novels are there for our selection, enjoyment and sometimes rejection. Some we like and some we don't. The purpose of this article is to present some approaches to interpreting historic house museums: approaches that draw on an understanding of the relationships that people may form with these places.

Try to remember your childhood when you were first becoming an independent reader of literature. There were stories read at bedtime, in the classroom and on TV. As you read and were read to, an understanding of the 'ingredients' of these stories would have grown. In these stories you went to places, you met people and interesting things happened. And as you matured as a reader, labels were found for these ingredients.

Any novel has some standard ingredients:

- *Characters* are the players.
- *Plot* is what happens.
- *Setting* is where and when the action takes place.
- *Language* is how the story is told.

Historic house museums have all of these things. Visitors encounter characters from the past and present. Many of these characters are known, with famous names and faces. Others are hidden, largely anonymous characters that lurk in the background. Historic houses have stories to tell about these characters: stories of relationships, events, tragedies and triumphs. These stories are told within a setting: a place set within a historical context or across a passage of time.

In novels, the stories are told using a language concocted by the author and engaged with by the reader. Our museums also have a language. Sometimes it is found on signage, display panels or in brochures, but it is often said that the most eloquent speakers are the buildings and collections themselves.

If you ask young readers 'What was that story about?', they'll probably answer in terms of the above four characteristics: characters, plot, setting and language. However, as readers become more sophisticated, they are encouraged to recognise that a piece of literature is about more than these elements, and that these elements actually create and reflect ideas. These ideas are called *themes*— the ideas and notions that are generated and reflected through the interaction of characters, plot, setting and language.

So where do Guides and interpreters fit in to this analogy? There is a school of thought among many museum professionals that a well-curated museum space will speak for itself, and yes it will. The characters may well be in evidence, elements of the story and setting will be clear, and the language of the house and its collection may be legible. But what we need to acknowledge is that people connect with, or *read*, the language of a museum in different ways. Individuals will bring to a museum (and to a piece of literature) their own reading experiences and capacities. Some people will read intuitively, some with a deep knowledge of the genre, some with confidence and some with apprehension, and some will read lazily and others diligently. So even a competently curated exhibition or room won't be read and understood in the same way by different visitors.

And it is this that makes the role of the Guide so important. We too are a part of the language of our museums that help visitors make meanings and develop understandings from the experience.

Just as a parent or teacher has a role in helping students access and comprehend a novel or poem or play, museum interpreters have a role to play in helping people when they visit a museum.

It is usually a matter of time for interpreters to become familiar with the characters and stories of a historic house, and to be able to explain the collection. It is equally important to consider the many themes that are generated by the place, and to use these themes for effective and exciting interpretation and communication. A tour of a historic house that relies only on the content of facts, dates, names, stories and knowledge of the collection will always run the risk of being a tour that leaves the visitors out. They can become the passive recipients of expert information held by the Guides. To engage the visitors to your museum, a 'theme-based' approach to Interpretation may be a better choice.

A simple way of getting started on this approach to theme-based tours is to make a theme list. With as many staff as possible, including property curators and experts on the history and collection, explore the setting of your historic house museum. Identify and list the themes that emanate from the spaces, and from the facts and dates and character stories that are already well-known by staff.

As an experiment for this approach, select just one object from your collection and try to extract from it as many ideas as possible. In the example opposite the simple object of a clay smoking pipe was examined in this way by a team of Historic Houses Trust Guides.

Health and hygiene	Leisure
Class	A clay smoking pipe	Technology
Transplanted customs and habits	Gender

The team was not concerned with the provenance or condition of the clay smoking pipe, but rather with the themes that could be suggested by it and subsequently used to move elsewhere in the collection. This approach requires some lateral thinking, but if one object can suggest several themes, imagine what your entire property and collection might suggest.

You can use this technique with any part of the building or grounds, for example a gate, door, garden bench, tree, staircase or fireplace.

Consider the example of the doorstep below, which was also discussed by a team of Historic Houses Trust Guides following a lateral and non-lateral train of thought. Where can this lead? By pointing out, for example, that the step is worn partly as a result of the long history of visitors to the house, one could establish a simple and accessible theme to be pursued through a tour, that of 'visitation'.

The house could be explored within the thematic context of visitation, looking into the spaces to which guests would have been welcomed, and contrasting these to the private family rooms. Following this theme, the house's family members can be placed imaginatively into the role of host, and stories of special guests or occasions can be woven through the theme. Objects (menus), furnishings and fittings (servants bells, dinner settings) and props and devices (place cards, period music) are able to be selected to complement the tour.

Also sitting comfortably in this theme of visitation is the role of Guide (host) and audience (guests) who represent the currency of an idea that has been explored historically. Of course, you could just as easily focus on one of the other ideas to explore the same house but in a new and fresh way. Once again, the approach helps to engage the audience with *ideas*, and avoids the prefabricated, content-driven tours that rely solely on the privileged knowledge of the interpreters.

Master and servant		Formality and informality
Guest and host	A worn front doorstep	'A passing parade'
Coming and going	'Following footsteps'	Continuity and change

It's a good idea to experiment with single items and objects, and then progress to the house as a whole. Using a floor plan, try to identify some predominant themes for each room. Perhaps the kitchen reflects informality, functionalism and domestic service, whereas the drawing room might reflect formality, aesthetics, gentility and particular manners. Into all spaces, characters and stories an analysis of selected items can help explore the selected ideas. Threads through a guided tour can then be created by identifying the themes that complement or support, or even contrast with, each other.

Selecting and using the themes that resonate through your historic house museum can benefit you and your visitors by:

- *Helping you structure your tours.* By identifying and articulating key themes that can be explored through a visit, you will orientate the visitors and provide a clear 'notional' direction for the tour. The visitors will develop an appreciation of the visit as an exploration of ideas, and not just information.
- *Creating threads.* Creating thoughtful and thought-provoking *threads* through your tours might avoid the 'spot-talk' or 'inventory' approach to guiding (something that can be tiresome for both the Guide and visitor).
- *Providing new ways of reading the museum.* You could enrich the visitor experience by providing new ways of reading the museum. Pursuing a theme of 'domestic labour' or 'childhood experiences' or 'master and servant' could provide a fresh perspective on the rooms and collections within.
- *Helping you to be selective of content.* Any historic house will simply have too much content to interpret. (Have you ever been on a tour during which the Guide tries to cover too much content?) Having a theme or two will help you be selective of the content available.
- *Creating a 'level playing field'.* By selecting themes as universal as 'family life' or 'the childhood experience' or 'leisure at home' or 'changing technologies' or 'manners', your tour should be intellectually accessible by a wide range of visitors including culturally diverse groups. People will be better and more appreciative readers of museums if they are invited to use their own experiences and understandings and language to make sense of these new and wonderful things around them.
- *Providing variety.* You can provide a variety of perspectives and approaches to your guiding beyond the delivery of expert information. Of course, people do like to encounter the new and unfamiliar (that's a major reason people visit), but let's not also make these things alien or alienating. We can place new and unfamiliar characters, events, times and places into familiar thematic contexts.

Of course, not all ideas and themes will be appropriate for guiding, some possibly being too obscure and tenuous. But you may also be surprised at the number of strong, resonant themes you find that can be used to generate and sustain visitor-friendly, engaging and comprehensive historic house tours. Your visitors, like the readers of a good book, will leave the experience enriched and appreciative of the characters, plot, setting, language and themes they've encountered along the way, and hopefully wanting to 'read' more.

ACTIVITY: Think about the item below. What ideas or themes are suggested by it?

| A child's alphabet reader |

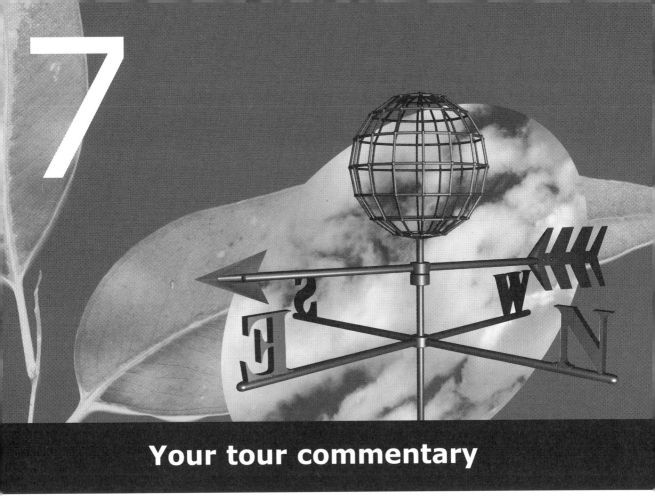

7

Your tour commentary

What are the learning outcomes for this chapter?

By the end of this chapter you should be able to:
● Identify the elements of a commentary.
● Describe the stages in building a commentary.
● Select and organise appropriate information to meet the needs of specific customers, operational contexts and timing restrictions.
● Identify the need to present current, accurate and relevant information within commentaries, and to use language appropriate to the customer group.
● Identify and develop possible themes and messages for a tour activity.
● Capture the attention of your audience.
● Demonstrate techniques for making your commentary relevant and interesting.
● Use presentation techniques to enhance the quality of the experience for the customer.
● Develop a tour activity according to interpretive principles.
● Demonstrate the use of words and descriptive phrasing for enriching your commentary.

WHAT IS A COMMENTARY?

A commentary is often considered to be any information you provide to your audience. It can be delivered in a variety of situations including:

- when leading people on a site tour;
- during meet-and-greets, and arrival-and-departure transfers;
- on a coach tour;
- as part of pretour and specific-event activities.

Within this book we will consider a commentary to be the information you provide during the tour which supports the theme of the tour and which highlights the message(s) you are trying to promote. Information provided in the following situations will not be considered to be part of a commentary: information provided during the start-and-welcome stages of the tour; information provided during any pretour briefing; and any information provided for logistical and operational purposes.

Commentaries and tours are immensely variable, as are the range of approaches for delivering a tour and its commentaries. The following model is one approach. While this model focuses on one subject area/theme, it can suit a variety of situations including the conducting of extended tours or the conducting of multisite tours.

STRUCTURE OF YOUR COMMENTARY

As mentioned in Chapter 6, the commentary occurs within the middle section of your tour and builds on the credibility, rapport and audience interaction which you would have established during the start of the tour. The middle section of your tour has three segments—the introduction, the body and the conclusion—with the commentary providing a unifying thread throughout each segment.

The introduction:

- captures audience attention;
- outlines the theme of the commentary and the tour;
- provides your audience with direction and an idea of what's coming up.

The body:

- fleshes out the theme of your tour;
- introduces a chosen list of key ideas and messages and extends them.

The conclusion:

- wraps up the main points.

BUILDING YOUR COMMENTARY

Building a commentary is like cooking a meal by following a recipe. You first decide on what type of food you'd like, you gather the necessary ingredients, you prepare and cook the ingredients to your chosen recipe, you eat the meal and then you reminisce on how it tasted.

Building a commentary is also like creating a story, in that they both follow a particular line of development. Whether the story is expressed in theatre, opera, song, dance or as a fireside tale, there will always be a sequential flow of events which develops the story.

To weave a story together you begin by asking a variety of questions. What is the story going to be about? In what period does the story take place? Who are the characters and what are the relationships between themselves and their environment? What are the objectives within the story?

The structure of an interpretive commentary should include:

- a focus on a particular topic;
- a theme;
- a message;
- a particular story-line (that is, sequential development);
- information and activities which are relevant to your audience and which provide a sense of context in addressing the whole 'big picture' perspective of what you are focusing on;
- information that is clear, concise, accurate and interesting;
- opportunities to reveal, provoke and evoke.

It is by working with commentaries that you address the interpretive principle of 'revealing meaning and significance' (pages 5 and 6).

CONSIDERATIONS IN BUILDING YOUR COMMENTARY

The following are some of the contextual elements which you might consider when framing and building your commentary:

- length of the tour and itinerary—there is a close relationship between itineraries, timings and your commentary;
- tour route and site characteristics;
- mode of transport, for example walking, coach, four-wheel drive, public transport or a combination of these;
- audience characteristics—what they find interesting, useful and valuable (what would I want to know if I were a member of the audience?);

- number of people and their mobility, educational levels, expectations, needs and interests;
- purpose of the tour—your tour objectives (refer to Chapter 6);
- physical, social and environmental opportunities and constraints.

DECIDING ON THE COMMENTARY TOPIC

The initial step in building your commentary is to decide on the topic of your tour. Topics are broad subject areas which provide an initial focus for the tour and which answer the simple question: What is this tour about?

Topics can focus on:

- the place—physical characteristics such as landscape, buildings, streetscapes, habitats and vegetation;
- people—historic characters, social times in the past and/or the present, and what the future holds for the people of an area;
- events and processes—some of the influences and events which have caused an area to change.

Within these categories possible topics could include the following:

Natural	Cultural/social
● Marine environment	● History of Melbourne
● Coastal reef platform	● Colonial life
● Sandstone bushland	● Indigenous culture
● Bush birds	● 19th-century military defences
● Rainforests	● Architectural styles
● Plants of a bushland area	● Lighthouses
● Animal habitats	● People and the social history of a place
● The life of little animals in a suburban backyard	● Technology
● Erosion	● Navigation
● Evolution	● Governing Australia

Topics will obviously be influenced to a large degree by the area you will be working in. Within a historic house tour, topics might include styles of architecture, periods of dress, furniture and interior fixtures, and construction methods and materials. For tours within a national park topics might include habitats, ecology, flora and fauna, and land management. Topics might also be influenced by the design of the tour and whether it is part of a package, whether it is a specific audience-requested activity, or whether it is part of a product-development initiative. Topics could also be influenced by audience feedback, which might require you to change topics halfway through your tour because of lack of interest.

Once you have decided on a topic you begin your specific researching efforts. You start to gather information on the particular site and/or events you will be visiting, and research what will be relevant to your identified audience group. Ideally, you would already have a researching method in place and have built up a filing and resource database of information.

This research element is essential as you need to ensure that your information is accurate and up to date. If you are ever in doubt about any information included in your commentary, either leave it out or spend more time finding out. Never make up any information, unless it's part of the activity or the audience knows that it's fabricated and have given you permission to deliver this information. An example of the latter would be when working with stories and creating fantasy worlds for your audience.

The same principles and attitude apply if you are asked a question and you do not know the answer. Never make up an answer—just admit that you do not know, and ask whether anyone else in the group knows and, if not, offer to find out at a later stage. Perhaps you could carry some reference material with you so you could look up the information during a rest stop. There are many knowledgeable people who travel and attend tours. All it takes is one occasion in which you provide inaccurate information and you can lose your status, respect and standing within the group.

With multisite tours the challenge is to find a common and consistent topic which can unify your commentary between sites. The concept of perception layering discussed on pages 153–6 can assist with this. Otherwise, you might need to develop unique topics for each site.

ACTIVITY:
1. You are about to plan a program of ten separate tours. Select a unique topic for each tour.
2. Spend 30 minutes exploring the Australian Museums and Galleries Online website (www.amol.org.au).
   (a) List six features of the website which you could use when planning tours.
   (b) How would you use these features?
   (c) Find six attractions which have websites that are linked to the AMOL website.
   (d) List at least four of the discussion groups on the AMOL website.
   (e) What assistance could these groups provide when you are planning tours?

DECIDING ON THE COMMENTARY THEME

The next step is to select a particular angle within this topic. If the topic is history, then what aspect and angle of history are you planning to share with people? If it is architecture, then what is it about the architecture?

By answering the question 'So what?' you are beginning to develop a theme for your tour. By doing this you tighten the focus of your topic and what you want people to know about this topic.

What is a theme?

The theme is the story-line and unifying thread for the tour. It is the theme which frames your activity, and which organises and connects the various elements of your tour.

A theme allows information to be systematically incorporated into your activity so that it is presented in digestible amounts. People remember the broad concepts and clusterings of information.

As an analogy, imagine entering a museum with an amazing collection of photos, priceless artefacts, tools and other historical objects. Imagine that there is no signage or complementary information provided about the collections. How would you be able to make sense of the mass of information being presented? Unless you have a specific interest and understanding of the objects this would be an extremely difficult undertaking.

Now imagine that prior to the collections going on display, they were grouped into relevant subject areas, for example tools used by the early pioneers of the area, and clothes worn by women, by men and by children. Complementing these groupings of collections is additional information which helps to associate the objects with some framework, and some context that assists in creating meaning.

In which scenario would you expect to gain a greater understanding of the collections? Most likely it would be in the second scenario. Why? Because the information is ordered, it is grouped and categorised, and it is complemented by additional information. This is the way the brain likes to work—it likes to be able to associate and allocate information into relevant 'mind slots'.

The theme is what helps the mind allocate information into relevant slots, and to complement its function as a self-organising system. At the same time it prevents you from showering your audience with seemingly unrelated and irrelevant information.

The theme reveals the overall purpose of the tour. It reveals what is unique and special about a particular site and/or event. For example, what is unique about Fremantle compared to Perth, or about Launceston compared to Hobart? It can also provide regional significance of an area and its relationships to surrounding areas; for example, Ku-ring-gai Chase National Park within the northern areas of Sydney as a Hawkesbury sandstone park.

The theme packages the main messages you want to promote to your audience, and it is these messages which people take away. You plan on these messages being positive and hope that your audience will share them with other people and/or apply them to other situations at later times. In this way a theme should be able to answer the question 'What sense of meaning do you want your audience to gain from coming along on your tour?'

Think of the last time you saw a movie or read a book. What were they about? In the majority of cases what you remember will be closely related to the theme or story-line of that movie or book.

By taking the time to think through your commentary and construct a theme-based approach, you are demonstrating your commitment to ensuring people have a great time, and that what you have to say is worth thinking about.

Theme statements

Themes are best expressed through theme statements. As an example, let's say you are planning a tour of Adelaide. You decide the topic to be 'The European history of Adelaide'. To arrive at your theme you now ask 'So *What* about the European history of Adelaide?' This could generate several possible themes including the following:

● It was the industries which grew and flourished within Adelaide in the 19th century which contributed to Adelaide becoming a major Australian settlement.
● The significant periods of Adelaide's European development are expressed through the architecture of its streets.

Another example might be a tour focusing on the topic of vegetation within a national park. You ask '*So What* about the plants?' and generate the following possible theme statements:

● There is an intricate and interdependent relationship between plant types and soil types.
● There is an intricate and interdependent relationship between vegetation and animals.
● Indigenous people used native vegetation for food and to make shelter.

The following are further examples of theme statements developed by David Newton in a workshop he conducted in 1994 called 'Storming the Pipes'.

Topic: Habitats
Theme: The diverse habitats represented in Victoria's national parks are shaped by the land and depend on our understanding for their survival.

Topic: Recreation zones
Theme: Management in Victoria is a careful balance of nature and recreation.

Topic: Backyard bandits
Theme: Many backyard plants and pets can endanger our native bushland.

What are the elements of these theme statements?

● They answer the question *So What?*
● They provide a tight focus for your planning and delivery efforts.
● They have an action element.
● They are a complete sentence, which means they include the all-important verb.

Selecting your theme

You can base the selection of your themes on a variety of criteria including the following:

● Assess and determine the significance of an area, and then decide on a theme which would best highlight/promote this.
● Choose an area of special interest.
● Respond to an audience-requested activity in which the audience specifies a particular theme.
● Conduct a tour which remains true to any relevant promotional material. The teaser lines associated with these promotional materials are generally based around the proposed theme of an activity. For example, if a tour package has promoted the living stromatolites (cyanobacteria colonies) of Western Australia, then you can be reasonably certain that this is what people will want to find out about.
● Research outcomes can be useful. An example of the latter is the work of Gianna Moscardo (2000) in surveying visitor attitudes and understanding of the environmental and human impacts on the Great Barrier Reef. This research indicated the need for tours to incorporate themes based on 'the human impact on marine environments'.
● By considering the tour from the audience's perspective, and by asking the following questions:
  —What information would your audience find interesting, relevant and useful?
  —What would your audience most want to know about this site and/or event?
  —Why would this information be useful?

As with topics, themes will also vary depending on your type of operation. An ecotour operator conducting bushwalks might focus more of the tour on the natural landscape while a cityscape walking tour might have a social history focus. It would obviously be irrelevant to talk about the evolution of Australia's mammal fauna while leading a snorkelling trip.

The Australian Heritage Commission has published a booklet titled *Australian Historic Themes*. This is an excellent resource for preparing themes, especially if you are interested in leading tours around heritage places. Contact the Australian Heritage Commission (details in Bibliography). Appendix 3 outlines other thematic approaches. (For further information on themes refer to Sam Ham's book *Environmental Interpretation* listed in the Bibliography.)

Fleshing out the theme

Once you have established the theme, you need to start developing a skeletal structure and then padding it out. You need to start thinking about what content, ideas, events, information and activities are to be included in the tour, how the tour will unfold, and in what sequence this will happen.

You can use a headline and point-form technique to assist in this process, which should be linked in with the itinerary timings. This technique is similar to the process of writing an article or book in which headings and subheadings are used to break up the text and present it in a packaged form for easier reading. Using the headline and point-form technique provides you with an outline of your tour and the opportunity to present and develop ideas one at a time.

The first part of the skeletal structure and of the headline and point-form technique is to develop a list of headlines or key points which you would consider to be a list of 'must-knows'.

Topic: Vegetation
Theme: Plants need homes, which are called habitats.
Headlines (your must-know key points):

- the three main habitat types in this area;
- characteristics of wet forest habitat;
- characteristics of dry forest and how they are different from wet forest;
- characteristics of heathland and how they are different from forest habitats.

Topic: History
Theme: Stepping into the alleyways of any city reveals many stories of its past.
Headlines (your must-know key points):

- alleyways—they preserve history;
- types of alleyways;
- what lays beneath all the manhole covers of an alleyway;
- changing use of alleyways;
- keeping safe when visiting alleyways.

A first part of the skeletal structure is to develop a list of headlines that relate to a list of 'must-knows'.

Once you have started to frame up your skeletal structure with a list of must-knows you can extend on your headlines with subheading pieces of information (these are the points within the headline and point-form technique). When developing these subheadings try to incorporate a variety of information forms and delivery methods. Add a little information spice by sprinkling in anecdotes, hands-on sensory experiences, questions and interactive activities, opportunities for people to be reflective and ponder, and use analogies to explain concepts and ideas, and involve people in demonstrations (see pages 181–88. Vary the style of information delivery by using the presentation techniques discussed in Chapter 5.

Most people find it easier to write the Introduction and Conclusion after they have completed their headline, point forms and associated information. Experiment and do what works for you.

When building your commentary the skill is in extracting information and focusing on that information relevant to your tour, while leaving some opportunity for people to discover things for themselves. The best Guides are not those who are the most knowledgeable but rather those who can bring the tour to life with a skilful use of communication and group-management techniques.

The following is an example of using the headline (must-knows) and point (subheadings) technique. (Appendix 5 includes an activity planning template used by the WA Department of Conservation and Land Management.)

Topic: Social *Theme:* Streets and their social history *Theme statement:* Drust street is an integral part of Riggybaa's social fabric. *Venue:* Drust Street in Riggybaa *Length:* 60 minutes *Audience:* Mixed group of 22 people—travellers from within Australia *Meeting place:* Shydog Park		
Body: must-knows	• Streets have individual and unique meanings. • The initial history of Drust Street. • The uses of Drust Street have changed with time. • Drust Street is part of people's sense of place, and this is reflected by the gardens and architecture along the street. • Final must-know (for you to write)	
	Must-knows Streets have individual and unique meanings	**Subheadings (blending a variety of information spices and delivery methods)** • Ask people to remember their favourite street (*group involvement and working with questions*). • Share a few of these memories (*group involvement and interaction*). • Streets are a personal thing (*group involvement in asking people to reflect*). • Provide 'formal' definition of a street (*facts and objective information*).

	The initial history of Drust Street.	• Describe when the street was built (*facts*) and the subsequent celebrations of local townsfolk (*anecdote*). Tell any other stories which occurred during the street's construction (*stories*). • Why was it built (*relationship and purpose, reflection*) and how (*processes*)? • What did it look like (*imaginary, sensory language*)?
Information spices and delivery	The uses of Drust Street have changed with time.	• The method of transport of people and goods has changed (*historical photos compared to current landscape*). • Play and leisure uses of the street have changed. Ask people to remember what activities they enjoyed in their local streets (*group interaction, working with questions*) and how their streets have changed (*reflection*). Share the changes in Drust Street through the memories of an elderly resident (*oral history*).
	Drust Street is part of people's sense of place, and this is reflected by the architecture along the street.	See no. 1 in the Activity section below.
	See no. 2 in the Activity section below.	See no. 3 in the Activity section below.
Conclusion—your wrap-up statement	'Well, that brings us to a wrap for this tour. I hope you enjoyed the walk along Drust Street and discovered just a few of the fascinating insights into this town. Before you leave I would like to ask you for a favour.' *Silence—scan the group.* 'It's only a small favour and it takes place right in	

	your own locale. Would you ring a close friend who you haven't seen for a while and take that person for a tour of your favourite street, perhaps doing what we did today or doing it in your own way, but just spending time enjoying what the street evokes.' *Silence*. 'Thanks again for taking the time to share in the stories of Drust Street. All the best.'
Introduction—opening statement	See no. 4 in the Activity section below.

ACTIVITY: Complete the above table using a similar format by doing the following:
1. Write subheadings for the people's sense of place.
2. Complete the final must-know point.
3. Write subheadings for the final must-know point.
4. Write your introduction to this tour.

Your commentary needs to be clear, concise and not too wordy. It also needs to be kept logical and sequential. The success of any story relies on the ability to sequence its development towards a climax and end. The same effort applies to tours.

THINKING SEQUENTIALLY

To assist you to think sequentially, use the dimensions of time and space and their related variations. It is these dimensions which provide the framework for all movement. For example, you could develop your tour from:

- a chronological viewpoint—past to present to future, future to present to past, or movement through time periods such as seasons, months, days or hours;
- raw materials to finished product;
- simple to complex;
- spatial—near to far, narrow to wide, expansive to concise, up to down, or national to regional to local to site specific;
- size—small to large;
- movement—fast to slow, or slow to fast;
- known to unknown;
- general and broad to specific;
- common to unusual;
- cause to effect, or effect to cause.

You can make up your own variations provided they follow a logical and sequential order.

Having sequence and logical flow to a commentary allows you to refer to previous elements, while providing for progression from one key point to the next. It makes it easier for people to store, remember, process and organise information. This increases the potential for keeping people's interest—the more you can ensure people's understanding, the more chance you have that they will enjoy your commentary and find the information interesting.

Generally, it is best to provide a broad, overall view of the topic and then bring your focus into more specific information, which would be provided in bite-sized chunks. And in this process what you leave out of your communication process will be just as important as what you include.

THE BEGINNING AND END OF YOUR COMMENTARY

The beginning and end of your commentary should be concise and serve to emphasise the main points made in the body of your commentary. While the ending is a summation of the main points, the introduction would provide a glimpse of what's in store. Avoid using phrases such as 'I would like to introduce the following . . .' or 'And in conclusion . . .', but rather try to be poetic and creative when writing your introduction and conclusion. The following is an example of an introduction.

The beginning of an interpretive tour within a small rural town

Let's imagine you have a particular interest in promoting your local town. You decide that the topic of your tour will be history. Next ask yourself what aspect of history interests you, and you may decide to focus on the derelict buildings in the town. You then choose to develop the tour on the theme statement: 'Derelict buildings are significant representations of the town's heritage and should be conserved.' To support this theme you choose a building which although derelict is still safe to visit. You also start to consider what relevant props you could use and begin collecting historical photos, oral histories and personal diaries.

You plan and promote all the relevant logistical details of the tour and feel reasonably confident that this will attract only those visitors who are really interested in coming along to this tour.

After you greet your audience, you invite them inside for the 'introduction' to your tour.

Hi, for those people I did not meet outside my name is Jack. I extend to you a warm welcome from the town of Redlore and thank you for taking the time to visit this cute and quaint cottage.

A cottage which has been home to many people over the years. A cottage whose walls, floors and ceilings are now considered redundant. Derelict. Amazing that word 'derelict'. That a cottage which boasts proud memories and echoes with the sounds of so many stories, that stands with delicate pride and spirit—is now called derelict.

And to many of us it may appear derelict.

By the end of this tour I hope that you will share in the spirit which still holds these walls intact. I hope that we can close the doors with a feeling that you would wish to return. I hope that you attribute a great sense of worth and value beyond the word 'derelict'.

Once again, welcome to Inns Cottage.

 ACTIVITY: Which part of the above passage do you believe expresses the theme and what do you think is the take-home message?

DELIVERY OF YOUR COMMENTARY

Presentation techniques for delivering your commentary are discussed in Chapter 5. In summary ensure the following:

- Information is accurate, relevant and takes into account cultural and social sensitivities.
- You use appropriate language.
- Your non-verbals support your presentation—this includes appropriate grooming, facial expressions, movements and mannerisms, and other body language.
- There is variety in your delivery styles and vocal techniques.
- You are enthusiastic, friendly and professional.
- You are natural and relaxed in your delivery.

EVALUATION OF YOUR COMMENTARY

Evaluation techniques and strategies are discussed in Chapter 6. It is important that you spend time evaluating your commentary. Note any questions which people ask, especially those you could not answer. Every time you do not know an answer treat it as a learning opportunity. Be objective in your appraisal of how it went. Ask yourself:

- Could you have incorporated any other props?
- Was your delivery clear?
- Was the commentary presented in a sequential and logical order?
- Did your audience know the theme and take-home message?

BUILDING THE COMMENTARY—A SUMMARY

This process of developing a structure for your commentary might well require a few drafts, but the effort will ensure you have a commentary that is clear, makes sense, and is sequential and logical. This effort will also boost your confidence.

An analogy to the above process is composing a song. Before a popular song is released musicians will decide on a particular key, for example the key of G. This decision will be based on the style of the song; for example, a minor key would be the most likely choice for a sombre piece of music while for an upbeat rock song it would be a major key. Once the musicians have decided on a key, they select and compose those chords and notes which provide the appropriate melody and harmony within this key. Next comes hours of rehearsal before the song is released.

There is an analogy with interpretive activities and listening. One of the roles of effective listening is to determine the meaning within communicated messages. Likewise, an environment will offer the audience a variety of messages—you are selecting a particular message and then facilitating the listening process for your audience. You are getting to the guts of it. Developing an activity is the same process as you are continually digging deeper and deeper, focusing on selected layers of your environment to select those which support your theme and message.

ENRICHING YOUR COMMENTARY

Whenever possible, strive to enrich your commentary by incorporating a variety of delivery techniques and approaches. This is essential within all interpretive activities as you seek to capture, engage and involve your audience. It's best to try to avoid your commentary becoming a 'gawk and talk' session, in which you rattle off a string of information while expecting the audience to politely take it all in.

Seeking and maintaining the involvement of your audience can be related to the adage: 'Don't sell. Create a desire to buy.'

Some of the ways you can create this desire include:

● capturing the attention of your audience;
● delivering information in a variety of forms;
● making your tour interesting, relevant and meaningful for your audience;
● incorporating props.

CAPTURING THE ATTENTION OF YOUR AUDIENCE

To capture attention you can incorporate subject matter which has some of the following characteristics:

● It is topical, has novelty value and includes provocative information.
● It focuses on social information and human interest.
● It includes humour , for example 'like the time you were enjoying a special moment and then the mosquitos arrived'.
● It includes mystery, suspense, drama and perhaps a shock element.
● It relates to something that works, something that your audience can observe in action. For example, consider a group of people on a bushwalking tour who stop alongside a trigger plant. The Guide can name it as a trigger plant and provide a

few additional bits of information or can demonstrate the way it pollinates by delivering the following presentation:

While you are watching the trigger plant I'm going to demonstrate the fascinating way it pollinates. An insect lands on the plant here, and triggers this part of the plant (the pistil) which dusts the insect with pollen. The insect, now covered in pollen, goes off to visit another trigger plant and guess what, it brushes the pollen onto a ready and waiting female plant part, the stigma, and pollination takes place. Fascinating, yes!

Showing is much more powerful than saying. This relates to other aspects of life in which it is so much easier for people to make promises and say things they will do and won't do—but it is much more powerful when they actually show us in their behaviour.

- It is fascinating and/or unusual and/or challenges myths. For example, few people know that people from the Ukraine immigrated to Australia as early as the 1840s, or that Chinese immigration to Australia was quite active as early as the 1820s. What about including information about amazing feats, for example birds which migrate for thousands of kilometres and return to the same roost, the mortality rate and longevity of animals, how long it took an artist to paint a particular painting and how much paint was used, and the fact that swifts fly for nine months without landing. The following is an example of challenging myths: most people believe that Australia's native mammal population is dominated by marsupials, and yet approximately 50 per cent of our native mammals are placentals (25 per cent bats, and 25 per cent native rodents).

- It is entertaining, which does not necessarily mean it has to involve jokes. Seek out ways to incorporate humour and light-hearted fun into your activity, while always making sure it's appropriate and respectful.

- It is interactive, for example asking questions, involving people in holding an object while you demonstrate how it works, or encouraging people to 'have a go' such as using binoculars or playing a simple game or trying an activity. For example:

Before we start our tour I would like you to observe the houses along this main street. Notice their different architecture and their unique styles. What do you think is the average price for these houses? $600 000? $800 000? Well, around 200 years ago this whole peninsula was bought for approximately this amount of money (*holding up a 50c coin*). That's right—the Balmain peninsula sold for 5 shillings. Now I think that this is amazing, and I would like to share with you on this tour the story of Balmain from the time it was sold for 50c to today when 50c doesn't even buy you a decent bar of chocolate.

- It uses spontaneous situations and emphasises being 'in the moment'. Relate to what people are experiencing in the moment.

Be alert for spontaneous situations which you can incorporate into your tour...

- It relates to a 'props bag' with items you can pass around such as artefacts and historical photos.

You can also capture the attention of your audience by demonstrating a genuine and honest interest in their well-being, in their interests, in satisfying their needs, and in providing exceptional customer service.

MEANS OF DELIVERING INFORMATION

Information can be delivered in a variety of forms including those listed below. The more you can incorporate information spices and variety into your tours, the greater the opportunity to capture and maintain the involvement of your audience, and assist their understanding of what it is you are trying to communicate.

- *Anecdotes and stories.* Anecdotes should be used as appropriate and not overused as too many can overwhelm your audience. Remember to let people know that they are anecdotes and not necessarily facts, and keep in mind that they need to be told in a manner which is appropriate to the audience. Anecdotes are just one form of story which can be incorporated into your commentary; other forms include personal experiences, oral histories, myths and legends, and humorous tales.
- *Ask questions and/or pose a problem.* Ask questions, for example you suddenly emerge from a woodland vegetation and are now standing in heathland, and there is a clear and divisible line between the two. You could ask your audience: 'Well, here we are, standing in a vegetation type called 'heath'. You notice that it is much

shorter and denser than the woodland vegetation we have just been walking through. If both these vegetation types have been here for thousands of years, why is it that they appear not to encroach on one another?' While looking at a building with intricate decorative features on its external parapets you could ask: 'How do you think workers in the early 19th century managed to decorate this building with those features?'

- *Facts and statistics and analogies and metaphors.* When using statistics and factual information try to disperse them throughout your commentary rather than as one clump. And try to research the interesting and unusual statistics which can generate a 'wow' factor. When statistics are difficult to comprehend it might be best to incorporate them within a metaphor or analogy. These help to simplify complex principles, making it easier for the audience to make sense of them. The more the audience can make sense of them, the more they will remain engaged rather than switch off because it is too much hard work to try to understand. They can also be fun. For example, if you were trying to explain the speed of light to a group of people, you could say, 'As I mentioned before the speed of light is 300 000 kilometres per second. That's pretty fast, but to give you an idea of how fast it is let's pretend we are all standing on the equator. What we're going to do is travel around the equator at the speed of light. How many times do you think we could go around in one second? Once . . . halfway . . . three times? Well, get ready, because here we go. Ready, here we go and run . . . (one second later) . . . Stop. Congratulations, you have just run around the equator seven times in one second by travelling at the speed of light.'
- *Mix up the 'what' elements.* You can mix up the 'what' elements within your presentation with descriptive words and active phrasings, expressive verbs, short sentences and long sentences, and varying adjectives and adverbs. For example, 'The *thump, thump, thump* of a wallaby', 'Wallabies love to *munch* on grasses' and 'Thornbills are those small little brown birds *flirting* with the tree canopy'.
- *Mix up the senses.* Incorporate visual media such as comparing old photos with a current landscape, and encouraging people to look at things in different ways. Incorporate auditory media such as poetry, music and songs. Encourage people to smell and sniff, and if possible to touch and taste. Following on from the preceding example, you could use a variety of sensory-based language. We receive information from our environment through our senses, so the more you can engage the senses of your audience—especially their non-dominant senses—the more information you can work into your tour as a resource.
- *Demonstrations.* Show people how things actually work (e.g. the trigger plant).
- *Testimonials.* These can come from famous people or locals, for example 'Today we will be walking through an area which all the rangers rate as their favourite part of this national park. And we'll be finding out just why they like it so much'.
- *Examples, illustrations and case studies.*

- *Meter and/or mnemonics.* Find poetry and other forms of information which include meter and/or mnemonics.
- *Games and quizzes.* This can require you to ask people questions.

MAKING YOUR COMMENTARY INTERESTING, RELEVANT AND MEANINGFUL

The more you can make your commentary relevant and meaningful for your audience, the greater the chance they will find it interesting and remain engaged in your delivery. Some of the ways to do this include:

- Make it enjoyable, and create a positive and comfortable environment. You need to be flexible in how you deliver your tour to accommodate diversity within the audience and/or the environment.
- Make the tour relevant to your audience and seek ways for them to make a personal connection—this can be achieved through satisfying the needs, expectations, interests and motivations of your audience. It can also be achieved through the human element—that is, by you being empathetic, enthusiastic and inspiring; and by ensuring that the content, level of information and style of delivery is appropriate to your audience. One way to make it personal is to use names, and incorporate personal words and phrases such as 'you', 'everyone here', 'remember when we all saw that building before . . .', 'I am going to ask you to remember back to . . .', 'I am going to ask you to think about . . .', 'How many people here love the taste of ice-cream?', and 'How many people have . . .?' You can make it relevant to people from different cultures by making connections to places with which they are familiar such as their town, region or country, and by

referring to the origins of relevant words used in Australia. For example:

—German origin—nickel, shale, kindergarten, seminar and waltz;

—Spanish origin—guitar, embargo, sherry and cask;

—Italian origin—traffic, umbrella, opera and studio;

—Dutch origin—buoy, dock and deck (these all reflect the maritime culture and heritage of the Netherlands).

- Inject your enthusiasm, which can become contagious; if you are not enthusiastic, how can you expect your audience to be?
- Provoke attention—work with contrast, challenge the senses and make it relevant. Stimulate people by provoking thought beyond the objective information you are providing.
- Engage the affective domain through beauty, evocative words and images, and stories.
- If you are stopping to talk about an object, make sure everyone can see it. Never simply identify an object unless asked and especially if there is nothing interesting to say about it.
- Cater to different learning styles (refer to pages 147–52).
- Provide a context (big picture) to assist people to make sense of, and integrate, the information you will be delivering. Provide structure to your tour (refer to the section on 'Building your commentary' earlier in this chapter). An example is the use of signposts. These indicate to the audience what is coming up. For example: 'During the next part of this tour I would like to share with you three of the most unusual happenings ever heard of in this part of the country.' And then you would go on to share these three happenings. Another example would be: 'As we walk down Collins Street, I would like you to notice the changes in architecture which occur on each cross street.' By saying this you are encouraging people to remain alert on the cross streets. Once you have completed this section of the walk you could then ask your audience what changes they noticed on the cross streets.
- Keep it current. Take a leaf from the news regarding how a 'disaster' is more newsworthy than prevention efforts which were implemented to avoid that disaster. The reason is that there are more emotions involved, that it is immediate and is happening now, and that it's in your face.
- Exaggerate items such as time and space. An example is condensing geological time of hundreds of millions of years into a 24-hour period and another example is the analogy of the speed of light described earlier.
- Compare items/events with other items/events you have been discussing with your audience, especially if you can demonstrate and discuss any process of cause and effect.
- Work with paradoxes, which are contradictory statements, as a way of adding colour to your word phrasings, for example 'warm ice', 'dry rain' and 'calm storm'.
- Ensure diversity and variety. Use different presentation methods and incorporate

vocal sounds into your commentary. For example, if you were talking about transport in the 19th century, you might make the sound of a steamship to incorporate an auditory component, or perhaps bring along a steam whistle as a prop. On a bushwalk you could incorporate animal sounds such as those of birds, and encourage your audience to practise the same.

Using words and phrasings to evoke and 'paint' mental pictures

- Leave out rumours and gossip.
- Relate what you are saying to something within their own experience. This could be as simple as the following:
  —Reincorporate any points made by members of your group, for example: 'A few minutes back I was talking with Ms Paperworm and she told me that she grew up in this area. And that . . .' (obviously check with Ms Paperworm that it is okay to share your conversation).
  —Reincorporate any answer provided, for example: 'Mr Sillworm asked that interesting question before about how the style of architecture is different. Well, that's what we are looking at now. The building on the right is . . . and the building on the left is . . .'
  —Repeat any questions people ask for the benefit of the rest of the group.
  —Praise and thank people for their contributions. And if you deliver a compliment let people know why. For example, 'Thanks for that. What a great story, I never knew that this site had such a rich history' or 'Thanks for being so helpful. We should now be able to leave on time'.
- Provide opportunities for silence and reflection.
- Keep your words and phrasing simple. Words and language become more interesting with precision and not length.

Seek to present a whole rather than parts—to generate a holistic experience, a holistic viewpoint or a holistic story. This is the beauty of stories: they have a beginning, middle and end; they are complete and whole; and they provide a complete picture.

Your audience is attending your activity to experience the site/event—your commentary is one of the main ways they can achieve this aim.

INCORPORATE PROPS INTO YOUR COMMENTARY

Props are a great resource to enrich your commentary. They provide an additional delivery strategy which increases the chances of appealing to people with different

reference books.... hand lens, binoculars, magnifying glasses...

booklets...

learning styles. Props can include:

- other speakers and Guides/specialist speakers;
- blindfolds;
- magnifying glasses;
- booklets and reference material such as field guides;
- artefacts;
- cupping ears for sound and curling hands for telescope;
- telescopes and star charts;
- models;
- audiovisuals (e.g. if leading a tour in a museum, take advantage of any short audiovisual presentations; or at the start of a walk show a short orientation video);
- dioramas;
- maps and diagrams;
- music;
- worksheets;
- experiments.

Special Focus

The wonderful World of Words

Sandra O'Neil
Consultant, Learning and Development

INTRODUCTION

Each of us lives in many worlds. At various times and in various circumstances you might inhabit the world of reality or fantasy, your internal world or the world external to yourself, the separate worlds of sounds or sights or sensations, or all three.

As an oral communicator, we also have a World of Words. This is the world created by the way we structure and use sentences, phrases and words. It is shaped by the variety of words we use (or make up), the creativity with which we string them together, their aptness in conveying the message and the images they conjure for our listener. Depending on our skill in navigating, exploring and traversing it, the World of Words can literally be a *wonder-full* place!

Your personal World of Words is a vast reservoir from which you can pick up drops of pure gold to enrich your oral communication. You can probably think of situations where you would like to be more eagerly listened to; where you could be more articulate, elegant and accurate in your speaking; where you could ensure your meaning is clearer; and where you are able to say more with less. Your World of Words is the resource which provides for all these needs.

Of course, almost everyone uses words to speak, and willy-nilly creates their own World of Words. Usually, however, this world is built up with no great awareness of its potential potency. Words strung together may indeed communicate a message, but the effect may be limited to the most basic comprehension of bare facts. This style of using words may be adequate for giving instructions, relaying data and minimising misinformation; however, when the listener is not involved, intrigued or entranced, it lacks the magic needed for engaging the soul and capturing the imagination.

It is noticeable that some people (including some storytellers) are more interesting to listen to because of the way they use words. They may be more entertaining, more clearly understood and more persuasive than other speakers. And yet, they may not necessarily have a wider vocabulary than your own. Somehow these people have developed the ability to use words, tap into their power, turn loose their images and forge strong connections between their messages and their listeners.

Your vocabulary does, of course, play a role in your personal World of

Words. However, more important than the number of words you know is the skill of using effectively the words you do know—and this skill can be learnt. This article provides eight basic techniques for enriching the World of Words you inhabit. Learning and applying these techniques will help you to make connections with your listeners that resonate with meaning, power and relevance.

However, before introducing the eight techniques, let us say a few words about vocabulary, grammar and rhythm.

VOCABULARY

It is worth noting that you probably already have a much wider vocabulary than you give yourself credit for. Typically, your normal World of Words is like a familiar home. Just as you spend the most time in the comfortable, well-lit, well-used rooms of the home, so also you tend to use comfortable, well-known, familiar words. However, if you choose to sweep out some of the less frequently visited corners and crevasses of your vocabulary, you will find a treasure trove of words ready and waiting which can amplify, colour and particularise your world!

For example, how many of the words below do you know?

- cavalcade
- offbeat
- secretive
- vigorous
- wheedle
- asinine
- glowering
- deft
- earnest
- disreputable
- misadventure
- reinforce
- trample
- waif
- bonanza
- dredge
- jagged
- quaver
- euphonious
- inquisitive

You can probably understand and define at least half of the words in this list. Although you may not use them often, they and many more are there in the corners of your mind, ready to be brought into the light and to play their role in enhancing your enlarged World of Words. Develop the habit of sweeping out those seldom-visited corners of your vocabulary.

Here's a useful exercise to recall lost words which are lurking in the crevasses: imagine a scene in your mind; take the time to see it in as much detail as you can; hear whatever sounds it produces; notice any sensory aspects such as smells or tastes; and get a sense of the ambience or feeling of what is taking place in the scene. Then sit down and write a list of all the words you can think of which describe the people, characters, things, noises, smells, tastes, actions and emotions of this scene. Don't try for descriptive sentences; simply write down appropriate words. Write quickly; go for quantity, not quality. Give yourself at least ten minutes. At the end of this time, review your list. You will undoubtedly see many words which you have not used recently, but which were there waiting for you to rediscover!

In addition to the vast reserve of 'official' words which currently exist, however underutilised, in your vocabulary, there is also an endless variety of words you can simply make up. These can be fanciful or serious, derivative or original, and they are often onomatopoeic. Perhaps one of the best known made-up words, from *Mary Poppins*, is 'supercalifragilisticexpialidotious'. Another, from *Alice in Wonderland*, is 'curiouser'. Another, from Shakespeare's *Hamlet*, is 'nighted', referring to dark-coloured clothing. Some made-up words have so caught the imagination of audiences that they have passed into the language to become official, such as 'serendipity', 'Shangrila', 'charisma' and 'fair dinkum'.

The aim when making up words to add to your own World of Words is to make even clearer and more particular the meaning of your message. Therefore the new words must be capable of being understood, even if it is the first time a listener hears them. The context in which they are used, or the sound of the words themselves (onomatopoeia), must give strong clues about the word's meaning. For example:

- 'The stone *ploshed* into the stream'
- 'The undulating meadow *greened* away into the distance'
- '*Chirruping* to his horse, the man drove the wagon on'

Continue to enlarge and enrich your own vocabulary. Rediscover those familiar words hidden in the dark corners of your vocabulary; create new words to serve your purposes; and, of course, take every opportunity through reading or listening to others to add new words to your repertoire. Words are the raw materials you use when applying the techniques which shape your World of Words.

GRAMMAR

While not advocating a complete disregard of the rules of grammar, it is true to say that oral communication is less bound by them than written literature. This article focuses on your oral World of Words as a highly imaginative place, and this may mean you sometimes take liberties with the strict rules of sentence construction and grammar. This is fine, as long as you observe that the effect on your listener is even more attentiveness to your colourful, innovative expressions. Language that confuses or fogs the true meaning should be avoided, of course, but be prepared to experiment to find the best, the most evocative way of using words, without being hamstrung by traditional grammar.

ABOUT RHYTHM

Several of the techniques discussed in this article for enriching your World of Words are based on variations on the use of rhythm. Rhythm is a satisfying combination of regular sounds and beats in speech. It can be achieved by repetition, and by arranging words into stressed and unstressed sequences or into long and short syllables. Even non-words can create rhythm. For example:

- 'Dum diddy dum, dum diddy dum'
- 'Dum diddely-um-pum, dum dum'

When used with real words, rhythm makes them memorable. Crafted in a way which creates rhythm, words stick!

TECHNIQUES FOR ENLARGING YOUR WORLD OF WORDS

1. Patterns of rhyme

The use of rhyme is a time-honoured way to create rhythm. It evolves as a function of the regularity of the rhyming sounds (e.g. 'The cat sat on the mat'). It is well known that, once learnt, the words which are strung together in doggerel, rhyming songs and poems stay with us—sometimes for a lifetime! The memory-jogger which starts, 'Thirty days has September . . .' is only one of many verses from childhood which prove the usefulness and longevity of rhyme as a technique.

There are many patterns of rhyme you can choose, but for oral communicating simplest is best. Rhyming couplets will usually get just as effective a result as a limerick or a poem in iambic pentameter. Also, since oral communication often needs to be flexible and spontaneous, rhyming couplets may be easier to create on the spur of the moment. For example:

- 'If it is to be, it is up to me'
- 'I'm a poet and I didn't know it'
- 'Use it or lose it'

In most oral communication, unless the whole speech is in the form of a poem, patterns of rhyme work best when used:

- at the beginning, to open in an arresting manner;
- during, to make specific points stand out from the rest of the content;
- regularly during, as a refrain (see below);
- at the end, to achieve closure in a satisfying way.

2. Alliteration

Alliteration is the use of the same letter at the beginning of several sequential words, or at the start of each stressed word in a phrase or line. This emphasis provides a beat to the words, and helps to develop rhythm. Examples of alliteration abound in literature, and it is a relatively simple task to use it spontaneously in spoken communication by selecting words with similar start sounds. For example:

- 'The wonderful World of Words'
- 'Round the rock the ragged rascal ran'
- 'Keep it clean'

With alliteration providing the rhythm, listeners have a repetitive sound to aid their recognition and connection with the message. In addition, more of what is said is likely to be remembered.

3. Repetition

Repetition is exactly that: saying the same word or phrase more than once. The oral strength of repetition comes from the neurological impact on our awareness and memory which infers that:

- once is an event;
- twice is a coincidence and a rhythm has begun to appear;
- three times indicates a pattern and the rhythm is recognisable;
- finally, four times is undeniable.

Repetition usually occurs in a very close time sequence. In oral communication, repetition can be extremely powerful for emphasising important points or strongly felt emotions. For example:

- 'Don't go out that door,' he cried. 'Don't go out!'
- 'I've had enough. I've had enough!'
- 'It just keeps pounding, pounding, pounding in my head'.

However, care must be taken not to overuse this technique. Too many repetitions, and boredom and a sense of predictability set in. It may also imply that you don't think you're being listened to! As a general rule of thumb, three times repeated is the recommended maximum.

4. Refrain

Normally the term 'refrain' refers to a regularly recurring melody, such as the chorus of a song. In oral communications, however, it refers to any regularly repeated saying or idea. It reinforces a key message and reminds listeners of how this message links with other parts of the speech. It keeps everyone (including the speaker!) on track with the main point of the story.

A refrain is similar to basic repetition in that it creates a regularity that gives a certain rhythm to speech. It differs from basic repetition in that the refrain can be widely spaced throughout the speech sequence. For example:

- 'I'll huff and I'll puff and I'll blow your house in!'
- 'So one door closed, but another opened' (said several times during a talk or story)
- 'I confess: that was the *[first/second/third]* mistake I made' (said sequentially through the story)

Note that a refrain loses power if you don't use exactly the same non-verbal signals each time (that is, identical vocal tone, gestures, posture and so on), so be sure to tie in these elements every time you return to your refrain.

5. Rule of three

It has been suggested that people operate in three-quarter time; that is, that they respond to three beats in a bar. If you consider many common abbreviations —such as ABC, IBM, MBF, AGC, TNT—you can almost 'hear' the satisfying rhythm making itself felt. Conversely it has been noticed that fluorescent lights, which many people find uncomfortable, unsatisfying or worse, have an electronic pulse of four-quarter time. Clearly the human system appears to respond better to the count of three.

This brings us to the rule of three. The rule of three is saying a descriptive word three times. However, unlike repetition where exactly the same word is repeated, in the rule of three you use a different synonym each time. For example:

- 'It was a beautiful, warm, sunny day'
- 'He pushed, shoved, forced his way through'
- 'I was amazed, impressed, delighted'

In oral communication, three seems to be a magical number in many ways. It creates the right balance between just enough to make a forceful point, but not so many that the message becomes predictable. There is a satisfying lilt and swing to the rhythm of three. And it allows nuances in the three synonyms used which add richness and detail to whatever is being described.

6. Parallel sentence structures

The technique of parallel sentence structures builds on the rule of three. It refers to grouping together three sentences which support the same message. Effectively they are reinforcing essentially the same thing, but using three different phrases to do so. Unlike the rule of three which uses simple word synonyms, parallel sentence structures use full sentences. For example:

- 'The sky was clear. The breeze was soft. The flowers were sweet.'

Parallel sentence structures gain potency when they are constructed using similar numbers of words, tenses and beats—all of which aid rhythm. Notice how this simple alteration to the example makes it much less rhythmic and more awkward:

● 'The sky was clear. The breeze was soft. The flowers smelled beautifully.'

Research indicates that different individuals use different sensory modalities as a way of processing information, with visual, auditory and kinaesthetic being the most common. People with a visual orientation relate best to words which describe 'seeing' experiences, for example colours or words such as 'clear', 'focused', 'sparkling' and so on. Similarly, people who process in an auditory way respond best to words which describe 'hearing' experiences, such as 'ring', 'buzzing', 'chime' or 'murmur'. People with a kinaesthetic orientation relate best to words which describe feelings, sensations or movement of the body, such as scents, tastes or words like 'rigid', 'tingling', 'hot', 'gripping' and so on.

Therefore another way to add power to parallel sentence structures is to design them to appeal to two or more of the physical senses. The first example given above does this. Other examples are:

● 'My legs, crippled by terror. My eyes, blinded with tears. My heart, throbbing in my ears.'
● 'The air smelt musty. The light was dim. The house echoed empty.'

Choosing words which relate to different senses will ensure you capture the attention of people who rely on different sensory modalities to process meaning. This tip adds not only to the effectiveness of parallel sentence structures, but also to any oral communication.

7. Analogy

An analogy is a comparison which describes similarities between two different things. The use of analogies enhances your World of Words by clarifying the meaning of what you say, enabling better understanding by your listener. They also allow you to embroider the image, creating a more vividly imagined picture for your listener to link into.

The simplest form of analogy is a *simile*, which uses the words 'like' or 'as' to link two disparate items. For example:

● 'She was pale as the dawn'
● 'His fury was like a lightning storm, slashing and thundering'
● 'She sang like a bird'

Another type of analogy is the *metaphor*, which indicates similarities between two different things without using 'like' or 'as'. For example:

- 'the blood-red rose'
- 'the frog-leapt over the fire hydrant'
- 'Ice-cold, his thoughts snailed their way to the obvious conclusion'

While your World of Words may not yet display the poetic skill of, say, Shakespeare, who was a master at manoeuvring words to create analogies to illustrate and magnify his meanings, you can begin by making simple but interesting comparisons when describing things. And it's helpful to remember that it's possible to compare anything with anything!

ACTIVITY: Look around you and select three common items within view. Then for each item, complete this sentence: 'Life is like this (*cup/pen/ring/chair*/and so on) because . . .'

With practice, you will soon be able to draw quick, accurate analogies to strengthen your World of Words too.

8. Six words or less

A sentence made up of six words or less is, by definition, relatively short. To remain under the six-word limit requires considerable refining and careful pruning of the unnecessary, superfluous or less meaningful elements. However, the distilled results are often very powerful indeed.

When 'six words or less' sentences are used in oral communication, they are very obviously contrived. The listener can tell words have been deleted; they don't sound quite 'natural'; and the rules of grammar have usually been bent or broken. Thus when several of these 'six words or less' sentences are used together, they form a small identifiable whole just for themselves, differentiated from the rest of the speech. For example:

- 'Canada. Crisp, cold Christmas night. Walking off the huge Christmas dinner. Brisk along the whitened road. Snow crunching underfoot. Breath huffing through face scarves. Distant merriment. But over all, a hush. At last, time and space. After a day of excitement, peace. I return to the Christmas truth.'

Because the 'six words or less' technique sets the content in a completely different rhythm from the rest, it is very useful for creating a change of pace, mind-set or emotional state in the listener which is different from what comes before or after.

However, always limiting sentences to six words or less tends to make them seem abrupt, staccato and even harsh. The benefits of regular rhythm disappear. Therefore it is counterproductive to keep using the technique indefinitely. Use it instead for emphasis, highlighting and state changing.

PUTTING THE TECHNIQUES INTO ACTION

It is rare for any of these eight techniques to just 'be there'. Though some may seem more readily usable to you than others, they all require planning, rehearsing and exposure to real listeners to become a seamless and integrated part of your World of Words.

However, as with any new skill, the more they are practised, the more easily and naturally they flow. You will even reach the stage where, on reviewing a talk or story or address you have given, you realise you have spontaneously and unconsciously included them in your World of Words.

A word to the wise: do not try to develop your skills in all eight techniques all at once. Rather, select one or two which seem appropriate to your communication style and content, and focus on becoming comfortable with using these. Take every opportunity, use them whenever you speak—informally or formally—to friends, colleagues or family, and when you're serious or light-hearted. Only move on to another technique or two when you sense the first ones are fully embedded into your oral repertoire. Keep going until you feel you have mastered all eight!

CONCLUSION

It is true that there are many worlds to inhabit, but in most of them words are used, either mentally or aloud, to help make meaning of life, to explain, describe, instruct, convince and inspire. Whether you are dealing with questioning children, difficult customers, confused clients, fractious colleagues, people you want to entertain, or those you want to influence or persuade, you have countless opportunities to practise oral communication and thereby enrich your World of Words.

This article has outlined eight techniques, together with suggestions to sweep the dust out of your vocabulary and grammar, to create a richer World of Words. Your enhanced World of Words will stand you in good stead whenever you want to create the magic of engaging the soul and capturing the imagination.

It's a wonderful world, the World of Words. Go on and enjoy it!

Sandra O'Neil can be contacted on Tel: 02 9525 9958.

Special Focus

Interpretation in the marine environment

Alice Crabtree
Tour Guide, Great Barrier Reef

BACKGROUND

The Great Barrier Reef is the world's largest coral reef system, consisting of a magically diverse and intertwined complex of coral reefs, lagoons, seagrass, and mangrove and island communities that cover an enormous area (nearly 350 000 square kilometres). Its majesty and magnificence helped gain it World Heritage status in 1981, and this explains the multitude of visitors eager to experience its wonders first hand (1.6 million in 1999).

Visitors to the reef can experience its magic through a bewildering variety of interpretive experiences, ranging from an idle beach ramble and pottering around in glass-bottomed boats or semisubmersibles to the drama of bird's-eye views from a thundering helicopter or full immersion in a snorkel tour or scuba dive. In this article I will focus on the particular challenges and trials of snorkel tours—providing some information not only on a specialised form of marine Interpretation and the trials, tribulations and joys of an interactive 'adventure' experience, but also on some insights into Interpretation in general.

SNORKEL TOURS AND SKILLS AND QUALIFICATIONS REQUIRED

A basic snorkel tour on the reef involves a Guide taking a number of visitors (who may not have any prior snorkelling experience) on an in-water and (hopefully)interpretive experience. As with all 'adventure' activities/sports, and especially so when water is involved, risk management and mitigation are fundamental. A concise but important briefing to your clients on the fundamentals of fitting and operating the equipment (mask, fins and a snorkel), safety procedures (such as buddy pairings, buoyancy aids, medical cautions and potential hazards) and 'rules' must be conducted. Thorough operational guidelines ensure that a safe as possible working environment exists with relevant, appropriate and rehearsed emergency procedures in place.

Tours may involve travel in a smaller boat away from the parent vessel to more exclusive or exciting sites, but the actual in-water activity rarely lasts more than an hour (in winter or rough weather much less, as the cold or sea conditions saps away your clients' comfort). As the Guide you are responsible for the safety, ease and elucidation of your clients.

This means Guides need to be multiskilled: at the very least qualified life savers, competent at first aid (preferably familiar with oxygen administration), and skilled at handling small boats. Depending on the boat and the operational structure you might require a coxswain's ticket, and need to be willing and able to act as crew (deckhand, host *and* cleaner!) for the 'mother' ship—and a radio licence would never go astray.   Being qualified at scuba or preferably as a snorkel instructor (with the patience and teaching skills to facilitate your clients' snorkelling ability) and having detailed knowledge or raw content on at least some of the huge amount of information on the reef at your fingertips is obviously also important. Last, but by no means least, is the ability not only to guide by keeping your group physically together but also to provide Interpretation. Interpretation is not the icing on the cake—it is the most vital, most important and most essential skill of a special Guide.

SO, WHAT IS 'INTERPRETATION'?
It is so much easier to say what Interpretation is not. It is not 'how big' or 'how tall' or 'how old'. It is not facts and the figures, despite the fact that they are every Guide's raw material and the building blocks that help them build messages and effectively communicate. Insufficient, unverified or badly researched information means you have poor materials to work with and even the best workmanship means that you can only build structures that collapse or rapidly crumble.

Interpretation to me is the attempt to build a structure that not only endures, but also is a thing of wonderment and inspiration. I need to take my raw materials, gather my tools and employ every trick of my trade to build effective messages, communicate and teach, so that my visitors remember long after the holiday has finished. I might only achieve embedding a basic grasp of the defence mechanisms of marine invertebrates or the myriad of possible reasons behind the kaleidoscope of fish colours, but I may also provide another nail that supports and strengthens a belief in conservation or a determination to help protect the environment.

GUIDING ON THE REEF
It is easy with even the most basic knowledge of the reef, simple skills in communication and an ability to snorkel to give your visitors a great time. The reef is a fabulous environment—you don't have to look too far or delve too deeply to find something of interest to the most jaded of palates. It is thus all too easy to become complacent about your guiding abilities—it's very hard to give a 'bad' tour. You should measure your success as a Guide not on the brochure days of sun and technicolour glory, but also on the days when the wind howls, the water clarity is such that it is hard, if not impossible, to see the bottom, and your visitors can barely swim, let alone snorkel! On the days when most of your passengers are involuntarily feeding the fish (and not with raw marine products!) it is all too easy to blame the weather for your lack of success

or sparkle. Be honest, appraise yourself and think what sort of tour you give.

It is tempting, on the reef, to fall into the trap of 'gawk and talk' or 'regurgitation' tours. The ever-changing scenes, the multitudes of willing actors on parade, the scenery and the sheer spectacle mean that you can easily flit from topic to topic. Your visitors are content—despite the hotchpotch of unrelated and indistinguishable facts—for they are often far more intent on looking at the wonders laid out before them than your gems of wisdom.

To attract and hold their attention (if for no other reason than to keep the group together for safety) is hard. Sure, you don't get any complaints, but are you being an effective communicator? Are you imparting a message, sowing a seed, providing them with anything besides a quick and easily forgotten litany of facts? If all they remember is the wonders of the reef that they could have obtained without your information, surely you have failed.

HOW TO MEET THE CHALLENGES

One of the biggest challenges on a system as dynamic and bountiful as the reef is what to leave out, what not to speak about, what to ignore or gloss over. Your challenge as an interpreter is not to end up just employing the big and the beautiful and the obvious, but injecting wonder and appreciation of the mundane and perhaps not-so-unusual by exploiting the twists, the specialness and the unusualness of the usual!

For example; why are there so few plants seen on the reef? You have to inject some magic—take them on a journey from the known to the unknown, from simple to complex, and from the mundane to the extraordinary. We see so few plants on the reef not because they are not there, for the reef (like all ecosystems) depends upon the plants to fuel it. We just can't see them or don't recognise them. We assume that 'green plus leaves = plants' so the reds and blues and pinks spread over the coral in an amorphous mass that look as though someone has had a tantrum with some paint pots defy our senses and understanding. Plants are here and here in abundance, but are often hard to see not only because they don't look like traditional plants, but also because they are microscopic (in the plankton) or found in a tight-knit symbiotic relationship actually hidden away inside the corals.

Another major challenge, particularly if you are snorkelling or diving, is the fact that you are taking your clients out of their comfort zone and into a less forgiving environment. Risk mitigation and safety concerns tend to jump to the foremost of your mind when the weather turns less than perfect, or the current speeds up or a large animal happens to drop by. Carefully rehearsed themes and set 'trails' rapidly become dismantled and a decline into 'gawk and talk' can totally destroy the messages you wanted to deliver as head counts become more frequent and your shepherding skills are stretched to the maximum.

THE TOOL KIT

To meet the challenge of attracting and keeping the attention of your visitors in a situation where for many the underwater world provides sights where everything is novel, every creature they see fantastic and all the landscapes bizarre, you *do* need to work. Pull out those all-important interpretive tools: use themes, make it fun, make it relevant and use vehicles.

Themes

To be effective at leaving behind something worthwhile in your visitors' heads, you must communicate well. To do this most effectively you should use themes. These force you to select from the myriad of animals, landforms, landscapes, facts and figures and by so doing give you direction and assist you to cut to the chase rather than allow you and your visitors to become distracted by the noise of the reef. Themes will let you weave a story that spellbinds and allows you to intensify your message.

Make it fun!

This is a cardinal rule of all guiding, for your visitors are on holiday, but it is doubly important on a snorkel tour. You are competing with one of the wonders of the world. If you want to bring your visitors with you—both literally and metaphorically—you have to have them *wanting* to hear you. You will not succeed if they are nervous or you are boring. Get the baseline right to start (by choosing an appropriate site for their snorkelling skills and abilities), and make sure your customers are as comfortable as possible. Keep close to the ones who are still nervous of the equipment or being in deep water, and use mermaid lines or flotation devices when necessary. Then worry about making it fun.

How can you fail with such a wealth of raw material and wonderful stories? Overlay the fascinating array of facts with some *humour*. Did you tell them the one about the fish that heard about women's lib? Or the clown fish that not only has a harem of males but also takes henpecking to the extreme (psychological castration)! Did you tell them about the damsel fish that gardens, the cleaner fish that not only gives its clients a very good dental check-up but also the very best in personal grooming, the sit-and-wait predators who mainly wait and miss, or the juvenile turtles that lope around waiting for adolescence to disappear? Don't lecture them—get them involved. You have an advantage as in snorkelling they are immersed and forced to *interact*—but play with their weightlessness and three dimensions. Teach them how to duck-dive. Get them to fondle soft corals waving in the current, find a mushroom coral, and name that fish from its shape or behaviour.

Make it relevant

Ensure you make your guiding *relevant to the site*. Concentrate mainly on the things that are common and that you can almost guarantee to see, yet are high reward. Sure, you've seen more parrotfish than you can poke a stick at, but who can fail to marvel at their kaleidoscope of colours, or fail to notice the fused teeth that give them a beak, or their flapping fins that make them look as if they are clumsily flying, not swimming, through the water? Mushroom corals—a dime a dozen—but how many other corals are not attached to the bottom? Why not marvel at their limestone sculpture and artwork of their skeleton?

Make sure your guiding is *relevant to the audience* as well. Tailor your tour, make it personal by referring to things that strike a chord with your audience. Show you have done your homework—you are interested in them and not just their money. This might be as simple as using measurements they are familiar with, or giving examples they can relate to. For example, the area covered by the Great Barrier Reef Marine Park is equivalent to the states of Tasmania and Victoria combined or, to show we can't win them all, about half the size of Texas.

Use vehicles

To work with the lavishness of the reef you need to be larger than life. You can afford to match the exuberance all around you with colourful, descriptive language. Use strategies to make a story more entertaining by telling it from an unusual context or viewpoint: use an overriding analogy; personify the fish and their behaviours (as I have already been guilty of doing); focus on an individual; exaggerate size or time scales; and use strong human-interest themes. You can weave useful, accurate and authentic information about some potentially dangerous animals by relating some of the fascinating horror stories (or myths and legends) of attacks and survival. What about the visitor who was intent on collecting shells despite being warned this was not allowed within the park with a particular zoning, who thought he had escaped penalty by hiding a particularly beautiful shell down his swimming togs, but was actually lucky to escape with his life as it was a rather irate and overheated cone shell!

To conclude

The overriding goal of Interpretation is earnest and serious, but Interpretation cannot be. It needs to translate the unintelligible, the technical and the indigestible into something that is fun, easy to understand, and both relevant and compelling. Not an easy task. I often fail to reach my stated goal of providing an enduring structure, or implanting and nurturing the seeds of a conservation ethic. But I hope I don't fail in providing stimulating experiences and imparting my passion for the very special world of the reef—because that is very easy.

8

Working with tour groups

What are the learning outcomes for this chapter?

By the end of this chapter you should be able to:
- Identify techniques for remembering people's names.
- Demonstrate techniques for engaging in conversation.
- Provide high-quality customer service.
- Identify opportunities to enhance the quality of service to people on tours.
- Maximise customer service levels by effective liaison with your colleagues and audience.
- Balance the needs of individuals and the group when managing tours.
- Demonstrate the use of conflict-resolution techniques to manage conflicts and difficult situations.
- Initiate short-term action to resolve the immediate problem where appropriate.
- Identify and manage a typical range of problems which arise on tour.

REMEMBERING PEOPLE'S NAMES AND ENGAGING IN CONVERSATION

A tour is a social activity. And a central element within any social activity is getting to know people.

REMEMBERING PEOPLE'S NAMES

As discussed in Chapter 3, your audience arrives with a range of needs, expectations, interests and motivations. They also arrive on your activity with a name, and one way of enriching the experience of a visitor is to spend time remembering that person's name.

Most people love to have their name remembered during conversation and whenever they are the focus of attention, for example after asking a question: 'Thanks for that question Bill. For those who did not hear, Bill just asked a question about the European settlers of this site . . .'

Remembering names also helps when you need to instruct people, for example when giving directions and when gathering the group together.

Remembering people's names is a blend of skill and attitude. And like any skill it requires practice and a few pointers. When remembering people's names you are stretching and building the capabilities of both your short-term and long-term memory.

Attitude and rewarding your memory

Attitude is extremely important—you need to want to remember a person's name as using your memory often involves work. You also need to reward your memory when it does remember rather than give it a roasting when it forgets. Imagine if each time you got something right you were ignored but whenever you erred you were scolded. It's so simple to reward your memory—simply praise it each time you remember something. Test your memory—look in your local phone directory and with the following techniques practise remembering names and then reward your memory for it.

Focus

Make a point of wanting to remember a person's name. Unless you are focused on actually wanting to remember a name your mind is busy with other things. and the last thing it is focused on is this activity. If remembering names in succession (eg people in a group) you might need to slow down your introductions and pause between people. Avoid distractions.

Repeat their name

When you hear the person's name repeat it aloud and then repeat it to yourself. For example, someone introduces himself as Paul. Your response:

● Said aloud—'Hi Paul, thanks for coming along.'
● Silent—'Paul is a biggish guy with big eyebrows wearing a dark blue jumper.'

Working with the SEAM technique

The SEAM technique in summary is as follows:

- Seek a feature.
- Exaggerate the feature.
- Add movement.
- Make a link in some way to the person's name.

When you meet a person search his or her physical features for some interesting or unique or unusual feature, perhaps big ears, warts, freckles or a particular hair style. You can also use changeable features such as clothing or earrings, but remember that these might change during your time together.

Now exaggerate one or more of these features. With Paul (above) you noticed he had big eyebrows so focus on these. Exaggerate them so that they cover his whole face. You can exaggerate colour, shape, size, composition and texture. Also add movement which helps your memory in its task. For example, see Paul's eyebrows growing around his head and creating a turban. And every time he reaches up to his face, the turban vanishes and the process starts again.

Next you need to peg this feature to his name, which requires you to make a link. Paul sounds like ball. So we image a ball sitting on top of his hair which is shaped like a turban.

Obviously Paul does not know the technique you use to remember his name. He just enjoys and feels quite chuffed that you took the time and effort to remember it.

Difficult names

Some names can be difficult to pronounce let alone remember—this situation can be quite common on some tours with the variety of multicultural visitors. Some suggestions to help you remember names in these situations include the following:

- Break the name into phonetic groupings.
- Ask the person to repeat his or her name if you are unsure and then repeat it back to the person slowly.
- Do not become condescending.

Practice is a key skill/element and the more you become familiar with unusual names, the more of these names you will already have locked in your memory. To assist you, read foreign newspapers, watch foreign movies and do some research.

ENGAGING IN CONVERSATION

As mentioned above, a tour is a social experience and part of any social experience is dialogue and conversation. In fact most of the tour will be dominated by members of the audience getting to know other members of the group, which will include the Guide. And most of this occurs during informal conversation.

Qualities of a Guide

Engaging in conversation should not be undertaken with the attitude of being solely a time filler but with a genuine and sincere interest in wanting to get to know the other person. Value the other person's comments and qualities.

Considerations when seeking to converse

Is the environment conducive to conversation? Trying to hold a conversation when you need to travel single file through the tight spaces of an underground cave tour might be a little difficult. Is the other person interested in conversation? Perhaps that person is coming along on the tour for a bit of solo downtime and the opportunity to get away from the social scene. Some people are shy and retiring and prefer to enjoy the experience on their own. As discussed in Chapter 4, remain alert to non-verbal signals which provide an insight into how the other person is feeling and responding to the situation.

Starting a conversation

One of the best places and times to start a conversation is during the staging periods of your activity. When you are greeting people during this period:

- Adopt a positive attitude—you need to have a sincere and genuine interest in people, to be courteous and caring, and to employ effective listening techniques.
- Take the initiative.
- Focus on the benefits of this interaction.
- Introduce yourself and have a few follow-up lines to promote a level of conversation. This could relate to the situation, the environment, the person or to yourself. As a question: 'Hi, I'm Jack, welcome to the tour. How did you hear about the tour? Are you here on your own?'
- Being able to maintain a conversation is made easier when you keep up to date with current events—read the paper each day, keep abreast of current events around the world, listen to radio and TV, be well versed and well read, and collect cartoons, articles and stories.
- Do not be rude, abusive, short-tempered, impatient or racial, and never criticise or embarrass other people.
- Notice whether there are any people on their own and not in a group. Can you introduce these people to others?
- At the same time avoid breaking into an obvious in-depth conversation with another person.

The introduction is a great way to get a glimpse of the other person's personality and insight into who that person is.

Using questions is one of the best ways to get a conversation moving. And the more relevant the question to the other person and the current situation, the more likely it will generate lengthy discussion. We can ask either closed or open-ended questions (refer to Chapter 4).

Of course, just asking questions can lead to an interrogative and one-way conversation which might cause the other person some discomfort. When engaging in conversation you need to also incorporate your thoughts, ideas and comments. To assist this and boost your knowledge, stay up to date with the latest news and happenings, develop an interest in sport, politics and world affairs, relive some of your travelling adventures to keep them fresh in your mind, or visit a comedy club to pick up some humorous angles on current events.

The following are a couple of examples of the use of questions to kick-start a conversation, both of which would occur at the start of a tour.

You:	Where are you from?
Other person:	Tasmania.
You:	Great place Tassie. I did a motorbike trip there a few years back and it was awesome. You certainly have a great state. What are some of your favourite spots around Tassie?
Other person:	I love the west coast and the central mountains
You:	Are you travelling around at the moment? (*or* What's it like down there this time of year? *or* Where are you off to for holidays?)
Other person:	Sure am.
You:	What areas are you visiting?
Other person:	Well, we just arrived from the *Spirit of Tasmania* and then we'll be travelling . . .
You:	Sounds like a great trip. If you're interested I could give you a few other suggestions.

During the start of a tour around the city of Melbourne:

You:	Are you from Melbourne?
Other person:	No, from Queensland.
You:	How long have you been down for?
Other person:	A couple of weeks.
You:	Any highlights so far?

If you are leading a tour focusing on a specific topic of interest you could ask people how they developed an interest in this field/subject area.

Starting off a conversation by talking about general topics is usually the safest way to go. Then focus on specific areas of interest and relevance. The skill is to be able to engage in a conversation so that it just seems to flow. For some people this is a natural skill; for others it requires practice and more practice.

ENSURING SATISFACTION THROUGH HIGH-QUALITY CUSTOMER SERVICE

THE CUSTOMER AND CUSTOMER SERVICE

Who is a customer?

Customers are those people who use your services and products. They are people with a set of needs, expectations, interests and motivations who seek to have these satisfied. Some people pay for these services while other people take advantage of free offers provided by relevant organisations and/or individuals.

Customers can include people travelling from overseas on a package tour, locals visiting their regional museum or people making travel inquiries. Customers are also your colleagues in the tourism industry. For example, if you are a Driver-Guide and utilise the services of a particular motel then you are their customer.

 ACTIVITY: List the main customer groups you would liaise with when planning and delivering tours.

What is customer service?

Customer service is the process of ensuring that your customer is satisfied.

It is the customer's impression that the service provider has done something worthwhile, in the way the customer wants it done.
NSW Department of Fair Trading, 2000

High-quality customer service is not just providing a service to a customer, but rather providing a service that ensures the customer is satisfied. And to provide exceptional customer service, you would provide a service that exceeds the expectations of customers.

Customer service is not just the tour but what comes with the tour—the empathy, the commitment, and the enthusiasm and desire to help and provide a high-quality experience. Remember that your customers have rights, always, regardless of whether or not they are right.

We can provide this customer service through two dimensions—procedural and personal. Procedures relate to all those activities which provide the infrastructure, framework, support, products and services for your customer. The personal dimension is when your customer interacts with you or your colleagues. When providing high-quality customer service you depend on both dimensions complementing and supporting each other, and working in harmony. The best product in the world cannot overcome poor customer service delivery standards, and likewise the best customer service people can only do their best if they are supported by the relevant infrastructure.

Why do we provide customer service?

Ensuring your customers are satisfied is critical to the success of your tour and associated operations. Customers are the sole reason there is a tourism industry. Without customers there would be no tourism industry—it's that simple.

There are numerous benefits in providing quality customer service:

- Quality customer service ensures the tourism industry is seen to provide an exceptional service to all its patrons.
- It leads to continued employment.
- It provides a competitive edge and can lead to increased business through repeat visits, referrals and/or recommendations.
- There is satisfaction in a job well done.
- The workplace environment is happier.
- Customers find it easier to deal with you and in having their needs met.
- The number of complaints is reduced.
- Marketing costs and other costs in running your business are reduced.
- Efficient and effective operations are ensured by focusing on the expectations, needs and interests of your customer rather than on your assumptions of these elements. This reduces wastage of effort and the need to redo work.

OPPORTUNITIES FOR DELIVERING HIGH-QUALITY CUSTOMER SERVICE

Basically, anywhere and anytime you interact with your customer is an opportunity to provide high-quality customer service. These can include:

- providing product and service information;
- answering the phone;
- meeting people at the start of your tour;
- at any point throughout your tour;
- liaising with industry colleagues;
- assisting people with physical and language difficulties at meet-and-greets;
- identifying opportunities for people through effective listening;
- going the extra distance for people;
- offering to follow up with information after people ask questions you cannot answer.

How you can ensure a high quality of customer service

You provide high-quality customer service by perceiving, identifying and satisfying the needs and expectations of your customers.

The first step is to perceive customer expectations to see if there is a gap between these and their actual experience. You can be pro-active and assess all aspects of your operation and all customer contact points. Can any of these be improved? Can you improve the frequency and level of providing 'moments of truth', that is those moments when you have an opportunity to provide high-quality customer service? You can also be reactive and respond to customer feedback. It is important in all phases of customer service to maintain effective listening skills and an appropriate level of assertive behaviour.

If you identify a gap, is the gap positive or negative and do you need to do something about it? If it is negative, you definitely need to do something, so identify what you can do to ensure your customer is satisfied. Listen to your customer, assist them the best you can and work together to assess possible solutions. For additional techniques review pages 213–21 on managing difficult situations.

If the gap is positive, can you improve your level of service? You can never remain complacent in this ever-changing world; otherwise, you will be left behind. You need to continually update and reassess the effectiveness and efficiencies of your operations, which includes those processes and activities related to customer service. One way to continue to evaluate your level of service is to conduct a service audit of all aspects of your operation. If this identifies the need to adjust your processes, make sure that they are processes which benefit the customer and also make sure that the customer knows about them.

The following are a few principles which can assist you to provide high-quality customer service:

- Be pro-active and always seek to improve all aspects of your operation.
- Have a positive attitude that is patient, respectful, courteous and friendly, and that says you love to help.
- Make customers feel special and seek to exceed their expectations, which might require you to 'go beyond the call of duty'.
- Know your customer—review Chapter 3 on audience characteristics.
- Know your product and service.
- Provide a service which is reliable, efficient and responsive, and which employs effective and appropriate communication skills.
- Demonstrate empathy for all people involved in the experience.
- Identify unstated needs.
- Build and foster rapport.
- Work to principles of best practice as identified by industry, work groups and/or your company.
- If you encounter a problem make sure you work towards finding solutions, and not towards seeking fault and more problems.
- Work with facts and objective data in preference to assumptions, hunches and guesses.
- Set and maintain appropriate standards of service, and seek to continually improve these standards. These standards might include ensuring:

—a level of service which is reliable, efficient, fair, orderly, polite and professional;

—customer requests receive a positive and prompt response;

—a high level of safety, security and comfort;

—information is accurate;

—all equipment and facilities (e.g, vehicles and coaches) are well-presented and maintained;

—staff present themselves in a neat and respectable manner;

—people receive a warm and courteous greeting and welcome, and that they are acknowledged and appreciated;

—people receive what was promised and do not receive any unexpected add-ons or hidden costs.

ACTIVITY: Consider the following scenario.

A lady telephones you to inquire about a tour. She is an independent traveller and is phoning from a phone box. You answer the phone and find it is extremely difficult to hear her. It is not her fault but that of the environment. You're in a hurry and are finding that you need to continually repeat yourself.

Consider the following two responses:

- *Response A*. You remain polite yet become increasingly irritated and frustrated. This is because you are in a hurry and yet need to keep repeating yourself.
- *Response B*. You display empathy and acknowledge that it is noisy, but despite this you remain patient and reduce your rate of speech, double checking that the lady hears all the details.

1. Do you agree that Response B would be the preferred manner in which to deal with this situation? Why?
2. Is it always possible to provide a preferred response? Give reasons for your answer.
3. Develop two similar scenarios based on real-life examples.

CUSTOMER SERVICE—A FEW POINTS

Customer service involves both the big things and the many little things—it's the 1 per cent improvement in 100 things as well as the 100 per cent improvement in one thing. As an analogy, it takes only one drop of dye to discolour and spoil a bucket of clean, fresh water.

Here is another analogy. There is a saying that if you wait until you are thirsty to have a drink when working and/or walking in remote bushland areas with water restrictions, then you are too late and your intake of water will be less effective in addressing your body's need for water. It is the same with poor customer service—if you wait until the complaints arrive or for tour sales to go down or patronage to decrease, then the momentum has turned against you. Positive customer service needs to be an integral part of your approach when managing tours and not a reactive response. It needs to be an attitude, belief and way of thinking that ensures a focus on the needs of the audience. Providing this customer service is about empathy. People love to feel good and one way to achieve this is through a positive experience that demonstrates empathy and respect.

The effect of a complaint (or moment of visitor contact) on the relationship between visitors and your organisation depends on how the complaint is dealt with. If positive steps are taken, the relationship is more likely to be healthy and might even improve. For example, if you excel in the way you handle a complaint or request for action, you have taken advantage of an opportunity to demonstrate the character of your organisation.

Customer complaints should be seen as opportunities as most customers who receive poor service do not complain (this has been estimated to be over 80 per cent). They simply go elsewhere. This latter fact lulls us into thinking all is well.

Customer service is about relationships, which once they begin never end. There will always be some point of reference for memories, feelings and thoughts related to that relationship. These points of reference may be negative, positive or indifferent. Obviously we are striving for a positive relationship.

When providing customer service think relationship and not 'snapshot service', as we are dealing with life and not 'still-life', with the whole and not a part.

The best exercise for the heart is to bend over backwards for someone else.
Anon.

Do all the good you can
By all the means you can
In all the ways you can
In all the places you can
At all the times you can
To all the people you can
As long as ever you can
John Wesley

The greatest unsatisfied need within the community today is the need for satisfaction—the demand is unlimited.
Jack Collins

ACTIVITY: Think of a situation in which you were extremely satisfied with the level of service provided by an individual. How did this individual achieve this level of service?

MANAGING DIFFICULT SITUATIONS

Difficult situations can be considered to be a form of conflict—it is when there is a disagreement between two or more parties (and where parties could include individuals, a group of people or an organisation). Difficult situations, customer complaints and conflicts are all normal elements within any tour operation. What is important is how they are managed.

MINIMISING THE OCCURRENCE OF DIFFICULT SITUATIONS
You can minimise the occurrence of difficult situations by ensuring the following:

- You spend the time and effort to establish rapport and a positive relationship with your audience.
- People know what is expected of them and are made aware of relevant rules, regulations and procedures.
- You confirm arrangements to ensure that what's expected will be delivered.
- You find out as much as possible about your audience so you can prepare for any specific interests and cultural considerations, and can pre-empt any potential misunderstandings.
- You observe and remain sensitive to the behaviour of people on your group, and check potentially difficult situations before they get out of hand.
- You set yourself up as the leader—a leader who is empathetic, fair and committed to the interests of all.
- You are well-prepared.

TYPES OF DIFFICULT SITUATIONS
Difficult situations can occur while managing a tour or liaising with colleagues or at any time in your working/personal life.

With a tour group
Difficult situations can occur with a tour group when:

- a person is dissatisfied with the quality of service or product;
- a person is dissatisfied with his or her accommodation, meals and other tour arrangements;
- a tour runs late;

- a tour leaves without a person;
- a tour is full;
- a tour might have to be cancelled;
- people might not have the appropriate equipment for a tour and/or associated activities;
- a 'group' becomes rowdy and self-indulgent without concern for the rest of the tour group;
- a person is told one thing by one industry colleague and another (usually conflicting) thing by another colleague;
- a person has just had a rude or discourteous experience.

With colleagues

Difficult situations can occur with colleagues when:

- deciding on shifts;
- sharing equipment;
- discussing operational procedures.

Universal (with colleagues or customers)

Difficult situations with colleagues or customers include:

- offensive body language, expressions and other non-verbals;
- culturally insensitive language, that is racist and sexist remarks and jokes in poor taste;
- racial and discriminating behaviour;
- inappropriate levels of formality and respect;
- environmental (including situational) pressures;
- different expectations;
- poor and ineffective communication, and communication barriers which get out of hand;
- clash of opinions, values and/or religious beliefs;
- lack of empathy and respect;
- need for attention;
- psychiatric disorders and intellectual disabilities.

In any of the above situations people can become:

- angry;
- rude;
- overly demanding of your time and attention;
- verbose and talkative;
- negative and pessimistic;
- unhappy;
- anxious.

TYPES OF BEHAVIOUR AND DIFFICULT SITUATIONS

There are three main categories of behaviour when dealing with difficult situations—submissive, assertive and aggressive—with assertive behaviour being the preferred.

Assertive behaviour

Whenever you are dealing with difficult situations it's important that you remain in an assertive frame of mind. This ensures that you do the following:

- Demonstrate a respect for your rights while respecting the rights of others.
- Provide the opportunity for others to respect your rights. (How do others know how to act/behave if you do not provide some opportunity for expression? Not everyone is a master communicator who can read all signals.)
- Say, think and feel without disregarding what the other person says, thinks and feels; and not sacrificing what you think, feel or want for others.
- Communicate and behave in a manner which takes responsibility for how you feel and think.

Submissive and aggressive behaviour

As mentioned, assertive behaviour is preferred to submissive or aggressive behaviour. The characteristics of these latter two behaviours include the following:

Submissive behaviour	Aggressive behaviour
Indicators	*Indicators*
Submissive people:	Aggressive people:
• show lack of respect for their rights, and sacrifice their thoughts, feelings, wants and needs in favour of others;	• show little regard for the rights of other people—that is, their rights are more important than those of others;
• are often timid and reluctant to express their views, concerns and feelings;	• express their views, feelings, thoughts and concerns at the expense of others;
• give permission for others to violate their 'personal space' whether this be physical, psychological and/or emotional;	• often display rude, loud and abusive behaviour;
• blame others for how they feel;	• often are controlling persons who want their own way;
• meet the rights of others at the expense of their own.	• make 'you' statements;
	• blame others for how they feel.
Negative consequences which people may experience when acting submissively	*Negative consequences which people may experience when acting aggressively*
• They often feel frustrated because their needs are not being heard, let	• They may suffer from a sense of failure when they lose control, and

alone met (usually because the person has not expressed them).

- They can cause frustration in others because of the inadequate disclosure of feelings, thoughts and concerns. People become frustrated in their attempts to work out the motives of a person displaying submissive behaviour.
- They lack the strength to make a decision, which can cause frustrations between themselves and other people.
- They say 'yes' or 'no' when wanting to say the opposite—this occurs as accepted practice within certain cultures.

Examples of this behaviour type
'No, you decide. I'll be happy with what you choose.'

Times when this behaviour may be useful
- The peace is kept until a later time.
- A situation might not be worth your attention and energy at the expense of the rest of the group.
- People's safety is threatened.

experience guilt, alienation from people who continue to be on the 'receiving end', and ill health due to the increased stress of maintaining this behaviour.

- They will usually have a low self-esteem, which they attempt to mask through aggressive behaviour.
- Aggressive behaviour can create its own opposition and foster its own destruction.
- Aggressive behaviour can result in a loss of control.

Examples of this behaviour type
'You do not have a choice because I have decided which attractions we will visit.'

Times when this behaviour may be useful
- People's safety is threatened.

MANAGING DIFFICULT SITUATIONS WITH ASSERTIVE BEHAVIOUR

Assertive behaviour is characterised by firm rather than dominating behaviour. It allows you to respect your rights while respecting the rights of other people. With assertive behaviour you seek to maintain the other person's self-esteem, and minimise the potential for any difficult situation to escalate into a major crisis. Despite these principles you need to be aware that sometimes assertive behaviour might be viewed by some people as aggressive.

The most effective means of assertive expression is to use 'I' statements. These tell the other person how you are feeling without blaming the other person or demanding that he or she change. You can never change the behaviour of another person, and in the same way that person cannot change your behaviour. Change comes from within but is often stimulated by external factors.

'I' statements take the following structure:

- 'When . . .'   = The action (a neutral and objective description of the other person's behaviour; be careful not to include any judgmental comments).
- 'I feel . . .'   = Your response (describe how it affects your feelings; again be careful not to express any judgmental or 'loaded' viewpoints).
- 'And what I would like is . . .' = Your response (your desired outcome).

Assertive statements let people know the effects of their actions. It is important to acknowledge that the behaviour of a person cannot impose a feeling on you. You experience the feeling because you choose to, because of the way it affects you as an individual.

You need to limit yourself to behavioural descriptions and never attack the identity, values, feelings, attitudes or character of the person. Make sure these behavioural descriptions are as objective as possible and not judgmental or subjective; that is, do not become sarcastic or exaggerated as this begins to enter the aggressive domain. For example: 'When you talk above the rest of the group and cut off the answer I was providing . . .' is a preferred response compared to 'When you were rude at the start of the tour'. You also need to be sure the person is actually causing trouble or disruptions and it is not your perception of the situation.

Avoid	Preferred words
You're crazy	I appreciate what you're saying and . . .
I know how you feel	It seems like this has caused you to become upset.
You're wrong	That's one viewpoint on the issue. Let's explore some others. (After more information is gathered the person might actually be found to be right.)
Rubbish	Let's take a break, while I find out more information which might assist us with this situation.
You're the one with a problem, mate!	Let's try to work this out together.

A person runs from a room within a building screaming 'Fire!'. The surrounding people respond with feelings of fear, excitement, curiosity and a mixture of these responses. The situation did not place these feelings within the people; it merely provided the stimulus to evoke these feelings. This is the reason you can never blame someone for making you feel a particular way. You must take responsibility, because it is you who chooses to experience a particular feeling.

Steps in working with assertive behaviour in managing a difficult situation

- Ensure you are in an appropriate state.
- Focus on the other person.
- Clarify the issue.
- Make an assessment and decision.
- Evaluate the process.

Ensure you are in an appropriate state
When managing any difficult situation ensure that you maintain a positive attitude.

- Remain courteous, calm, impartial and sensitive.
- Use a clear voice and attentive body language.
- Do not become personally involved—often the conflict is not to do with you.
- Do not become emotionally involved and, especially, do not argue.
- Remain balanced and assertive.

You need to ensure that you respect your rights as well as the rights of the other person. If at any stage you are being adversely affected by the situation, you might need to excuse yourself with comments such as:

- 'I'd just like to get more information.'
- 'I'll just go and get some paper to write this down.'
- 'What about if I make a quick call just to confirm a couple of points.'

Focus on the other person
This stage is concerned with building rapport and empathy with the other person. The first step is to focus on, and address any feelings being expressed within, the situation.

Feelings, especially if intense, increase the likelihood of irrational behaviour which is a barrier to good communication and to reaching an effective solution. Irrational behaviour also increases the likelihood of losing focus on the original issue.

Let the other person blow off steam—this often calms the person down.

Reflect and acknowledge the feelings and emotions of the person. Try to develop a degree of empathy with the person. How would you be feeling in the same situation? Reflect on how you believe the other person is feeling. You may comment on how you believe the person is feeling:

- 'This seems to have made you quite angry.'
- 'It's obviously made you upset.'
- 'You seem quite upset.'

During this phase you might need to pause and let things come back into context and focus. You might also need to move to a more appropriate location to ensure discretion, and to minimise the potential to disturb other people or evoke a reaction from additional people towards the same situation.

Throughout this stage reassure the other person but do not patronise. Continue to acknowledge his or her point of view and empathise with the effects of the situation until you develop some level of rational dialogue. Work towards making the other person feel better.

Throughout this stage use the 4 Fs—be frank, be firm, be friendly, be flexible. Never interrupt at inappropriate times; engage your effective listening skills (refer to pages 70–3).

Clarify the issue

As you continue to listen to the other person, make an assessment of what you believe to be the nature, details and cause of the issue. Listen beyond the emotive state to the objective cause—what is motivating this person(s) to act in this way.

When appropriate, summarise in your own words your understanding and assessment of the situation. This allows all parties to check in and make sure the same issue is being discussed.

Work out where the differences are by confirming the other person's position and how it differs from what you believe to be the person's desired position. Remember to always focus on the reasoning behind an argument and never on the conclusion of an argument.

This provides you more leverage in working towards solutions by exploring the line of reasoning. Is it valid? Is it accurate? Does it follow a logical progression to the conclusion?

Clarify details of the situation by asking:

- 'What happened?'
- 'When did it happen?'
- 'Who did that?'

Verify your understanding of the situation by saying:

- 'What I'm hearing is . . .'
- 'It seems that . . .'
- 'Would I be right to say . . .'
- 'I want to make sure I'm clear on what happened. First, . . . , and then . . .'

If relevant and possible, explain your side of the issue without denying the other person's. Provide the other person with organisational, operational or other relevant perspectives.

To obtain additional information you might need to talk with other people to gather further viewpoints.

Make an assessment and decision

Once you have gathered thoughts, ideas and other information, you need to make a relevant assessment of the situation and decide on a course of action.

If you are dealing with a complaint about a certain issue, ask yourself whether there actually is a real cause to complain or whether the person just wants attention. The issue might also be a clash of personalities. Separate the genuine complainers from the chronic whingers who find fault with anything and everything, and make sure you and other people know about it. With chronic complainers find out what the problem is, and remain focused on the issue or concerns. Do as much as you can without going too far. Are they attention seekers, rather than complainers?

If you or your company has made a genuine mistake, and you are in an appropriate position to do so, then apologise. We cannot always be perfect and mistakes are inevitable—most people accept this, especially if you take prompt action to do something about it.

Do you have the responsibility or authority to do something about this situation? Are there any relevant and appropriate organisational guidelines and policies which can guide you in this situation? Will you need to refer the matter to another person?

Together with the other person develop some possible options/solutions for the situation and decide on the best course of action. Seek areas of agreement. Ask the person what he or she would like. What outcome is being sought? Be clear about what the other person wants from you and what you want from the other person. You could say:

- 'What would you like me to do?'
- 'How would you like me to achieve that?'
- 'How could I assist you?'
- 'If I did . . . , would that help you?'

Then if you agree on an outcome tell the person what you will do and what he or she should do. And decide on whether the person wants to remain informed of the situation.

Evaluate the process

Evaluating the process of managing a difficult situation is an essential step, during which you have the opportunity to debrief with colleagues and friends, and address any heightened feelings and emotions. You can also use it as a learning opportunity for future situations. Ask:

- How do you feel about the process? Was it satisfactory? Could you have done anything different?
- Did the person seem okay and satisfied?

During this step you might also need to complete any necessary documentation/reports.

MANAGING DIFFICULT SITUATIONS—A WRAP

When managing difficult situations ensure you do the following:

- Go for the issue and not the person.
- Remain calm and do not become aggressive.
- Remain impartial and do not become emotionally involved.
- Remain open-minded about all sides of the issue.
- Never criticise, attack or comment in a negative manner about a person's identity— always focus on behaviour.

Attitude, attitude, attitude—it is so important in these situations. You cannot always change or influence another person's behaviour but you can change yours and make sure that it is appropriate to the situation. You need to manage your behaviour; and the other person might just model you.

Notice any escalations in people's behaviour. If at all possible deal with difficult issues before they blow up into major incidents. Generally, conflict situations escalate from periods of discomfort and tension before they blow up into major incidents. Listen to people's behaviour—nip it in the bud.

Be careful of the language you use when managing difficult situations and avoid using words that can escalate the feelings and emotions of the other person.

Nothing is ever gained by winning an argument, whilst losing a customer.
C.F. Norton

ASSERTIVE BEHAVIOUR IN MORE DETAIL

ASSERTIVE BEHAVIOUR WHEN DEALING WITH PERSISTENT PEOPLE

A typical example involving tours is the person who continues to ask questions and commands the attention of the leader. The following example is hypothetical and is being used as an illustration to demonstrate this technique. Other approaches to managing such behaviour from your audience would be to change your presentation techniques, the information you are providing and your commentary, and how you are managing the space and your group.

First response—empathic assertion

- 'It's obvious that you're interested in finding out more about this subject, and I would be happy to spend some time with you at the end of the activity and answer further questions. At the moment I need to also spend time with other people on this activity.'
- 'I'd love to hear more of your stories. Perhaps after the tour?'
- 'Thanks for sharing that story/comment/anecdote/question. Does anyone else have something they would like to ask/say/share?'

Second response—simple assertion

This is for situations when the person continues to command your attention. This response involves a simple statement of the situation.

- 'I'm finding it quite difficult to continually give you my attention because there are other people on this walk who also require my attention.'

Third response—direct assertion

This response involves using the 'I' statement.

- 'When you continue to ask questions and interrupt me I feel frustrated because my attention is not being shared equally among the group and I would like you to leave your questions until the end of the tour.' *or*
- 'When you continue to ask questions and interrupt me I feel upset and angry because it appears that you are not respecting my initial request, and I would prefer that you do respect the fact that I cannot continue to answer your questions. I would be more than happy to spend time with you at the end of the tour.'

In most situations it is best to talk to people on their own and not in the presence of the rest of the tour group.

ASSERTIVE BEHAVIOUR WHEN DEALING WITH CRITICISM

Being able to handle criticism is essential if we wish to keep communication channels open. We all make mistakes and are responsible for mishaps. It is part of life and an essential ingredient of learning.

To handle criticism in a constructive manner make sure that you:

- clarify whether there is a real or conceived issue;
- keep emotions at a manageable level;
- keep discussions rational.

When criticism is correct

When the criticism is correct, acknowledge the situation. It may not be viewed as a criticism by the critic making the statement. Here are the steps you could take:

- Say, 'You're right'.
- Reflect the criticism so that the other person knows you understand the nature of the criticism.
- Thank the person (if appropriate).
- If appropriate, provide an explanation of your actions. (Do not apologise—an acknowledgment is enough.)

For example:

Criticism: I wish you'd stop leaving your things everywhere when we make camp.

Response: You're right. I should not leave my things all over the camp site. I'm sorry if they got in the way.

This is all that needs saying. The respondent has acknowledged the critic for picking up on an annoying habit.

When the criticism is partly correct

This is when the criticism has a variety of false accusations and only some truth. Follow the steps as for the 'acknowledgment approach' illustrated above, except you usually have to pick out which statement contains the element of truth.

For example:

Criticism: You're always late. I've been waiting here for hours. We're going to miss the tour.

Response: You're right, we are going to miss the tour. I'm sorry; perhaps we can go on the next tour.

The respondent ignores the 'always late' because this is the first time he or she has been late. The respondent also ignores the 'been waiting here for hours' because the critic was waiting only for 20 minutes. However, the respondent does acknowledge the objective information of missing the tour while offering an idea on how to improve the situation.

When the critic is vague

These situations require you to do a little probing. You need to clarify the exact nature of the criticism. Effective listening skills are required so that you can seek further information in a neutral and non-argumentative manner.

Use phrases such as:

- 'Which part of the tour did you . . . (like?) . . . (dislike?) . . .'
- 'What is an example of my incompetence?'
- 'What exactly did I do to upset you?'
- 'What was the specific behaviour I did while leading the tour that . . .?'
- 'In what way do you believe . . . ?'

Criticism: Can't you ever get it right?
Response: What exactly would you like me to get right?

When the criticism turns nasty

Assertive behaviour is also useful if criticism comes in the form of an abusive and aggressive attack, where the person is making it quite clear you are the problem. Obviously if your safety is being compromised, you may need to remove yourself from the situation rather than rely on 'I' statements.

Consider the following steps when dealing with abusive and aggressive behaviour:

- Do not retaliate with your own abuse—this only meets aggression with aggression.
- Deal with the critic's emotions. Let the person know you understand the criticism and how it appears to be affecting him or her. The critic may be shouting and raving, in which case remain calm. Say, 'It's obviously caused you to become quite mad' or 'I can see how much it has affected you and how frustrated you are'.
- After reflecting on the critic's emotions acknowledge where the criticisms are coming from. Check in and acknowledge the other person's point of view even though you may not necessarily agree. The important element is that the other person knows that you understand his or her point of view.
- Is the cause of the critic's anger obvious? Do you need to find out more about the real issue? Is there a deeper issue at play? Perhaps you need to introduce some delicate probing (discussed previously).
- After acknowledging the point of view of the critic present your side.
- Work together to achieve a solution and discuss how the situation can be improved.
- If the situation continues without improvement go back to active listening.

A simple approach

If it was obvious that you caused this situation it could also be handled with an assertive yet sincere apology. Think of the time someone caused you to become upset and just when you wanted to unleash your snarling vengeance he or she shrugged his or her shoulders, turned his or her palms upward, tilted his or her head slightly to one side and with sincere facial expressions said: 'I'm sorry about that!' This usually calms you down enough for you to become rational and be able to discuss the issue without flaring tempers.

CONTINUAL INTERRUPTIONS BY AN INDIVIDUAL WHEN WORKING WITH GROUPS

With group situations when you are being continually confronted by an individual, ask yourself the following questions:

● Does the person attack me (the leader) continually; that is, is the person consistent?
● Does the rest of the group acknowledge the person's reaction; that is, is there consensus?
● Do I know of the person confronting other leaders and/or people; that is, is this situation distinct?

If you answer 'yes' to the first and third questions above, you most likely have a troublemaker. That is, the person is consistent and does it with others. (See the above section, 'Assertive behaviour when dealing with persistent people'.)

If you answer 'yes' to at least the first two questions above, perhaps you need to reconsider your actions and how well you are leading the tour. That is, not only is the person confronting you but the group is right behind that person.

With the latter situation adopt an assertive approach and engage active listening skills to find out what it is you may be doing that is causing the confrontation.

(While on tour if you experience the situation of people chatting in the background keep in mind their rights as individuals. It is their tour and if they want to talk it is their right. However, when this right compromises the rights of the group and has an adverse effect on the tour, you as the Guide have a responsibility to manage the situation.)

ACTIVITY: Decide which approach (aggressive, submissive or assertive behaviour) is illustrated by the following statements.
1. I'm okay with a compromise rather than go looking for a completely satisfying solution.
2. I'll admit to being wrong just to keep the peace.
3. I'll give in rather than try to change another person's opinion.
4. I look for a solution which is of mutual benefit.
5. I'll avoid any controversial issues.
6. I make sure the other person knows my side of the issue, and I'll listen to his or her side of the issue.
7. I try to win the person to my point of view.

PEOPLE AFFECTED BY DRUGS AND/OR ALCOHOL

Situations in which you suspect a person of being affected by drugs and/or alcohol can be extremely sensitive and can introduce a range of liability issues. You need to be absolutely certain of your suspicions, and even if you are certain you need to manage the situation with diplomacy, professionalism and discretion. If possible liaise with other work colleagues (not members of your group) to assist you in the situation.

People affected by drugs and/or alcohol need to be spoken to as soon as possible. Everyone loves a good time and you do not want to be seen to be a party pooper, but if their behaviour is adversely affecting the group, it needs to be dealt with.

Speak to the person and try to confirm your suspicions. Try to do this in a non-threatening manner; for example, by making the following neutral observation; 'Hi, you seem a little tired. Are you okay?' or 'I've noticed that you seem to be having trouble keeping up with the group; are you alright?'

Always maintain a professional attitude. If you suspect illegal substances, you need to seek additional assistance. If possible, seek assistance from colleagues.

ACTIVITY: Reflect on the information provided in this section, and then describe how you would address some of the different types of difficult situations that are listed.

Reflect on how you like to be treated when attending tours.

WHAT TO DO WHEN THINGS GO AWRY

THINGS THAT GO AWRY
Lost passport

When someone loses his or her passport inform the police immediately and contact the relevant consulate. If the person has to leave the tour to visit the relevant consulate that person is usually responsible for all expenses. This might vary between tours but check with your tour operator and ensure that before leaving that person has all the necessary documentation including a copy of the police report. As the Guide, assist that person with travel arrangements as much as possible and leave contact details so he or she can rejoin the group.

Lost baggage

Lost baggage normally occurs during flights (although it can happen en route to hotels) so follow normal airline procedures. The person might need to buy ancillary items while waiting for luggage, especially if the wait will be extended. In these cases you might need to assist the person to liaise with the relevant airline for some form of compensation.

One of your audience members becomes ill

If a person becomes ill, attend the nearest medical centre and seek professional assistance. If that person cannot continue with the tour, make the necessary arrangements regarding forward bookings. You might need to supply the person with a letter or other signed correspondence stating the relevant circumstances. Any hospital and medical bookings should be in the name of the person concerned and not in your name or in the name of the company/organisation you are working for.

If a hospital stay is required you will need to pack the sick person's belongings (in the presence of the coach captain, hotel staff or other relevant personnel). Check whether the person had any belongings in the hotel safety box. You might need to arrange storage of the belongings if not required at the hospital. If the person is seriously ill, you might also need to contact the relevant consulate and notify next of kin. It is best to be guided by the situation and by the relevant medical staff.

HOW TO AVOID THINGS GOING AWRY
Other situations you might need to plan for to avoid things going astray.

Situation	Possible action
● Person turns up:	
—without water (for a daylong walking tour)	Take extra water for the person to carry or offer alternatives.
—without sunscreen	Ensure you carry some in your car, coach and/or backpack (or other carry pack).

—without proper footwear	Discuss safety issues with the person. Suggest that the person obtain appropriate footwear if it is possible within the timeframe. Be assertive and if there is a potential safety issue inform the person he or she will not be allowed to attend the activity. Suggest alternatives.
—without a hat	As per water.
● Know-it-alls/hecklers/continual chatterers/smart people	Work with them, ask them questions and allocate them a task. Ask yourself why they are heckling—perhaps they have something interesting to say, perhaps they are active talkers, and, of course, perhaps they just love the attention. Move closer to hecklers and when possible walk with them to discuss relevant ideas and issues. Other approaches to consider: —Relate to their feelings. —Never embarrass or belittle them. —If appropriate, share in their humour and try not to take the situation too seriously. —Talk to them as individuals.
● Outrageous expectations	Ensure expectations are explained/outlined at the start of the activity.
● Medical problems	Talk with the person and make an assessment of the person's condition. Is it safe for the person to attend your tour? If not, inform him or her of your decision. If it is okay, keep a check on the person throughout the tour.
● Not fit for activity	Ensure expectations are made clear. Offer alternatives.
● Shufflers, fidgeters	Introduce kinaesthetic activities. If the majority of the group adopts this behaviour it might well be time for you to change your style of delivery.
● Question for which you do not know the answer	Ask your audience. Find out. Never make up an answer unless the audience knows and has given you permission to do so. Sometimes you can respond with a humorous comment which is in good taste but obviously incorrect.

Special Focus

Interpretation in ecotourism

Sabina Douglas-Hill and Rafferty Fynn
Wilderness Guides Australia Pty Ltd
Kangaroo Island, South Australia

We believe there is a fairly convincing argument that ecotourism isn't ecotourism unless there is both an interpretive and an experiential element in it, the aim being to have a positive influence on the attitudes of an audience and to enrich their level of environmental awareness.

The recent effort to separate the market of 'nature-based' from 'ecotourism' is a very wise move. There is always going to be a market for 'feel-good' outdoor-oriented tourism with a taste of natural environment and an emphasis on wildlife, spectacular scenery and physical activity. This can be both a stand-alone experience and a stepping stone to ecotourism, depending on the motivations of individuals and the skill (and motivations) of the tour operator and/or Guide.

Feel-good ecotourism (the inspiring scenery, the astonishing wildlife, the unique tastes and smells, and the bush camaraderie) is valuable insofar as it heightens the visitor's receptiveness to ecological values. When that point is reached ecological messages can kick in, cause shifts in understanding and catalyse attitudinal change.

People generally seek ecotourism experiences to better understand their environment. And Australia is packed with wonderful natural environments, brimming with first-hand accessible nature experience, facilitated by locals who truly love and largely understand their patch and at a price that on international markets is vastly affordable.

There are literally hundreds of interpretive themes and take-home messages relevant to ecotourism-based activities. These include:

- When is an environment that looks okay, not okay? Learn to spot the indicators.
- Let's share and compare human influences on nature at a global scale.
- What's the difference between traditional ecological knowledge and Western ecological knowledge? The impact of human resource management is all about scale.

In working within the Australian landscape let's look at our uniqueness. Do many Australians truly understand just how special Australia is or why? Sure, everyone tells each other, but there's very little understanding behind the rhetoric. The truth is that the things that make Australia different are a gold mine for attitude-altering interpretive messages:

- Let's use the geological concept of continental drift to explain not only the uniqueness of Australia's flora and fauna but also the interconnectedness of Gondwana continents such as Africa, Australia, South America and Antarctica.
- Why is macropod (kangaroos and others) propulsion the most energy-efficient form of transport? (What has hopping got to do with nutrient and water deficiencies?)
- Where did all the eucalypts come from? (And why do we have such big bushfires?)

The interpretive opportunities are endless.

We find one of our greatest 'tools' is that of web-spinning. Our first job is to get people to see the links between apparently unrelated topics.

- Pick a site, or an animate or inanimate object.
- Pick a popular environmental topic.
- Pick an ecological theme.

Then dream up the gossamer that you'll use to weave the patterns and draw it all together into a story worth remembering. Deliver it with intrigue and magic and awe. Then draw breath; watch the lights come on!

Sounds easy, right? Well, it is for some people: the Davids—Attenborough, Bellamy and Suzuki to name a few. The rest of us have to work at it!

The important thing to remember is that no matter how committed you as a Guide and eco-interpreter are to the environment, people on holiday are primarily there to relax and have a good time—and that's what they are paying for. If you are an EcoGuide the trick is to find ways to engage travellers in learning and attitude-changing experiences in as many painless and fun ways as possible.

Lecturing is out. Guilt trips are out. Lists of do's and don'ts are definitely out! All these practices achieve is to diminish the visitors' willingness and ability to be open to new experiences and ideas. Think how you feel when you walk into a sports store, ready to spend, and the salesperson:

- advises you that you will have to leave your bag at the counter;
- reminds you that anything you buy will be non-refundable; and
- gives you a filthy look every time you touch a product display.

Our guess is that you'll have a cursory look around while thinking of other shops you'd rather be in, and then leave, wallet intact.

'Selling' environmental messages is no different. We're not suggesting that people on tour can be left to their own devices, no matter how damaging, but we believe there are more subtle and empowering ways to get the message across.

Wherever possible, provide basic information prior to the visit through the mail or on the tickets or in a welcome brochure. Make sure there is time at the start for people to review this. Establish simple instructive signs or posters about best behaviours where visitors can't miss them—in foyers and waiting rooms, on the backs of toilet doors and on the bus seat in front.

Instead of saying: 'Don't feed the kangaroos', say 'Kangaroos are wild animals and will become sick if they have access to human food scraps. Please use the sealed bins provided.'

Instead of just forcing an Aussie pit-toilet experience onto a visiting European, explain: 'Because effluent management is a major problem in remote locations we have designed clean dry pit toilets that do not waste water and that prevent contamination of underground water reserves and streams. Thank you for your help.'

Setting a good example is critical. You can influence nearly anyone by demonstrating and leading by example, but especially people out of their comfort zone and in a strange place. They will be watching you to see what you do. Where did you put your apple core? Where did you step? Did you rush up to the echidna or squat down in silence at a respectful distance? Demonstrating your organisation's and your personal environmental integrity is vital. If you're going to talk about it, be seen to do it! Avoid anything disposable; get people to re-use and wash their cups; use biodegradable cleaning agents, energy-saving equipment and fuel-economical vehicles; pocket your orange peel; and stay on existing roads and tracks . . . Better still, wherever possible simply follow the guidelines for best practice developed by the Ecotourism Association of Australia (see the Bibliography for contact details).

Use analogy and personal stories to explain why some rules or appropriate behaviours are necessary. Tell your visitors about wildlife found choking on bits of plastic and drinking straws. Stop when you see an ugly cigarette packet on the side of the road, pick it up and talk about how long it would take to break down. Tell the tale about that person you had on tour once who was stung by wasps because he refused to stay on the walking trail and crashed bodily into a nest. Poetic licence may be permissible if it achieves an environmental outcome!

Engage at a personal level with your clients—take time to ask what their work and interests and concerns are. Fill up your day's tool box with potential topics of common interest—points of reference that you can come back to later when you have specific information and messages to share. This is what famous politicians and foreign dignitaries do and you can too. If you can spend a few minutes doing this at the beginning of the day or activity you'll make your job easier later.

This does not require a memory like a trap or an encyclopaedic knowledge of global environmental issues. Ecotourists fall into a dozen basic employment categories, mostly professional and some students. Ninety per cent of tourists in Australia come from three continents and a few islands: Europe, North America, South-East Asia, New Zealand and Japan and our own fellow Aussies. Internationally, people are concerned to some degree by:

- population and urban sprawl;
- loss of biodiversity;
- reducing water supply and water quality;
- loss of arable land;
- pollution and chemical contamination; and
- greenhouse gases and the greenhouse effect

As a professional EcoGuide part of your job is to start learning about these things on your patch, at home in Australia and abroad. Watch TV documentaries, read good magazines, listen to intelligent radio—and keep notes. Best of all, listen to your clients, hear their stories and ask questions. Before too long you'll be in a position to chat informatively about key environmental issues in a relaxed way that deliberately relates to the places you visit and the sights you see. You'll be sending home important and attitude-changing messages by simply engaging people in individual and group conversations about stuff that interests them and that really, at some level, they already know about. You simply make the connections; weave that web we talked about earlier.

Rule Number One and One Hundred and One is that travellers are *not* stupid. If you treat clients as if they know nothing they will learn nothing from you. Simple really. However, if you work on the premise that everyone has some knowledge of abstract environmental issues and also some detailed understanding of topics particular to their home base (be it New York or Newtown) all you need to do is identify the links. You'll get the 'ah ha's' and the 'understandings' about that pit-toilet experience when you can show your visitors an unhealthy algal bloom in a wilderness creek and then find they are telling you about the dead fish in the Thames or the Hudson River. You'll know you've won when you can't find that last passenger because she's collecting dozens of soft-drink can pull-tops around the scenic roadside lunch stop and putting them in the bin.

CAPACITY BUILDING IN ECOTOURISM

In our business we train EcoGuides in Interpretive guiding and other guides (and commercial tour operators (CTOs)) in eco-interpretation. This may sound a bit pedantic but there are actually two quite specific tasks here. On the one hand, there are many experienced Guides, many who have been employed in the game for decades and have a vast knowledge of wildlife or ecology or indigenous culture, and so on, but who are not particularly switched on to the value of good Interpretation or the mechanics of interpretive techniques.

On the other hand, there are some fantastic interpretive Guides in the industry with magnificent communication techniques who simply need to increase their 'eco' content. This includes a range of very experienced Tour Guides who may have focused on other topics (built environment, history, art, and so on) and not had much cause to learn or convey ecological messages, or those Guides with a strong outdoor or nature-experience focus but without the appropriate messages in ecological sustainability.

The capacity-building workshops and courses that we run are either tailor-made to suit particular Guide groups or the specific needs of tour operators or follow national curricula as identified in the Tourism Industry National Competency Standards. We have a suite of sessions designed for flexibility and, in particular, a high practical, hands-on and field content.

We emphasise learning through experience, self-reflection and peer feedback throughout our programs and organise as much practice in the field as time and venues allow.

Another aspect of our work is to constantly advocate and promote the professional accreditation of operators and individuals through Ecotourism Association of Australia (EAA) programs including Nature and Ecotourism Accreditation Program (NEAP) and EcoGuide (Appendix 4). We wear our EcoGuide badges proudly and encourage all working Guides to make a commitment to continual personal improvement and accreditation with EAA as part of that commitment.

In finding ways to integrate our respective skills under the one operational umbrella we have had the opportunity to identify the things we each enjoy doing the best and focus on finding the work to suit. This approach allows us to maintain our enthusiasm and enjoyment of what we do and to avoid work that dampens our spirit. We hope this enthusiasm and belief in what we are doing is conveyed to the great people we end up working with both in guiding and in CTO training.

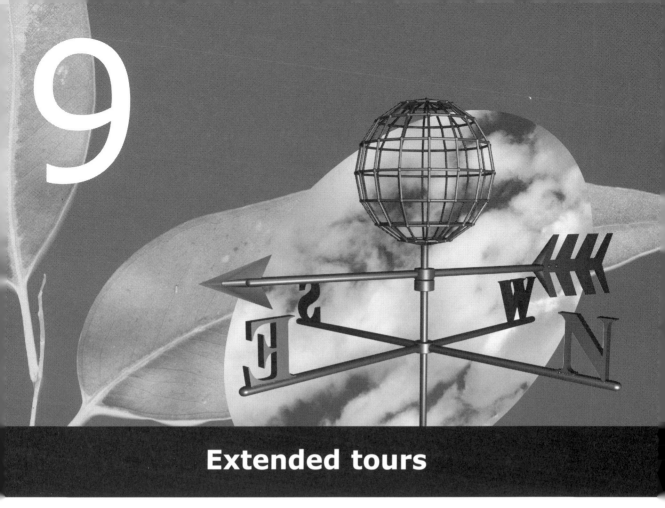

9

Extended tours

What are the learning outcomes for this chapter?

By the end of this chapter you should be able to:
● Identify the roles and responsibilities of working as a tour manager.
● Demonstrate the principles of working with coaches and buses.
● Identify the elements and stages of an extended tour.
● Describe the characteristics and challenges of leading extended tours.

Note: This chapter was written with the assistance of Vicki Longmuir, freelance tour manager and Tourist Guide.

WHAT ARE EXTENDED TOURS?

Extended tours are generally considered to be those tours which last for several days, weeks or months—that is, for an extended period of time. They often include visits to a variety of locales along a designated route, and include facilities and services such as accommodation, food and optional tours.

Travel modes for extended tours can be quite varied with some tours being solely coach-based while others combine coach, train and airline travel.

TYPES OF EXTENDED TOURS

The types of extended tours can include:

- package tours visiting a selection of Australian attractions and icons;
- sightseeing tours;
- special-interest tours (e.g. study tours);
- camping tours.

CHALLENGES AND UNIQUE CONDITIONS OF EXTENDED TOURS

Extended tours can be quite rewarding but they are also hard work. What makes it harder is the expectation from people that you are on holiday and that 'it must be amazing to travel to so many different places'. Tolerance, patience and stamina are essential qualities with extended tours as you are on call 24 hours a day. You are usually the last to go to bed and the first to get up, and in between you are always smiling and always cheery. The following are other challenges and unique conditions which you might experience if managing extended tours:

- You spend considerable lengths of time looking after the needs of people and being responsible for maintaining rapport, handling difficult situations, keeping people happy and ensuring they have a great time.
- Travelling through a variety of locales means you require broad Australiana-based information in addition to specialist information on the local and regional areas you visit.
- You are both the leader and manager when working on extended tours. As the manager you need to manage all aspects of the tour, including a diverse range of logistical activities and the activities of other people such as local Guides and coach captains.
- You spend a lot of downtime with people at airports and other transport modes, which can make it hard to relax and take time out for yourself.
- You manage people from a diverse range of nationalities, with a corresponding diversity of personalities and sociocultural backgrounds.

- You are expected to know everything. While it is unrealistic to know every single bit of information to answer every possible question, you must know how to find the information. And once you have found the information you are required to pass it on to the relevant person(s). Plan and pre-empt possible questions—if you are going to be travelling through desert country you can bet people will want to know about the arid areas, likewise if visiting coastal areas and regional towns.
- You are the leader when things go wrong. During these times the group looks to you to fix any problems. Some may hold you responsible regardless of whether or not it is your fault. You need to learn not to take it personally and not to lay blame on others. If you can sort it out quickly and efficiently, it will help you gain your group's respect and confidence.
- You need to be quick on your feet.
- You become a family for a temporary period of time, and so enjoy sharing a great time together; of course, it also means that it can become emotional when it is time to leave and say goodbye.
- Patience is tested on extended tours.
- Confidence is a big thing—keep confidence up and going.

BEING A TOUR MANAGER

DUTIES AND ROLES OF THE TOUR MANAGER

A Guide working extended programs is generally in the role of a tour manager, and thus has far greater responsibilities than a Tourist Guide. To reflect this role the classification of tour manager will be used for this section of the book.

The duties and roles of the tour manager during an extended tour include:

Duties and roles of the tour manager include...

- Check all necessary paperwork and documents including itineraries, passports and visas.
- Make and reconfirm bookings. Whenever you are liaising with other people it is important to always keep a record of the name of any person you liaise with, date and time of the call, and other relevant details, just in case things go astray.
- Find out about optional tours.
- Ensure availability of necessary equipment.
- Facilitate handling of luggage.
- Find out about financial matters—local currency, travellers cheques, exchange rates and credit cards.

- Liaise with local Guides.
- Find out whether there are any public holidays coming up.
- Get to know your audience. Will anyone be having a birthday while on tour? Do any close relatives of people on tour expect good news such as the arrival of a baby? Get to know their interests as people are impressed when you point out something especially for them.
- Manage individual needs on a daily basis, for example food preferences, accommodation requirements and other daily needs.
- Vicki works to the following philosophy: 'Confirm! Confirm! Confirm!' Never think everything is going to work out smoothly. If something can go wrong, it will. Always double check and check again. Never assume it will happen. Phone ahead to any accommodation or attraction establishments and confirm relevant details associated with your trip. This allows them to prepare for your arrival and to check and adjust for any unexpected changes. If you are travelling to unfamiliar destinations including accommodation establishments check the relevant facilities such as laundry, ATMs (automatic teller machines), Internet and phone access.

THE UPS AND DOWNS OF BEING A TOUR MANAGER

The positive aspects of being a tour manager on extended tours include:

- travelling to many wonderful places;
- enjoying lots of great food without having to cook and clean;
- meeting a wide variety of people, and learning about their unique cultural and social backgrounds;
- being presented with a learning experience each and every day;
- having the opportunity to manage a variety of situations and to build organisational skills.

The negative aspects of being a tour manager on extended tours include:

- You visit the same place time and time again.
- It is seen by others as always being on holidays.
- It is not as glamorous as it looks.
- It can be a lonely job.
- It is hard work as you are on call 24 hours a day.

THOUGHTS ON BEING A TOUR MANAGER

When working as a tour manager you need to be committed to the tour; otherwise, your lack of enthusiasm and commitment will show and will have an adverse impact on the tour. People taking part in extended tours are on holidays and your role is to give them the time of their lives. They should leave the tour with fantastic memories, and whenever they think back to the tour they should be able to recall what a great time they had.

As a tour manager you are not a passenger. You are the leader of the tour, always smiling, organised and confident, and a source of endless information.

WORKING WITH COACHES AND BUSES

The term 'coach captain' is used in this book as a generic term for those people responsible for driving coaches, but not all coach drivers go by this title. Some prefer bus driver, driver or Driver-Guide. Work out the title preferred by your coach captain.

It is important when working with coaches to establish a professional, positive and fun relationship with your coach captain. The same goes for any other staff who might travel with you such as a camp cook. You all need to communicate with one another and work together as a team. If there are any disagreements these need to be worked out away from the group. Your tour group will pick up on the mood of this working team, and will especially pick up on any tension which might be occurring. A successful working team promotes a happy, confident and relaxed group.

You also need to be aware of legal issues surrounding the length of time drivers are allowed to drive their coaches when planning your itinerary or activities during the day. This includes managing the tour group so that if the driver requires a clean break, the driver has a clean break and is not being requested to undertake any duties associated with the coach. Checking any planned schedules with your driver is the best approach and shows respect for your driver's knowledge and experience. At the end of the day it's also good practice to revise the itinerary with your driver for the following day and days.

CHALLENGES OF WORKING WITH COACHES

These challenges include the following:

- There is lack of eye contact and a reliance on your vocals when providing commentaries and other information while in transit.
- People are sitting in confined spaces for long periods of time.
- People become possessive of their seats and can compete for certain seats.
- Capturing and keeping the attention of people can be more difficult, especially when referring to items in the landscape whilst on the move.
- You have to ensure that your commentary matches what people can see out the window or can somehow relate to, such as a previous town or upcoming attraction.
- Timing is critical—that is, departing on time, arriving back at the coach on time, and arriving at an attraction or other destination on time.
- You have to adjust the heating and cooling levels to ensure it is comfortable for all coach passengers.
- Tours are either run by a Driver-Guide with the driver doing the commentary, or

the driver and tour manager work together in which case the tour manager does the commentary. In the latter it can be a challenge if the driver takes over the microphone and commentary. You need to ensure that roles are clear for each person.

STAGES OF AN EXTENDED TOUR

AT THE START OF THE TOUR

This is an extremely important period of the tour. It is critical that you get off to a positive start, and that you create an appropriate image of yourself as a knowledgeable, trustworthy, friendly, helpful and empathetic leader. The first few minutes is what sets the tone of the tour so if you start off positive and friendly the chances are that the group will pick up on and follow this same mood.

- Set up the ground rules for the tour which might include being punctual, encouraging people to get involved, being considerate and tolerant of others, being respectful of others, and accepting the seating arrangements. With coaches and buses there are generally allocated seats for the tour manager which normally are near the driver and have access to the microphone.
- Emphasise any 'coach rules'—changing seats, games, eating and drinking, smoking and use of the toilet. Check to see if the driver has any rules specific to the coach.
- Mention cultural customs—tipping, cultural greetings and behaviours, and shopping tips.
- Explain the do's and don'ts regarding photography.
- Do a head count, but be subtle so the group does not know unless you turn it into a fun activity.
- Do a luggage count and ensure that all members of the group sight their luggage before it is packed away.
- Obtain any information on special dietary requirements, medical needs, illnesses, allergies, medication and any other relevant information. This is best kept on a 'Personal information sheet' filled in by each person, and should also include details of next of kin and contact details in case of emergency. Keep these sheets confidential and stored in a safe place.

EACH DAY OF THE TOUR

- Greet visitors in the morning and answer any questions they might have for the day.
- Advise of the day's itinerary and whether there are any changes.
- Always introduce the coach captain (if new for that day) and local Guides and other relevant personnel.
- Liaise with accommodation staff as to any particular festivals or local events which would be worthwhile visiting and taking part in.
- Vicki's routine for each morning is to tell the group:
  —in detail what's happening today;

—less detail for what's in store for tomorrow;
—and an overview for the third day.

AT STOPS AND BETWEEN STOPS WHILE ON TOUR
At stops

- Welcome people to the site.
- Inform people of any relevant information: give a brief history and insight into the significance of the site; try to build curiosity and suspense for visiting the site; and explain the facilities and services, orientation information, and what to do if lost.
- Ensure people are made aware of any ground rules, for example littering, respect for the site, minimal impact activities and keeping to tracks.
- Always do a headcount.

The inconspicuous headcount

- Advise people of when they need to return, for example 'It's now 1.30. Please be back in 60 minutes so that we can leave at 2.30 pm' or 'It's now 1.30. Please be back at 2.30 pm, which gives us one hour to visit the gallery'.
- Assist people on and off the coaches and with any luggage.
- Let people know what there is to do.
- Ensure the safety of the group as they move away from and towards the coach.
- Whenever possible be the first person back on the coach to greet and assist people.
- Advise of any shopping tips—places to visit and places to avoid.
- Let the group know of any special arrangements at attractions, for example group entrances and group discounts.
- Explain what to do if they arrive back early.

Before leaving the stop
- Do a headcount to make sure everyone has returned.
- Advise of what's coming up.

Between stops
- Undertake any necessary logistical activities, including liaising with upcoming attractions and accommodation, and checking upcoming itineraries. Ensure that these activities do not interfere with the attention you provide your tour group.
- Complete any reports.
- Circulate among the group.
- Initiate and play games, puzzles, singalongs and other activities.
- Some of the activities which Vicki incorporates into her tours include:
  —Aussie singsongs with songs such as 'Home among the Gum Trees', 'Waltzing Matilda' and the Australian national anthem;
  —a daily Aussie word or phrase, for example 'fair dinkum' and 'flat out like a lizard drinking'.
- Vicki also encourages people from other nationalities to share their national anthem, and words and phrases from their language. She also encourages them to share their culinary customs and to compare different names for the same food, for example 'hot chips' in Australia and 'fries' in the United States.

At the end of the day
- Let people know the arrangements for the evening.
- Confirm the next day's arrangements including meeting times, accommodation requirements and itineraries.
- Let people know whether they will require any special items for the next day relevant to the planned activities such as sunscreen, hats or swimmers. They rely on you to ensure they are prepared.
- Pass around a day sheet for the following day (if required by the company) and advise where this will be left for further reference. A day sheet is the itinerary in detail for the following day. This enables people to check relevant times and activities, and what special items might be required for the following day.

AT THE END OF THE TOUR
- Wrap up the tour—thank people for coming along and discuss their highlights of the trip.
- Check people are okay with forward arrangements.
- Share a quiet meal or drink as a momento farewell.
- Organise any contact details and swap relevant contact details.
- Hand out and collect any relevant documentations, for example evaluation forms.

WHAT COULD POSSIBLY GO WRONG ON EXTENDED TOURS?

Things that can go wrong on extended tours include:

- transport strikes;
- public holidays—closure of certain services—and also country towns not being as equipped with facilities as larger towns and cities;
- mechanical problems with the coach and/or other forms of transport;
- theft and loss;
- accidents and illness;
- weather (e.g. severe weather in fires or floods);
- overbooked hotels or other accommodation;
- conflict between different people on tour or between tour members and other people (e.g. hotel staff, restaurant staff or attractions staff), and between driver and tour manager;
- conflict between audience and locals—either through misunderstandings, inappropriate photography activities or deliberate intentions.

Remember that it's inappropriate to have favourites on your tour—spread yourself around. Provide equal attention to all members of your tour group. And never share the secrets of one person with that of another person on tour.

If problems do occur with a particular establishment (e.g. attraction or optional tour) never complain to the group. Handle the problem in a professional manner, and prepare a report at the earliest possible time.

WHAT TO DO IF THINGS GO AWRY

- Communicate with your audience—they are generally considerate of the fact that it is not your fault.
- Always have a back-up plan.
- Be seen to do something about it and come up with some alternatives, but be careful about asking a group for a decision as it could split the group.
- Liaise with relevant personnel, such as your employer company, to amend the situation and/or work out alternative arrangements.
- Remain professional, calm, courteous and efficient.
- Remain focused on the needs and interests of your audience—and keep them updated of any progress.
- Adjust any forward bookings and other logistical/operational arrangements.
- Never lay blame and complain—work it out and move on.

Special Focus

Experience of an extended tour

Sharing an experience with *Lorraine Smith*

Why did you decide to go on an 18-day camping adventure package tour of north-west Australia from Darwin to Perth?
Some of my reasons included:

- I work full time so I didn't really have the time to organise my own trip. Because my time was limited I wanted to make sure that I could fit in as much as possible in the time I had.
- Letting someone else organise the trip and all the gear, food, accommodation and transport was great—that way I could just turn up and enjoy.
- I was also keen on the bus idea as it provided plenty of opportunities to socialise and meet other like-minded people, which makes it much more of an interesting trip.
- I have never been to the west coast before so I was keen to see this part of Australia and I didn't know where to go.
- It was also good value for money.

Why did you go for a camping-based tour?
I chose the camping trip because of my interests in natural areas and the outdoors. I've been on shorter camping trips in the past and like the idea of sitting around camp fires, eating outdoors and sleeping in tents. Also from my previous experience I knew that camping trips tend to attract more of a mix of active younger to middle-aged people, and probably like other package tours I knew that there would be a range of people from around Australia and throughout the world.

While on the trip I found out that a camping holiday promoted more opportunities to socialise, as when these long tours use hotels most people head off to their rooms after dinner. With camping trips people stay around the fire or the cooking area chatting and sharing stories.

How was the tour?
The Guide and tour company were great. Right from the start they looked after us by providing us with tour folders, maps and other tour information. Then each day they would provide us with coloured pens so that we could mark where we had been.

The driver was also excellent. At the end of each day he would run a competition to see who could guess how many kilometres we'd travelled that day.

Having said all this, it was not relaxing in the sense I could just pull up somewhere and stay for as long as I'd like. We were always on the go, always busy, always doing something. We were in the bus for a lot of the time.

What did you like about your Guide?

Her pleasant personality and good sense of humour. She was easy to get along with, even tempered and obviously quite experienced.

She was also quite knowledgeable and carried a resource portfolio with her, and a small library which she kept at the rear of the bus for anyone to use. And even though she was knowledgeable she used her knowledge and resources well—not giving us too much information but just enough and at the right times.

When we were approaching a particular place she would give us an overview of that place together with notes. She made it clear that if we needed any more information we could talk to her in private or read the books from her library.

She also played relevant music, for example when we were approaching Broome she played a John Williamson song, which I think was called 'Welcome All to Broome'. I wasn't much of a fan of John Williamson before the trip but now I've bought that CD to bring back memories of the trip.

At the start of each day she told us exactly what the plan for the day was— when we would be expecting to arrive at towns and stops of interest, toilet stops, coffee breaks, lunch stops and also what was expected of us.

When we were approaching towns she would provide us with a layout of that town, where to find ATMs, post office, coffee and food shops, and interesting places to visit.

She also made sure we were aware of optional tours. We were told of these before the trip but our Guide went through them again, so that if anyone was interested she could either make new bookings or confirm existing bookings. These optionals included flights over Purnululu (the Bungle Bungles) and Kakadu, and yachting around Monkey Mia.

How did she keep your interest and promote fun during the trip?

When we were travelling some of the long stretches she would play games, puzzles, brain teasers and trivia.

The seats were numbered, which she used to play seat number games to ensure we mixed ourselves during the trip. At the start of the trip she asked us to introduce ourselves by going to the front of the bus and using the microphone to speak to all the other passengers. This was excellent as we found out a few things about each other which we picked up in conversation later on in the trip.

Were there any mishaps?
The trailer we were towing behind the bus broke down.

How did the Guide handle that situation?
She looked after our comforts—made sure we had plenty of drink and food, seats in the shade and things to do, and also kept us updated with what was going on. She also worked well with the driver who spent most of the time under the trailer trying to fix the problem, while she liaised with her company to organise alternative arrangements.

What was your favourite time?
What I enjoyed most was the time we spent at Windjana Gorge. It was one of our longer stops and was absolutely beautiful. It was located in a wilderness area, and was completely different from anywhere else we had been. There was plenty to do including bushwalking and swimming and just being able to take time out and explore the area on our own.

Special Focus
Nature-based tourism in Western Australia
Anecdotes and tips

Kevin Coate
A longtime tour operator, tour manager and Tourist Guide

My definition of nature-based tourism
I define nature-based tourism as a flexible, relaxed and pleasurable experience, led by a person who knows the subject taking tours to relatively undisturbed habitats so as to personally observe intricate relationships between plants and animals in their natural environments, in an ecologically sustainable way, that is, with minimal impact to the environment.

Background
I have been involved in tourism since 1975 and was the first tour operator in Western Australia to run regular nature-based tours. This stemmed from a desire to combine my outdoor hobbies and interests with an occupation.

Initially it was difficult to gain acceptance. In the 1970s and early 1980s there was not the appreciation of natural history in the wider community as there is now. At this time nature-based tours had not been developed and the word 'ecotourism' had not been coined. However, I saw a market for this type of activity. Other tour operators thought I was crazy taking weekend and three-day trips to Dryandra State Forest, a diverse mixture of mallet plantation and shrub woodland in the wheat belt, about 200 kilometres south-east of Perth. They wondered what there was to be seen apart from bush.

From initial involvement in tourism concentrating on scenic and adventure tours, I could see from passenger appreciation of my bush knowledge and a more in-depth interpretation of the natural world that this was worth developing further, especially with a focus on natural history. At the time it was a novel approach.

Although this account is based on my own experiences, the aim of this article is to summarise these in some logical order so that others can benefit from my experience.

From the start I developed innovative nature-based tours and rarely went to an area for more than two successive years. New destinations and variety ensured repeat bookings by clients; some have taken over 20 trips with me and one person more than 30 trips. Our market developed from close association with natural history clubs, and personal contact was maintained by inviting participants and friends to slide evenings and reunions after each trip.

In 1978, I completed the first Tour Guide course conducted by the then Technical Education Division of the Education Department of Western Australia.

A unique location that interested me was the Pinnacles, now Nambung National Park, south of Cervantes. As there was no factual information readily available at the time, my wife and I researched and produced a booklet that explains these unusual pinnacle formations and contains background information to the area.

During the 1980s I developed annual expeditions with the Western Australian Naturalist's Club to the Kimberleys, and special-interest tours throughout Australia and overseas with the Bird Observers Club of Australia, the Western Australian Wildflower Society and other natural history groups. People were becoming much more aware of their natural surroundings and began to realise the fragility of the environment.

Type of tours and destinations

In the past, using either large or small coaches on camping or accommodated tours, I have taken adventure, botanical, ornithological, photographic, art, geological and general scenic type tours. I have also been involved with schools and young people who are unemployed, the purpose of which was to build up their self-esteem and imbue a sense of place. These days, of most interest to me are specific nature-based study tours requiring tight Interpretation and assisting in scientific endeavours, for example botanical tours or birdwatching to remote areas.

Topics I endeavour to focus on are natural history and pioneer history. The type of tour depends on clientele and destination. They range from day trips, accommodated tours, backpacking and camping safaris; these latter tours make up the bulk of tours.

For most groups, information is imparted in a general way during the day and is sufficient. For others with special interests, I usually take reference books to complement more in-depth discussions and stimulating conversation around the camp fire. It is essential for a tour operator or Guide to know the area well, so that participants have a quality experience. For assessment of a special-interest charter group, a briefing beforehand determines the level of material needed.

Those interested in a wide range of natural history topics are attracted to these types of tour where they will share the companionship of other enthusiasts. Our tour itinerary caters for all ages, and this varies from the teenager to those in their eighties, but predominantly middle-aged. An eye is kept on older participants in case the program proves too difficult.

For utmost enjoyment small groups are preferred, the size depending on the particular interest, for example smaller groups for birdwatching and larger groups for botanical exploration. For a quality tour, 10 to 14 people is ideal and allows for a more flexible itinerary and a more detailed level of Interpretation. However, numbers vary with charter groups, from a single person to 30 or more, in which case additional Guides are required.

Duration of, and intervals between, tours

Nature-based tourism should be planned on not-too-tight a schedule. Ideally duration should not be more than 12 days and should be flexible to allow time to observe individual pursuits. For extended interstate tours such as the Flinders Ranges or Kakadu National Park, about 23 days is necessary to avoid backtracking. On tours of this length it is necessary to be aware of possible stress and friction between participants and, should this occur, to alleviate it quickly.

Intervals between tours depend on the season, for example, during winter, the concentration of work is in the north of Western Australia. Apart from one or two special school groups, summer is usually free of tours and is a good time for consolidation and overhaul of equipment. On long-range excursions it is desirable for a Driver-Guide to have about four days between trips for relaxation and familiarisation of details for the following trip.

Involvement of tour participants

Tour-participant involvement is encouraged in some form or other. This may be in the form of collecting wildflower specimens for pressing and identification or making records of birds seen. Where clients have a deeper involvement it may take the form of keying out plants, trapping animals and so on. They know at the end of the trip they have contributed in a positive way to a study of the environment.

Individuals on tour have different expectations. I circulate continually, so that everyone has an opportunity to discuss their personal interests. I don't allow voluble participants to take control. If one person is constantly questioning, that's fine, but answers and comments are made relevant and audible to everyone. I avoid too much detail, unless it is on a person-to-person basis. Nothing is more boring than continually sprouting knowledge, for example scientific names or exact dates.

Discussions are always encouraged so that everyone feels that they are participating and contributing.

Preparation and Interpretation

Research and planning activities are essential before every trip. This includes the following:

- Research relevant topics such as historical background, early explorers, pastoral history, geological information, mineral surveys and fossils.
- Select books and references on the area, for example flora and fauna.
- Liaise with relevant departments including the Department of Land Administration (DOLA), Aboriginal Affairs Department, WA Museum, and the Department of Conservation and Land Management.
- Contact land owners for permission to go on their property.
- Make a reconnaissance trip. It is essential to visit the destination prior to conducting a tour to the area, preferably during the same season one year before the proposed trip. Potential logistical hazards and highlights are identified so that the practical side of the trip runs smoothly, leaving quality time for the group to conduct activities and enjoy the experience. A reconnaissance trip will hold good for one season only, but when not practical, additional information of the conditions should be sought, because a bushfire may have burnt out the tour area or floods could have washed away the tracks.

Logistics

- *Number of tours per year.* For small tour companies, the limit is about 14 scheduled trips, ranging from 4 to 21 days' duration plus charters.
- *Weather conditions, vehicle breakdown or accidents.* A contingency plan is always necessary in the likelihood of bad weather, for example change of route or possible alternative accommodation for those who want it.

- *Equipment.* This is as follows:
  —four-wheel drive vehicle/s (a small coach, e.g. 18–22 seater may be suitable for many areas) equipped with long-range fuel tanks and spare parts, support vehicle and camp kitchen;
  —camping equipment such as insect-proof tents, self-inflating mattresses and pillows;
  —safety equipment—expedition to carry a first-aid kit, satellite phone, Royal Flying Doctor radio, GPS (Global Positioning System) and CB radio;
  —chemical toilet, using biodegradable chemicals.
  Note: it is not necessary to own equipment, as tours can be operated by subcontracting or hiring the equipment as required.
- *Advertising.* It is essential to make potential customers aware of what your tour offers. An attractively designed brochure spelling out the style of tour and destinations should be available well before the start of the new year (preferably no later than the end of November) so that prospective clients with long-term commitments can plan their year. It should be mailed to all previous passengers and advertised towards niche markets, for example club magazines of groups with whom you have an affinity. Word of mouth is the best way of advertising and this is achieved by running a good operation.
- *Vehicle and equipment maintenance.* Most vehicle breakdowns can be avoided or fixed en route. In the case of a major hold-up, arrange prompt action for assistance or another vehicle by radio or telephone. Preventative maintenance is vital and should there be any doubts about any items or components, these should be replaced. It is expensive and inconvenient to order and courier parts to isolated regions.
- *Emergencies.* In case of a medical emergency, make note of the nearest airstrip. Use Royal Flying Doctor radio contact or satellite phone in case of accident, and bring into play first-aid skills. All tour operators need to have the appropriate first-aid certificate.
- *Licences.* A number of licences or permits may be required. These include Transport Commission licence, motor vehicle licence (tour category—TC plates), communication licence (e.g. CB radio and RFD radio), F Class driving licence, Conservation and Land Management (CALM) licences for entering national parks, and licences to pick up passengers in another state (e.g. Northern Territory).
- *Insurance.* Public liability insurance is compulsory for all operators. Participants are advised to take out their own travel insurance.
- *Items supplied by tour operators.* These are tents, mattresses, all necessary camping gear, a comprehensive library, all food and refreshments, catering

for special diets, cooking equipment and eating utensils. A checklist of suggested items is usually given to participants.

- *Items supplied by participants*. These are sleeping bag for camping tours, items of personal clothing and footwear, a small backpack with personal water bottle, insect repellant, camera, film and, above all, a sense of humour.
- *Hygiene*. This is one of the most important aspects of any outback tour and can have serious repercussions if a high standard of cleanliness, particularly with food, is not maintained.
  - —*For personal hygiene and cleanliness*. Basins of clean water should be on hand at all times and participants shown how to conserve water.
  - —*Drinking water*. In remote locations, if water is collected from creeks or waterholes, drinking water must be boiled and chlorinated with appropriate tablets (see camping supply stores).
  - —*Cups, plates and cutlery*. Participants should be given their own set of eating utensils and a wipex in a clean draw-string bag for the trip, and be responsible for the washing-up of the same.
  - —*Washing-up*. Three wash-up bowls are lined up—the first containing hot soapy water, followed by two of rinsing water, the last of which should include a chlorine-based disinfectant. These should be rotated and changed regularly during the washing-up process.
  - —*Rubbish disposal*. The old saying 'If you can cart it in, you can cart it out' is as relevant today as when I first heard it more than 40 years ago.
  - —*Toilets*. A tent specially set aside for the purpose, containing a bucket-type toilet is the most desirable. It takes little effort to set up and maintain, and is particularly appreciated by older people and those worried about going into the bush at night. Alternatively, if space is at a premium, a small shovel and roll of toilet paper can be made available and participants instructed on waste disposal.

Education

Education and accreditation is essential for operators and their staff, if participants are to receive a quality experience. This can be achieved by attending tour courses at tertiary institutions and seeking accreditation from recognised agencies. An awareness of our state's natural history would flow from this.

Since 1988 tourism has become an accepted subject of study in tertiary institutions and is seen as a growth area for university undergraduate studies.

With the large number of courses available, inevitably there will be differences in emphasis and standards. However, this is one area of education on which I feel there should be no compromise. Tour Guides need to be able to deliver reliable and factually accurate information to tour participants. Regrettably, there is evidence that this not always the case. To develop an appropriate standard of performance in the field, their training should include a period of practical experience with an accredited Guide. To be effective, this aspect of their training should be assessed rigorously as part of the tertiary course, before they become employed as Tour Guides.

An avenue where students may gain initial experience as potential Guides in nature or culturally based tourism is to join organisations, clubs or societies that actively encourage the study of environments, nature and culture. Another avenue might be a period of volunteer or work experience with authoritative bodies such as departments of conservation, forestry, geological surveys or wildlife services. A period as a Guide in a zoo, botanic gardens or museum would also provide good experience. As part of tertiary courses on tourism, it is important to inculcate sound habits of gathering correct information and the ability to impart it effectively.

This also raises issues of ethical standards required for tour operators and Guides. A unit in ethics could justifiably form part of tertiary courses on tourism.

The future

As remote localities become more accessible, there may be a need to limit tourist numbers entering fragile environments. Numbers are expanding rapidly, often to the detriment of the surrounding countryside; in some areas limitation of visitor numbers will be inevitable, and this is being done already in Queensland's Carnarvon Gorge. Having said this, new areas of outstanding beauty and interest are opening up and hopefully relieving pressure on other destinations.

The use of helicopters in remote areas to reach specific sites for particular interests such as backpacking, fishing and Aboriginal paintings will become more prevalent.

Some tour operators cater for 'tag-alongs' (a convoy following a lead vehicle) and this is another mode of tour organisation. This has a higher impact on the environment, but the advantage is that in less accessible areas, a larger number of participants and a wider range of interests can be catered for in a shorter window of opportunity.

From seeing some excellent wildlife documentaries on television and/or joining a naturalist group, people now are becoming more aware and interested in natural history. As a consequence, participants on nature-based tours expect more knowledge from the tour operator. I see those conducting tours becoming more conversant with the subject at hand, and having a far greater awareness of the environment and of the country traversed.

Credible nature-based tourism now needs younger, active people, particularly women who seem to be able to put their information across extremely well. Ideally, Tour Guides should have accreditation from universities or Technical and Further Education (TAFE) colleges that offer courses in nature-based tourism and the hospitality industries. A national accreditation system is currently being developed. Courses should be designed so that students receive practical experience during their training, by working with existing tour companies and operators.

Conclusion

The world has changed significantly since I first started in tourism 26 years ago; however, my focus still remains firmly fixed on nature-based tourism and I have great faith in its future. There are better vehicles, better camping equipment, better means of communication and better weather forecasting. Through television and popular literature, people are much more informed about the natural world and they understand much better the association between plants and animals and are more aware of the impact of people's activities on the environment. Consequently, participants are more knowledgeable and are more attuned to the various relationships and interactions in nature.

Nature-based tourism's broad appeal across many spectrums is its strength and will ensure its survival. Tour operators will be better educated and participants will be better prepared when going out on tour. I see nature-based tours becoming more specific with predetermined themes. Cultural tourism that involves Aboriginal culture, cave painting, rock art and the use of traditional food is a type of tour with great potential. It relates well to nature-based tourism and is becoming more popular.

The continuation of nature-based tourism, as distinct from ecotourism, will depend on attracting younger members to nature-based clubs and societies whose purpose is to observe, to educate and to record.

Source: Western Australian Naturalists' Club, 2001.

10

Working with stories

What are the learning outcomes for this chapter?

By the end of this chapter you should be able to:
- Incorporate stories into tours.
- Engage in creative communication techniques for interpretive activities including working with stories and storytelling.
- Create and present a story.
- Develop activities according to interpretive principles that engage and captivate an audience.
- Identify opportunities to access stories.

WHAT ARE STORIES?

The universe is made up of stories, not atoms.
Muriel Kukeyser

Stories have been shared by people for thousands of years—whether it be at school, home or work, or when socialising. Stories provide an immense opportunity to captivate, excite and enthral an audience; to arouse emotions within individuals; and to take people into realms of fantasy and beyond. Stories are about fostering connections between people. Stories also provide a record of past experiences, whether as historical events or as a special and moving memory shared with a loved one.

Stories surround us. Everything has a story; we just need to listen to the many forms of its voice.

Stories come in a variety of shapes and sizes including jokes, cultural tales, oral histories, expedition records, songs, quotes, poetry, movies, plays, anecdotes, fairytales, myths and the good old yarn. And they can vary in length from a short phrase to something lasting several days. They can either be prerecorded stories which you then pass on through your presentation, or stories which you create.

So what is a story? Helen McKay and Berice Dudley (1996) in their book *About Storytelling—A Practical Guide* define stories as 'a narrative or tale of real or fictitious events'. Within this broad definition we have a variety of specific forms of story including myths, jokes, anecdotes, historical accounts and ballads. One of the important elements of any story is that it has an emotive effect on the listener.

And who is the storyteller? This question was discussed at a meeting of the Storytelling Guild of Australia (NSW) in February 2002. The definition which gained general agreement was: 'A storyteller is an entertainer and educator who engages the heart and mind, and who transports the listener to another time and place'.

WHY WORK WITH STORIES?

Storytelling is one of the oldest activities of the human species; and for that matter so is guiding. In times gone by it was the storyteller who took the key role in preserving and passing on historical and current information, which might have included relevant laws, cultural traditions, or tales from nearby and distant villages.

Stories are not just about people hearing words and sentences and literary phrasings. Stories are about encouraging people to sense and feel, to imagine, to be moved and affected, to see the characters and events, and to experience the story far beyond the literary ingredients.

The following are some of the qualities of stories which make them so attractive and engaging:

- Stories captivate and evoke your imagination and curiosity, and bring events and places to life through active, descriptive and vivid imagery.
- Stories awaken feelings of awe, wonder, amazement and empathy.
- Stories involve the affective domains, provide touching insights into the lives of people, and reach the universal motivators of people. It is this connection with the affective domains that sets a story apart from other 'forms' of information.
- Stories create, build and foster relationships.
- Stories present a holistic rather than monocular viewpoint, in which the consequences of actions are explored in the context of their relationships.
- Stories feature simple words in straightforward and clear sentences, so it's easier to keep up with the story and where it is going, and you do not have to spend too much energy working things out for yourself.
- Stories follow a sequence and logical flow of events, which again helps you to keep up with the story.
- Stories provide opportunities for escape.

All of these intrinsic qualities are what makes stories so fascinating and memorable, and what provides stories with the ability to unify people regardless of their backgrounds.

Working with stories on the Australian Museums and Galleries Online website

Australian Museums and Galleries Online (AMOL) receives over 1500 unique visitors a day to its website. Some of the most popular sections of the site include the National Quilt Register, which is a database of historic quilts and oral histories (stories) about their makers' lives.

Although it is a very simple design, in 2001, people spent an average of 21 minutes on the National Quilt Register site. This is a very long time compared to similar sites. This proves the point that even with all the whizz-bang features of the Internet and new technologies, there's nothing like a good story to hold people's interest.
Lee Adendorff
Website Coordinator
Australian Museums and Galleries Online

Note: To read some of the fascinating stories on the AMOL website go to:
http://www.amol.org.au/guide/stories_index.asp

STRUCTURE OF A STORY

Most stories work to the following basic template:

- The situation involves a central 'goodie' character—the protagonist—with whom you can relate, sympathise and empathise. Not all protagonists need to be real-life people; they can be legends, mythical creatures and animals.
- An antagonist element creates drama and tension through a sequence of events that challenges the objective of the protagonist. This antagonist element can be a person such as a 'badie' or a force such as social conditions, economic times or a particular adverse situation. It is this antagonist element which provides the tension, suspense and conflict that brings excitement and suspense to stories.
- The sequence of events takes place in which the protagonist works towards solving these challenges.
- The resolution of the situation marks the end of the story.

Stories need to have a point. They have a climax and a theme. A great story goes somewhere...

Stories need to have a purpose. They also need to reincorporate events and characters throughout their development. For example, a narrative which describes a person who runs away from danger, then meets another danger and escapes, and then another danger and escapes is not a story but rather a collection and recounting of facts. You need to bring back characters, events and objects and not simply discard them. This is a techniques often used in films. For example, in the following films the events or objects listed appeared early in the film and were then reincorporated towards the end:

- *Cinema Paradiso*—pieces of film cut out by the local priest;
- *Dead Poets Society*—the phrase 'Captain, my Captain';
- *Bicentennial Man*—the doll horse which belonged to 'Little Missey'.

TENSION

The tangle of good and bad is what provides the tension within the story and gives it movement. All good stories have some degree of tension. Basically, what does the character want and why can't he or she have it?

The story of a character who has an easy path to reach his or her objective offers little interest and will soon become boring. It is through resistance and meeting objectives that you get to discover elements of a character, even when you anthropomorphise a situation (e.g. telling the story of a tree). A tree growing in the forest is interesting but when you hear about how the seed was one of several hundred to actually take root, then it survived the voracious appetite of rats, and now it has survived the ravages of fire—your interest goes up a few notches. It is a similar situation with other plants growing in a harsh environment having to adapt to cold and wind and rain. How do they resolve this situation? What unique adaptations allow them to survive while other species do not?

Tension need not necessarily be a stereotypical evil force. Tension could also arise from a conflict between values and actions, between lack of confidence and the need to act through necessity, between physical appearance and desire, and through hardship and human conflict with the elements. Depending on your story you can build this tension to a climax by progressively 'raising the stakes'.

One way to play with this element of tension is by creating a scenario using the simple progression—good to bad to good. For example, 'I was skipping down the path after hearing a piece of exciting news when I slipped and cracked my head on the gutter. I struggled to the nearest house. The ambulance finally came, took me to hospital and there I met a long lost love. We are soon to marry—and the rest will be history.'

An example of tension within a story is that of the Blessed Sister Mary MacKillop, an Australian who co-founded the Sisters of St Joseph of the Sacred Heart and devoted her life to helping others. What makes the story of Mary MacKillop captivating, moving and inspirational are the hardships she had to overcome— hardships which tested the resolve of her character and put her faith to the wire. And in the process she demonstrated the unending faith which will make her, when canonised, Australia's first saint.

TELLING THE STORY
WAYS TO TELL A STORY

There are many ways to tell a story, for example in dramatic form such as taking on a character, with the aid of props, in a conversational manner, by reading verbatim and by recalling a personal story. There is no right way, just a way which works for you, your personality, the audience and the situation.

An important element when telling your story is your enthusiasm, commitment and emotional involvement. In the words of John Hockney (Australian storyteller),

'Don't just like the story, LOVE the story.'

You can vary how you tell your story by switching between first person and third person, that is, by working in character and with narrative. An example of the latter could be the following scenario of a Guide leading a city-sights tour. While leading his group along the streets the Guide delivers a 'traditional' commentary with information relating to the history of the sites and attractions. However, he changes tack within several of the old buildings, where he asks participants to wait in predetermined spots while he goes looking for the nurse, the caretaker or the security guard. And, of course, when he returns he is no longer the Guide but the nominated character who shares 'their' stories of that particular area. When done well, such an approach offers visitors a fresh and enriching experience.

Telling a story is not mere recital of information or a narration of facts and figures. Telling a story requires you to be passionate, to breathe life into whatever it is you are sharing with people, and to bring to life the essence of that story. To learn storytelling you have to practise and then practise some more. It is a skill that cannot be prescribed.

Stories grow in the telling.
Peter Dargin

Where and when can you practise? You can practise with yourself using a tape and microphone, at social outings, or with your partner or children, or you could join a relevant organisation such as the Australian Storytelling Guild (see contact details in the Bibliography).

Researching the story will give it more depth and increase your confidence in telling the story. For example, say you want to include a myth you heard relating to the stars Orion and Scorpio. Then research both these mythical characters and also where they are in the night sky, and how they move in the night—get to know them.

The aim of storytellers is to tell their stories in such a manner that they evoke a sense of trance within their audience, and are not seen to be telling the story but rather that the story is telling itself. The storyteller is not the focus of the storytelling event but rather the medium.

Stories are also about the human spirit, and the human spirit is best evoked when sharing an experience with others, in person. This human element is a critical element of storytelling and is what differentiates it from reading books, watching TV and listening to songs on the radio. All these latter media contain stories and are telling a story, but that is different from storytelling.

So, keep all your TVs and radios too.
Your records and CDs, the odd book or two.
Just give me a fire with lots of wood in store
And a Storyteller with tales galore!
John W. Kelly

The storyteller is you and me; it is the person within us who is alive and who yearns for the opportunity to share their favourite stories.

IDEAS WHEN DEVELOPING AND TELLING A STORY

Here are some ideas which might help you when developing and telling a story:

● Be careful of inconsistencies in the story. For example, if you were telling a tale as a settler from the early 19th century, you cannot include metres to describe distance. Also, be sure that characters, events and situations are believable within the framework and context of the story, and that any rules, traditions and cultural norms which you apply to your story remain consistent for the length of the story and do not change unless you can validate the change and it remains in keeping with the story.

- Take your time—rushing the story might lose people. Remember that you control the order of information being presented and the speed at which it is presented.
- Keep out elements which slow down and/or have no purpose in the story; this includes long sentences, words and phrases.
- Keep it clear, concise and simple, and avoid confusing elements within the story— a common example is when there are too many characters in a story. When people read a story they can retrace their steps to clarify any points of confusion. With oral stories your audience does not have this opportunity; they must rely on their memory. The role of the storyteller is to ensure that the task of remembering details is made as easy as possible.

There are three things that never return—the spoken word, the spent arrow, and the lost opportunity.
Anon.

- Remember that the audience is listening to you and not reading what you say.
- Avoid any elements which might cause breaks in rhythm. That can include jumping between and around points in the story. It could also include inappropriate use of props such as puppets. Practise working with your props before you incorporate them into your public performances.
- Make sure the story is relevant to your audience, your tour and your situation.
- Seek balance in how much time you give the elements of a story, for example the length of time of scenes, appearance time of characters and depth of detail.
- Bring rhythm into your story through variations in tension, pace, volume, movement and energy. Attempt to match the language and style of the story with the intent of the story. For example, an exciting story would feature short and punchy words and phrases to keep the action flowing and the story on edge.
- Ensure your audience is relaxed. Ask yourself: Are people sitting if it's a long

story? Are they in the shade if it's a hot day? Are they in the sun if it's a cold day? Have you addressed all safety concerns? Have you addressed the needs of your audience? Are you running to time or are people anxious because the tour has run over time?

- Make sure people can see and hear you. Remain aware of how the sounds and noises within your environment might enhance or diminish your delivery.
- Involve your audience—make sure they can all hear you. Work their names into the story, and have them get up and pretend to be characters within the story.
- Ensure adequate group control. Are there people who might distract you during the telling of the story? Are people in a receptive mood?
- Do not tell people, show people. If you are talking about an old man, 'show' that old man through characteristics such as his use of a walking stick, crackling voice, softy spoken voice, coarse face and manner of ambling around his yard. If someone is feeling happy, what does this look like? Is that person whistling, skipping down the path and smiling although it's a grey and overcast day?
- It is the same with situations—show what it is like. For example, if it's hot, how can you express this in your characters? Are their shirts clinging to their backs? Are they trying to write a letter and the paper keeps sticking to their hands? Are they continually wiping their foreheads to remove the sweat? What about if it is cold? Does the character pull his collar tight and wrap his arms around his chest? Is he rubbing his hands and pacing, pausing every so often to cup his hands and bring them to his face to be warmed by a blast of his breath?
- Seek contrasts as it is these contrasting elements which give the story depth, colour and vibrancy. Contrasts can be in the differences between events, characters and moods. For example, James Barnet was a famous architect of the mid- to late 19th century who was responsible for designing a number of buildings throughout New South Wales. An interesting contrast occurs between his social and political standing and his rebellious and indifferent attitude to the government of the time.

The following anecdote from Australian storyteller Berice Dudley taken from the Australian Storytelling Guild (NSW) newsletter, illustrates the etiquette of storytelling:

> While in Alaska cruising with the East Tennessee State University Storytelling Group, I heard of a woman holidaying in Singapore who told one of Donald Davis's personal stories. She told it in the first person, representing it as her own and basking in the admiration of her audience. She was hugely embarrassed when an audience member commented how she had enjoyed the story almost as much as when she had heard Donald Davis first tell it back home in the United States.

The moral—never retell another person's story as your own. Always gain permission to retell another person's story. As a general rule you can share published stories within an informal setting but always credit the source. Sharing anecdotes such as what happened on a previous tour is acceptable but leave out any direct references to people, such as their names, unless you have their permission.

TELLING STORIES—A WRAP!

Enjoy yourself. Make sure they're appropriate. Be enthusiastic.

STORY FORMS

TYPES OF STORIES

The following provides a selected variety of story forms and their unique characteristics.

Personal stories

Personal stories are probably the most commonly used in guiding and can include tales associated with both the Guide and visitors. These include the old yarn, anecdotes, oral histories and life stories.

Personal stories are often the most emotive and engaging of all story forms because they are about real people being affected by real-life events. That's why mainstream magazines sell so well—they are full of stories (not always ethical or respectful) about people.

Life stories are the essence of what has happened to a person. A tighter focus within this is the oral history, which focuses on capturing, through oral form, a picture of the past in a person's own words. Oral histories could focus on the journey of immigrating to a new country, on the community spirit which brought life to a particular town, or on the struggles of life during an economic depression.

An oral history

Sharing stories about people

One of the essential ingredients of a great yarn is the personal and human element. One way to capture this element is with quotes, anecdotes, oral histories and/or your own experience. These human-based stories can be drawn from people who have attended previous tours, from other folk who might have worked in your area, from historical records or from friends. And, of course, any story of which you were a part is all the more vivid and real and powerful—so begin to develop a diary of stories you can share with visitors.

Sharing of stories should always be conducted within a framework of respect. And, of course, should always be relevant to your audience.

Myths

Myths are usually associated with the creation and make-up of the world, the landscape and its people, such as myths associated with the stars and those from indigenous cultures. Myths might also relate to your fabrication of fears such as those associated with snakes, insects and spiders, and urban myths which have grown from fabricated and exaggerated tales.

We can also work with myths through associations with language. For example, January is derived from the god Janus, a Roman god who guarded all entrances and exits to homes, buildings and public areas. He was also the god of beginnings and as a solar god he presided over the daybreak. He was honoured on the first day of every month and the first month of the year is attributed to his name.

Ballads and poetry

Ballads are often set to music, and are basically a narrative folk poem written in short stanzas. A classic example is the work of Andrew Barton Paterson. The unique feature of poetry is its structure of rhythm, rhyme and meter. You might recite a complete piece or a stanza.

Ghost stories

These are usually told as part of specific tours although they can be introduced into any tour, especially at night.

Tall tales

Tall tales are often stories based in reality but which have become more and more exaggerated, for example the famous fishing story of 'The fish we caught that year was this big!' 'How big?' These can also be related to the urban myths mentioned above.

Historical accounts
Historical accounts can be given of how certain objects received their names or the historical use of an area. You might enhance historical accounts with quotes, oral histories, journals and historical photos.

Other story forms
Other story forms include recollections or stories of current events, jokes and other humorous forms, bush yarns and folk tales.

Indigenous stories
Stories relevant to indigenous culture need to be told whenever possible by an indigenous person, although there are universal stories which non-indigenous people can share with their audience. If you are interested in sharing indigenous stories contact and develop a relationship with local Aboriginal communities (refer to the special focus article 'Interpreting Aboriginal heritage' in Chapter 1). Follow their protocols when sharing the story. These might include acknowledging the indigenous people of the area, and mentioning that permission has been obtained to share the story and that the story is one which is okay to be told.

An example of sharing a story pertaining to Aboriginal culture could be on an astronomy tour in which you include the telling of a myth surrounding the Southern Cross. As myths of the Southern Cross vary immensely across Australia you could share the story relevant to your area. The same tour conducted with a specific focus on Aboriginal myths should involve an Aboriginal person.

WHERE DO YOU FIND STORIES?
Stories surround you. They weave in and out of your life cloaked in so many forms. All you need to do is listen. And where do you start to listen? The following are a few ideas:

- from real events—either to yourself or someone you know;
- anecdotes;
- stories borrowed (with permission and acknowledgment) from other people;
- your imagination—create and fabricate your own story by tapping into your daydreaming capabilities;
- from published sources—newspapers, magazines, journals, television and documentaries;
- from pictures, cartoons and other visual media—use these to generate ideas.

You should check what relevant permissions might be required before sharing stories from a third source. Even if you create your own stories you might still need to consider who else the story involves and check with them. Or refer to people in an indirect and vague way without reference to names, places and organisations. For example, imagine you meet an elderly lady on your museum tour named Molly Screensaver. Molly has a personal connection with several of the museum objects and shares with you stories related to them. Rather than introduce her into your story by name you might just introduce her as 'a dear old lady', and tell the story as 'a dear old lady I met on one of my walks shared with me the history of this particular object . . .'

CHARACTER INTERPRETATION—TELLING A STORY IN CHARACTER

Character (or first person) Interpretation relates to occasions when working and telling stories in character, as opposed to reciting a story as told in historical reference material or personal anecdotes.

Working in character means taking on the characteristics of that character—the manner of speaking, dress, habits and movements. You can take on a character for a whole tour, a segment of a tour or perhaps as part of a group presentation within a visitor centre. In the latter example, the character could greet and orient people.

When choosing a character it is strongly recommended that you veer away from popular or well-known characters. This is particularly the case with well-known historical characters as there are usually quite firm historical perspectives and you run the risk of being 'incorrect' in your interpretation.

It is far better to create a character who would be able to represent the story and interpretation you are attempting to share. For example, if you wanted to tell the story of life in an early European settlement, rather than take on the character of a high-profile governor of the time, take on the character of one of the convicts, or a free settler or even a visiting sailor who has arrived on a whaling ship.

When working in character you need to be aware of your every movement and behaviour. How does it contribute to the story? How is it relevant to your situation? If you are a rebellious character who is leading an uprising, you need to move as this character. Or if you do not, then why not? Are you actually behaving as a submissive servant until you know enough to launch your attack? Do you become emotionally involved with one of the other servants and now begin to value life? Does this change your motivation to lead an uprising, and if so how does this affect the relationship with your followers? Whatever your movement and behaviour it must support the story and be consistent with its purpose. This reliance on effective movements and working with your body is one of the reasons telling a story in character requires a degree of training in the dramatic and public speaking fields (see Chapter 5).

Sometimes costumes and/or period clothing are used when creating characters. This is particularly popular with school and holiday programs at historic sites, botanic gardens and museums. If you work with character clothing then develop a connection and relationship with what the clothing represents. What fabric was used in making the clothes? How long did the clothes take to make? Who made them? How were they worn and why? How were they kept clean?

When working in costume with small children be wary of the potential impact of your character; they might not be able to distinguish between real and imaginary and might well become frightened or feel quite threatened. Older children and adults, while able to be drawn into a story and forgo the element of disbelief in a character, are more able to step outside this realm if threatened or frightened or whenever the telling becomes inappropriate.

When dressing others in costume be alert to the opportunities for people to take on the character being represented by that costume. At a historic locale, a school group was dressed in period costumes of the early 19th century. Between tour stops, the Rum Corps walked in the same manner and were treated the same as the convicts and free settlers. Why not have the Rum Corps maintain order among the convicts? Why not establish relationships between the free settlers and convicts? These insights enable increased opportunities for people to develop a greater depth of connection with a character.

ENJOYING CROW WHEN CREATING STORIES

CROW is an acronym for Character, Relationship, Objective and Where, and provides an approach to creating and building stories.

Character

It is the character who captivates you, who moves you and who evokes an emotional response. Exciting stories have rich characters. And to be rich, characters need to be affected by their circumstances.

Characters may change—coward to hero, confident to shy, humble to arrogant, young to old or old to young (rediscovering their youth). Everything in life goes through change—your story captures change relevant to your story.

What makes a character interesting are the mannerisms and odd habits, the peculiar traits and contrasting qualities. For example, a king who is high and noble might be interesting but to add a little spunk you might taint him with a mischievous streak, or a rebellious attitude, or an innocent and naïve quality which puts him at the mercy of scrupulous knights. In the same way a strapping young gentleman in a top hat and tails might be interesting but what if this same person was actually a cunning thief or a bumbling idiot trying to impress? And what about the hardened prisoner, convicted of murder, who develops a redeeming soul and becomes a priest?

Who are these people? The following questions can assist you when developing your characters:

● What time period are the characters from?
● What language would they have used? Read old journals and become familiar with the words, phrasing and language characteristics of the time.
● What status does the character hold with respect to other characters? Does this status change?

- What are some of the objectives of the character? To escape from prison? To be famous? To explore the unknown and beyond?
- How do the characters change and how are they affected by events which unfold throughout the story? It is often far better to prolong the suspense than initiate a fight scene. Once the fight begins, the story is limited in where it can go.
- What were their hobbies, sports and leisure pursuits?
- What physical hardships did they endure and how were these reflected in the physical features of their body?
- What relationships do the characters experience with their surrounds including other people?
- What fabrics were used in their dresses? How did they dress?
- What tools did they use? What resources did they have?
- What is in the characters' background that makes these people behave in a certain way? Are they of pessimistic or optimistic disposition?

What makes a character is the articulation and expression of the answers to these and numerous other questions. The more you can find out, the richer the character.

As mentioned in character interpretation earlier, seek out the lesser known characters. It is often refreshing to find out about the lesser known personalities, for example the women involved in early Australian politics. Characters are also more interesting when they feature unique idiosyncrasies, mannerisms, quirks of character and physical features. For example, the animated version of *The Hunchback of Notre Dame* is an uplifting and moving story of how someone with horrid features living under oppressive conditions could still be caring and loving to those around him. Predictable characters make it hard for a story to develop.

Watch people in the streets, in bars, in theatres and in other public places. What character traits do they express? How could you develop a character from a few of these traits? Can you mix the traits of several people to form a composite character?

The following are a few of the characters you could explore:

- miner—could be coal, gold or iron ore;
- surgeon;
- doctor;
- politician;
- shaker and mover and radical citizen;
- farmer;
- sealer;
- convict;
- ship's crew or ship's captain.

And taking an old prospector, some of his characteristics could include:

- an attitude which reflects his history and current mood;
- sore limbs;

- arthritic hands and joints;
- dusty clothes;
- drinker and so is found near the pub most times;
- lives alone but knows a lot of people;
- seen a lot/is wise;
- croaky voice;
- relationships—lost friends because of times, did not marry, lungs have given way, finds it hard to walk because of shortage of breath.

Some ways an audience can get to know your character include:

- *Physiology or physical make-up*. This is size, shape, facial features, weight, attractiveness and so on. How do these physical features affect your character, and build his or her personality and behaviour?
- *Behaviour*. This is the character's actions and mannerisms, gestures, movements, way of talking and what they talk about. What motivates your character—greed, jealousy, love, self-preservation? And where do these motivations come from?
- *Sociological perspectives*. These are found through other people and their perspectives. Thus we can get to know a character through the relationships with their parents, friends, workmates, lover and strangers.

Relationship

Stories are about relationships. These are relationships between all the elements within a story—the events, characters and setting. Without relationships you have no story.

Rich characters are rich only because of their relationships to the environment, to other characters, to circumstances, to their personality and to their history. And we make those characters rich by exploring how they are affected by these relationships.

Are the relationships between two or more characters flavoured by jealousy, envy, mateship or camaraderie? Do characters share a common history? Perhaps they share a common dream but with differing commitments so that one character has to take on the lead role and coach the other person forward through difficult and trying times. What is the status play between the characters? Does this change? And what relationships are there between the characters and their environments?

When introducing elements into a story be careful not to discard them once their moment has passed. Continually introducing new events without giving your character a chance to react to these events leads a story nowhere.

Objective

What is the objective of the story? What is the objective of your characters? What motivates them? And what obstacles get in the way?

For example, a story about a cute little girl ambling through the forest can be interesting but it will not hold your interest for too long unless something happens.

Something needs to get in the way of this little girl skipping through the forest on her way to her grandma's house. And, of course, we have the big bad wolf.

If we wanted to explore the story of a curator who devoted her life to seeking out the best collections for a particular museum, what could make the story interesting? What obstacles did this curator have to surmount in order to achieve her objective of a fascinating and valuable collection?

We can also explore the challenges of elements within the landscape, such as a tree and its struggles in growing on a rock surface with skeletal soils. How does it do this? Where does it obtain its moisture and nutrients? How can it appear so strong when its roots are exposed and not anchored in the soil?

Where

Where is the story taking place? What is unique about this place?

If it is in Australia, then where in Australia? What is the time period? What foods did they eat at this time? What did they call this food? How did people get around? Who are the people and what is the current state of play regarding politics, society and the economy? Is it on a cattle station in central Australia or in a penthouse suite in Double Bay? Just imagining these two locations would evoke two contrasting images in a matter of seconds. The 'where' assists with creating an overall context for your story.

How does the location of the story impact on your characters? What challenges does it present?

There is an extraordinary oral history at Gulgong Pioneer Museum (central New South Wales) told by an old lady. She recounted a time when as a young mother living in this locale in the 19th century she had to watch while her youngest son died after accidentally eating poison. What made the story so moving was that it took two days for the child to die. And all the while, she remained helpless. The reason—the family lived two days by horseback from the nearest doctor.

REVISITING CROW

To develop a feel for using CROW try the following time-traveller activity: Sit in your favourite chair. Become intimately aware of your surroundings—the clothes you are wearing, the sounds which surround you, the feel and fabric of the chair, and the style of your furniture. Now imagine yourself shooting back to the mid-18th century. How have your surroundings changed? What sounds can you hear? What can you smell? What lighting do you use? What does your chair feel like now? And then go forward 20 years. How has it changed this time?

Whenever possible ensure your stories are personal. If you are creating or researching stories then go to the local scene and talk to people from the area you are researching: visit the pub, the local hang-outs and the local shops. Encourage people to reflect on stories they have heard. Such effort does not have to be a full-scale oral history session—even a few minutes talking to a local while waiting in a queue might provide an invaluable gem. If you are genuinely interested and respectful, such effort will reward you with stories which are rich and relevant and real. They will provide you with an excellent opportunity to capture the essence of the landscape through the personalities of people who live in the landscape.

WORKING WITH STORIES—A WRAP

Stories provide an opportunity to enrich tours for both yourself and the visitor. There is no right or wrong way to tell a story—just a way that is appropriate to the situation. When working with stories it is important to develop your own storytelling spices—those which work for you and your style. The spices discussed above were focused on the content element of your stories; such spices—together with a heap of spirit and enthusiasm, rich sounding vocals and captivating physical movements—are some of the ingredients you can use when working with stories.

Special Focus

Bush magic

Dianne Eva and Nadia Lalak

Working with stories and characters is part of Willoughby Council's School Environmental Awareness and Bushland Education Program.
We are guided by the Confucian proverb:

Tell me and I will forget.
Show me and I may remember.
But involve me and I will understand.
Confucius

Our program aims to provide children with the opportunity to:

● have a direct and hands-on experience with the natural world (urban bushland/waterways);
● understand the interconnectedness of all living and non-living things and the child's place and responsibility within it;
● experience moments of enchantment and fun.

WHY IS STORYTELLING AND CHARACTERISATION PART OF OUR INTERPRETATION PROGRAMS?

The main reasons are that this approach provides opportunities to do the following:

- Have fun and use fantasy.
- Draw people in, capture their interest and arouse imaginations.
- Retain focus and maintain interest by plot and character development.
- Break down barriers.
- Provide a sense of the unknown and what's going to happen—a sense of anticipation and expectation.
- Interact and become involved in the story.
- Suspend belief and enter the world of the character, leading to a better understanding of the character and the situation.

We believe that storytelling is a wonderful means of communication because it taps into feelings, emotions and 'the heart'. It goes beyond intellectual reasoning; this can have a deeper impact and thus generate a more profound connection. With stories the message and understanding we are trying to convey will have a longer lasting effect and will stay with people longer.

EXAMPLES OF STORYTELLING IN ACTION
Bush Fairies Picnic

The Bush Fairies Picnic is a sensory bushwalk with a difference. It is an opportunity to extend children's connections with bushland by 'sensitising' them through the fairy's magic wand and (imaginary) fairy dust.

Children enter a nominated reserve and their anticipation is heightened by the sound of distant fairy music. They come upon fairies dancing, picnicking and frolicking among magic mushrooms in a picturesque spot. They are enchanted by gum-nut (pink), water (blue) and wattle (yellow) fairies who invite them into their world (bushland).

The children divide into small groups each led by a fairy to embark upon a walk of discovery. Each group is 'sensitised' by using a magic wand and imaginary fairy dust. The children seem to enjoy this and are comfortable in being encouraged in a deeper use of their senses so that the bush can be experienced on a different level. Their sense of wonder is encouraged and they make many discoveries. Activities on the walk may also include some poetry reading (fairy and bushland focused), spells, meditation (very basic level) and perhaps a fairy treat (fairy bread). If there is time children may be given the opportunity to record thoughts, poems or drawings on paper in a special place in the bush.

A wonderful closure to the activity is the forming of a magic circle within which a fairy, with the help of two children, makes a wish for the environment. A white feather symbolises peace and a green leaf the environment—these are waved over the earth (a large marble) while the children close their eyes and make a wish for peace, love and harmony for the environment.

Bush Xmas Walk

This is an opportunity for a fun bushwalk near Xmas time while raising awareness of urban bushland and catchment issues.

Each year we work to a different focus, for example 'Surfing Santa', 'Who Stole the Xmas Bell Flowers?' and the 'WaCCy Wizard'.

'Surfing Santa' highlighted stormwater and catchment issues and their impact on bushland, while 'Who Stole the Xmas Bell Flowers' dramatised problems of native flora and endangered species.

We worked with 'WaCCy Wizard' in 2001 to capitalise on the interest generated by Harry Potter and *The Lord of the Rings*. That is magic, mystery, mayhem . . . wizards, fairies, spells . . . (We try to find a theme that children will easily relate to.)

The story-line is that WaCCy (Willoughby City Council) stumbles upon a group of schoolchildren and while acting confused tells them that he's in a state because he has muddled up his Xmas spell (by losing pages from his spell-book). The result is that the bush has become topsy-turvy and a great muddle. The children are invited to participate in setting things right by finding the four missing pages from the spell-book, and making their way to the magic tree. As the wizard disappears the children are delighted to spot a fairy. She is dressed in black and is also puzzled by what's going on in the bush. She says the animals are doing strange things, and that her dress has turned to black and she's not sure whether she gave the animals the right Xmas presents. The children eagerly respond that they know what's wrong and they know what to do. They set off with the bush fairy to find the missing pages.

On the way to the magic Xmas tree they discover four animals (at intervals along the bush track) doing crazy things and using their (inappropriate) Xmas presents:

- whistling wobbling wallaby (eating fruitloops);
- crazy swimming cockatoo (eating fairy bread);
- silly knitting spider (using a can of flyspray);
- funky freaky frog (dancing and using soap).

The children have to work out what's wrong, and they discuss more appropriate behaviour and gifts. Each animal produces a spell-page and demonstrates action for the children to learn.

All make their way to the Xmas tree eager to share their discoveries with the wizard. The spell is broken when all the children recite and do the required actions of the missing pages together, while the wizard waves his wand and disperses magic. The animals return to normal and the fairy is transformed back into white! The animals then receive the right Xmas present—peace and harmony is restored to the bush.

A WRAP

Our experience has been that these bushwalks with a strong story-line have appeared to enhance children's connection with the bush. We see 'the story' in their faces and they eagerly await the next walk.

TILDEN'S SIX PRINCIPLES OF INTERPRETATION

I. Any Interpretation that does not somehow relate what is being displayed or described to something within the personality or experience of the visitor will be sterile.

II. Information, as such, is not Interpretation. Interpretation is revelation based upon information. But they are entirely different things. However, all Interpretation includes information.

III. Interpretation is an art, which combines many arts, whether the materials presented are scientific, historical or architectural. Any art is in some degree teachable.

IV. The chief aim of Interpretation is not instruction, but provocation.

V. Interpretation should aim to present a whole rather than a part, and must address itself to the whole man rather than any phase.

VI. Interpretation addressed to children (say, up to the age of twelve) should not be a dilution of the presentation to adults, but should follow a fundamentally different approach. To be at its best it will require a separate program.

Source: Tilden (1977) Copyright © 1977 by the University of North Carolina Press. Used by permission of the publisher.

TOURISM MARKETS

Tourism

The activities of persons travelling to and staying in places outside their normal place of residence for pleasure, business, holiday, recreation and to visit friends and relatives. It is also the business of providing goods and services to facilitate such activities.

Adventure tourism

Commercially operated activities involving a combination of adventure and excitement pursued in an outdoor environment.

Cultural tourism

Tourism that focuses on the culture of a destination—the lifestyles, heritage, arts, industries and leisure pursuits of the local population. It can include attendance at cultural events, visits to museums and heritage places and mixing with local people. Cultural tourism includes indigenous tourism.

Ecotourism
Ecologically sustainable tourism that fosters environmental and cultural understanding, appreciation and conservation. Its ecological and social responsibility and educational element distinguish it from other tourism which focuses on experiencing natural areas, such as nature-based and adventure tourism.

Heritage tourism
Activities and services which provide visitors with the opportunity to experience, understand and enjoy the special values of Australia's natural and cultural heritage.

Indigenous tourism
Tourism which provides visitors with an opportunity to appreciate indigenous cultures and places of significance or which is either indigenous-owned or part-owned or employs indigenous people. It can encompass a wide range of products and services including cultural heritage and nature-based tours, visitor/cultural centres, educational programs, production of art and craft, performances, events, accommodation, transport and hospitality.

Nature-based tourism
A broad term that includes a range of tourism activities and experiences which occur in natural areas, or are based around experiencing and learning about aspects of natural heritage. It can include ecotourism and adventure tourism, and aspects of cultural tourism and indigenous tourism.

Source: Australian Heritage Commission 2001b. Reproduced with permission.

INTERPRETATION AS AN INTEGRATED PLANNING ACTIVITY

A CONVERSATION WITH BILL NETHERY
Mitchell, Nethery Associates Heritage Presentation

Heritage Presentation focuses on the activities, programs and services that bring the public into contact with ecologically and culturally significant environments. Planning for Heritage Presentation acknowledges the multiple functions of heritage resources in the recreational, cultural and economic life of the community. A key role in approach is the exploration and sharing of 'significance' with target audiences.

Interpretation is a vital component of Heritage Presentation along with conservation planning and business planning. Interpretation is one of the means by which Heritage Presentation activities 'explore and share "significance" with a target audience'. Heritage Presentation is more extensive in that it addresses the resource in the following three ways:

1. *Physically: conservation planning.* How is significance embodied in the actual place? That is, *what* do we want to preserve that visitors will encounter?
2. *Intellectually and affectively (emotively): Interpretation planning.* What personal programs, non-personal media (in this book non-personal media are referred to as 'interpretive media') and communications techniques will best convey understanding and appreciation of significance (historic, scientific, social and aesthetic) to visitors (and potential visitors), given what we know about who they are? That is, *how* will visitors encounter significance?
3. *Logistically and economically: business planning.* Open hours? Parking? Toilets? Ticketing? Security? Benches/seating? Group numbers? Accommodation? Refreshment? Merchandise? Transportation? Limits of acceptable change? Maps? and so on. How much will all this cost? How will it be paid for? Who are our partners/stakeholders/competitors? What can we charge? What should we charge? That is, *on what terms* will the place and its significance be accessible?

Heritage Presentation then is the means by which these questions are productively answered through a multidisciplinary approach, involving people who understand, respect and support the vital contribution that each discipline makes to the sustainable survival of significant places.

Traditionally, the primary concerns of organisations involved with heritage resource management focused on conservation in isolation.

Although conservation planning establishes the significance of the resource and preserves the physical evidence of that significance, business planning identifies the opportunities for cost recovery and revenue generation. Interpretation, which actually promotes and delivers popular and political support for continued conservation, was regarded as something to be addressed later, if at all.

In current practice the value of Interpretation is being recognised and is increasingly becoming an integrated element within any Heritage Presentation planning efforts. And so it should. For how can you plan for 'Presentation' without incorporating interpretive principles and techniques which focus in their entirety on giving effect to the significance of a resource by communicating it to the public?

Not all Heritage Presentation plans need to incorporate guided activities. It depends on the site, resources and other contextual elements. However, when guided activities are appropriate, planning efforts should reflect an integrated approach and ensure that all aspects of conducting a guided activity have been integrated into a holistic planning effort. This ensures that messages and operational elements associated with business, operational and conservation activities are aligned with those involved with delivering high-quality Interpretation programs. How else can efficiency and effectiveness be achieved in the allocation of resources required by an Interpretation program?

ACTIVITY: How does Heritage Presentation relate to you as a Guide? Do you ensure a holistic approach to your tour planning efforts?

Appendix 3

AN APPROACH TO DEVELOPING KEY INTERPRETIVE MESSAGES

FROM A DISCUSSION WITH CATH RENWICK

When developing Interpretation plans for heritage places Cath Renwick (who manages the landscape Interpretation consultancy 'Out in the Open' and has extensive experience in the Interpretation field) focuses on the reasons the place is important enough to keep. The following sequence illustrates her method.

- *Place*. First, establish the boundaries of the place and the interpretive resources available on site. Establish an inventory of resources and rank them according to their accessibility, legibility, robustness and, most importantly, their relative significance. Having defined the scope of the place, the next vital step is to research all aspects of its significance. This requires an open mind and a willingness to undertake an extensive research effort to generate all the significant topic options. This research also helps to refine the significance of the place.
- *Topics*. Develop a broad range of possible topics which could relate to historic heritage, natural heritage, indigenous heritage, and community significance as well as contemporary significance.
- *Theme*. Create themes within these topics (refer to Chapter 7 for discussion on themes).
- *Key messages*. Develop one distinct key message for each theme—that is, the one most important message to get across.

An example of the above approach is provided in the following outline of an Interpretation and recreation master plan for Wonnangatta Homestead Flat. This is an example of working with interpretive media rather than face-to-face Interpretation. However, the principles and approaches are similar, and often guided activities are developed following projects focusing on interpretive media.

With this project the key messages are based on, and guided by, a set of principles in a similar way to the guiding principles outlined in Chapter 3. The interpretive key messages combine with a set of contextual messages which relate to promoting management ideals for the site.

INTERPRETIVE THEMES AND KEY MESSAGES

Wonnangatta Valley is important to the people of Victoria and it can tell many stories of the past. The interpretive themes have been based on the Australian Heritage Commission's recently released *Australian Historical Themes* Framework (Australian Heritage Commission 200la) and on the principles mentioned above.

Themes	Topics	Key messages
Natural wonders Appreciating the natural wonders of Australia	● Landscape of the valley; ● The Viking; ● Kangaroo grassland with the Wonnangatta orchid.	This valley is cherished by all those who know about it—it has unusual features, especially the view of The Viking, and the kangaroo grassland provides a home for the rare Wonnangatta orchid.
Earliest inhabitants Living as Australia's earliest inhabitants	● Gunai-Kurnai; ● Taungurong; ● Natural pathways provide access; ● Good mild climate; ● Ceremonies and trade; ● Grassland and river provided access to food, clothing, medicine and tools. (These topics were identified by Aboriginal people as appropriate)	Aboriginal people used Wonnangatta Valley because of it rich resources, mild climate and open grassland.
Finding land Finding land with agricultural potential, developing primary production and struggling with remoteness and hardship	● The resilience of the Smith and Bryce families demonstrating the experiences of 19th-century homesteaders.	The resourceful Smith and Bryce families lived and worked in this valley for more than 50 years, growing, making or trading everything they needed for life on the land.
Enjoying the environment Enjoying the natural and cultural environment, forming associations and making Australian folklore	● Recreation in the valley; ● Associations for recreational activities (FoW, ADA and 4wders); ● The folklore surrounding the unsolved murders; ● The new folklore in John Marsden's 'Tomorrow' series.	Now that the valley is in Alpine National Park, it has become a much-loved destination. Parks Victoria continues to manage the area around the homestead with help from the Friends of Wonnangatta and other groups.

ORIENTATION AND MANAGEMENT KEY MESSAGES

These messages and themes are an integrated part of broader contextual messages that promote an accepted level of behaviour with the target audience. With guided activities such contextual messages would be demonstrated by the Guides in how they lead the activity and in how they model appropriate behaviours.

Parks Victoria, the client for the Wonnangatta Valley project, believes these management messages are extremely important in changing the habits of long-term users of the place:

- Respect Alpine National Park.
- Look after this precious valley by respecting the heritage it holds.
- Stick to existing tracks—don't make unnecessary vehicle tracks (not even when collecting firewood).
- Take your rubbish away with you—it is too far for a garbage truck to visit. Remember metal, glass and plastic do not burn. (Drop your rubbish at [suggested site/s] on your way home.)
- Conserve trees and the wildlife that live in them by collecting firewood outside the valley—do not use standing wood for fires and do not use your chainsaw within 200 metres of any camping area.
- Respect others—most people come to Wonnangatta for relaxation and rejuvenation. Wonnangatta Valley is a popular place for families. Consider others by keeping noise down and making sure the valley is safe for everyone.

RELEVANCE TO GUIDING ACTIVITIES

The above approach provides a working example of how themes, topics and messages are integrated into the management of a specific site. This same approach can be used when developing guided activities.

 ACTIVITY: Develop an outline for a two-hour guided walk which incorporates the above themes and their associated messages.

Appendix 4

THE ECOGUIDE CERTIFICATION PROGRAM

AN EXAMPLE OF A CERTIFICATION PROGRAM FOR THE GUIDING INDUSTRY

The EcoGuide Certification Program is an example of a certification program initiated by industry with the aim of setting a benchmark standard of guiding in the natural environment. It was launched in October 2000 as a voluntary certification program for Nature and Ecotour Guides, and is run under the auspices of the Ecotourism Association of Australia (EAA) with a multistakeholder panel. This program is a reflection of the increasing efforts being injected into the tourism industry to raise the standard of guiding.

The EcoGuide Program is not designed to train Guides, but to improve guiding standards and encourage professionalism among Ecotour Guides through a process of assessing and recognising the skills, knowledge, attitude and behaviour (the competence) of Guides.

The program continues to be driven by industry and to involve key industry stakeholders.

A background

The EAA is the peak industry body for ecotourism in Australia. It includes representatives from the tourism industry (operators and Guides); protected area managers; academics; consultants; and representatives from non-governmental organisations (including conservation group interests), local councils, and government and tourism commissions.

The EAA has two flagship products—an operator accreditation program 'Nature and Ecotourism Accreditation Program' (NEAP) and the EcoGuide Program. NEAP accredits products in the sectors of nature or ecotourism accommodation, attractions and tours. This has been up and running since 1996 and not only was a world first but also has been remarkably successful in Australia with product accredited from all states and territories. NEAP has recently formed an alliance with Green Globe 21 Asia Pacific to develop an international ecotourism product certification standard.

The EcoGuide Program is linked to and nests under the NEAP program—but is still autonomous and remains the only national Guide Certification program. The program grew out of research conducted by Alice Crabtree and Betty Weiler in the mid-1990s. The EAA gained funding assistance from the Office of National Tourism to develop the program in conjunction with a multistakeholder steering group.

Who are Ecotour Guides?

An Ecotour Guide is a person who leads tourists around an area or site of natural and/or cultural significance while adhering to ecotourism and sustainable tourism principles.

'They communicate and interpret the significance of the environment, promote minimal impact practices, ensure the sustainability of the natural and cultural environment, and motivate tourists to consider their own lives in relation to larger ecological and cultural concerns.' (Black & Mackay 1995).

Ecotour Guides may be employed by a variety of organisations including tour operators, land management agencies including national parks and forestry departments, adventure travel companies, non-governmental organisations and educational institutions.

The benefits of the EcoGuide Certification Program includes:

- *For Guides*. Certified Guides have a competitive edge by gaining industry-based recognition within the tourism industry, and links to the national training and qualifications framework set up within the Tourism Training Package.
- *For tour operators*. Tour operators who employ certified Guides are maximising the opportunity of working with people who are committed to quality tourism experiences. There is also the benefit of using certification as a benchmark for training purposes, and greater product appeal by employing and promoting the use of bona fide Nature and Ecotour Guides.
- *For visitors*. Visitors attending tours led by certified Guides have the reassurance that these Guides are committed to providing quality nature tourism and ecotourism experiences in a safe, culturally sensitive and environmentally sustainable manner.
- *For the environment*. Environmental benefits flow from improved guiding practices that lead to fewer negative environmental and cultural impacts.
- *For protected area managers*. Certification can assist protected area managers in the review of permit applications for sensitive areas by being able to identify operators who employ staff with the appropriate training and qualifications.

How it works

People who are interested in receiving certification can obtain the relevant details from the Ecotourism website or contact the EAA direct.

Certification is based on benchmarks provided by:

- national tour guiding competencies;
- a range of additional competencies specific to nature-based/ecotourism activities including minimal impact procedures, Interpretation skills, ecological and land management knowledge, and nature-based knowledge;

in addition to:

- guiding experience and currency of this experience;
- a demonstrated commitment to ongoing professional development.

On entry to the program, Guides declare their intent to provide high-quality nature or ecotourism experiences in a safe, culturally sensitive and environmentally sustainable manner through signing a professional code of ethics.

The certification process involves Guides demonstrating their competence through a portfolio of evidence (based on the criteria outlined above). Guides who are eligible for certification might also be eligible for the national qualification of Certificate III or IV in Tourism (Tour Guiding).

Qualified assessors assist applicants collect and produce evidence demonstrating they have the skills and knowledge as well as the attitudes and behaviour necessary to their job as a Nature or Ecotour Guide.

The EcoGuide Program recognises that Guides gain their competence through a number of very different ways; hence, the portfolio of evidence the program needs to collect will vary from Guide to Guide. At least some of the evidence must be collected through some form of workplace assessment.

Certified Guides receive:

- a package containing numbered certificate and Guide badge;
- automatic membership of the Ecotourism Association of Australia (Associate) with reduced fee upgrade to Professional membership;
- *Ecotourism News* (monthly by email or quarterly in hard copy);
- access to reduced-cost training materials;
- listing on the Association's members search database;
- networking and professional development opportunities.

Source: Reproduced with permission of the Ecotourism Association of Australia. For updated information, see website at www.ecotourism.org.au

INTERPRETIVE ACTIVITY PLANNER

TITLE

THEME/MESSAGE

The theme is your intended message for clients to take away with them.

TOPIC

Natural values
  Landscape/seascape/processes
  Plants
  Animals
  Ecology

Cultural values
  Aboriginal/history/heritage
    Lifestyle
      Customs
      Religion
      Law/lore
      Entertainment
    Resource use
      Land/water/sea
      Food
      Tools
      Shelter
      Clothing
  Management issues
    Visitors
    Fire
    Ferals
    Weeds
    Wise use

CAPTION/SLOGAN FOR ACTIVITY
(OPTIONAL)

DESIGN TECHNIQUE

Talk
Walk/drive
Wildlife observations
Concept exploring
Arts and craft
Sensory
Problem solving

INTERPRETIVE ACTIVITY PLANNER

THE EXPERIENCE

Use as many learning styles as possible. What will participants:

See?

Hear?

Do?

Make?

Feel? (emotionally)

AUDIENCE

Consider 'visitor profile' (country of origin; cultural preferences; special interests)

❑ Children 6–10

❑ Children 11–12

❑ Teens 13–17

❑ Young adults 18–25

❑ Adults

❑ Family

❑ Groups

Maximum

Minimum

OBJECTIVES

These are your desired outcomes.

What *knowledge* will participants gain?

What *skills* will participants gain?

What *attitudes/values* will be discussed/ integrated into the activity that the clients can take away with them?

What *actions* will participants be able to take as a result of the activity?

INTERPRETIVE ACTIVITY PLANNER

OUTLINE	SITE

OUTLINE

The major points that hold the activity together—include introduction, activity steps or points, and conclusion/theme.

Introduction

Body

Conclusion

SITE

Describe site essentials.

❏ Map attached (optional)

TIME LENGTH

TIME OF DAY

❏ Morning   ❏ Evening

❏ Afternoon   ❏ Anytime

PROPS

For leader to supply

For participants to bring

PROMOTION

What? (write the advertisement)

When/where? (state time and place)

How? (the media)

INTERPRETIVE ACTIVITY PLANNER

BUDGET	**Self-evaluation**
	Which objectives did you achieve?
PARTICIPANT COST	
THE SCRIPT AND TIPS FOR GUIDE	
❏ Completed and attached	
EVALUATION	
Number attending the activity	
	How could you improve your activity?
Age groups	

❏ 6–10   ❏ 18–25

❏ 11–12   ❏ 26–60

❏ 13–17   ❏ 61+

Overall audience response

Participant evaluation survey

❏ Attached

REVISED ACTIVITY PLANNER

❏ Revised planner attached

Source: Department of Conservation and Land Management, Western Australia (2000)

Bibliography

Absher, J. 1997, 'Introduction: Interpretation as communication', *Trends: Park Practice Program*, vol. 34, no. 4, pp. 2–3.

Aiello, R. 1998, 'Interpretation and the marine industry, who needs it? A case study of Great Adventures', *Journal of Tourism Studies*, 9, pp. 51–61.

Ap, J. & Wong, K.K.F. 2001, 'Case study on tour guiding: professionalism, issues and problems', *Tourism Management*, 22, pp. 551–563.

Arnould, E.J. & Price, L.L. 1998, 'Communicative staging of the wilderness servicescape', *Service Industries Journal*, vol. 18, no. 3, pp. 90–115.

Australia ICOMOS Inc. 2000, The Burra Charter: the Australia ICOMOS Charter for Places of Cultural Significance, Australia ICOMOS Inc. Victoria.

Australian Heritage Commission 2001a, *Australian Historic Themes*, Commonwealth of Australia, Canberra.

Australian Heritage Commission 2001b, *Successful Tourism at Heritage Places—A Guide for Tourism Operators, Heritage Managers and Communities*, 2nd edn, Australian Heritage Commission, Canberra.

Australian Heritage Commission 2001c, *A Guide—How to Find Your Heritage Places. Migrant Heritage Places in Australia*, Canberra.

Australian Heritage Commission 2001d, *A Handbook for Group Coordinators. Migrant Heritage Places in Australia*, Canberra.

Australian Heritage Commission and Commonwealth Department of the Environment and Heritage (Environment Australia) 2001, *Protecting Heritage Places—Workbook*, Australian Heritage Commission and Commonwealth Department of the Environment and Heritage (Environment Australia), Canberra.

Australian Tourism Export Council/Tourism Queensland 2001, Code of Conduct—draft 2001.

Australian Tourism Export Council/Tourism Queensland 2001b, 'Issues for the Regulation of Tourist Guides in Australia', compiled by Margot Homersham.

Beck, L. & Cable, T. 1997, *Interpretation for the 21st Century: Fifteen Guiding Principles for Interpreting Nature and Culture*, Sagamore Publishing, Champaign, Illinois.

Beckmann, E.A. 1992, 'Environmental interpretation for education and management in Australian national parks and other protected areas', unpublished doctoral thesis.

Black, R. & Mackay, J. 1995, 'The Australian Alps: Getting the messages across', in E. Beckmann and R. Russell (eds), *Interpretation and the Getting of Wisdom*, Conference papers of the Fourth Annual Conference of the Interpretation Australia Association, Interpretation Australia Association, Collingwood, Victoria.

Bolitho, A. & Hutchinson, M. 1998, *Out of the Ordinary*, Canberra Stories Group, Canberra.

Carnegie, D. 1962, *The Quick and Easy Way to Effective Speaking*, Dale Carnegie & Associates, Inc. New York.

Carter, J. (ed.) 1997, *A Sense of Place*, Tourism & Environment Initiative, Inverness, UK.

Cassady, M. 1992, *The Art of Storytelling*, Element Books, UK.

Cheatley, B. 1994, 'Managing the visitor experience: Knowing your current and potential visitors is the first step', in E. Beckman and S. Hull (eds), *Interpretation Attached to Heritage*, Papers presented at the Third Annual Conference of the Interpretation Australia Association 1994, Interpretation Australia Association, Collingwood, Victoria.

Cohen, E. 1985, 'The tourist guide: The origins, structure and dynamics of a role', *Annals of Tourism Research*, 12, pp. 15–29.

Commonwealth Department of Tourism 1994, *A Talent for Tourism—Stories about Indigenous People in Tourism*, Commonwealth of Australia, Canberra.

Commonwealth of Australia 2000, *Australian Standard Classification of Occupations*, Australian Bureau of Statistics, Canberra.

Commonwealth of Australia, *Register of the National Estate*, website www.environment.gov.au/heritage/register/index.html.

Cornell, J. 1989, *Sharing the Joy of Nature*, Dawn Publications, Nevada City, California.

Cornell, J. 1998, *Sharing Nature with Children*, Dawn Publications, Nevada City, California.

Dargin, P. 1997, *Making and Telling Stories*, Development and Advisory Publications, Dubbo, NSW.

De Bono, E. 1993, *Serious Creativity*, HarperCollins, New York.

Department of Conservation and Land Management 1996, *Running Activity Programs. A Guide to*

Interpreting the Natural and Cultural World for Visitors, Department of Conservation and Land Management, Como, Western Australia.

Department of Conservation and Land Management 1998a, *Best Recipes for Interpreting our Heritage*, Como, Western Australia.

Department of Conservation and Land Management 1998b, *Designing Interpretive Activities Workshop*, Leader's Manual and Participant Workbook, Department of Conservation and Land Management, Perth.

Department of Conservation Western Australia 2000, *Developing Ecotours and Other Interpretive Activity Programs*, Gil Field and Lotte Lent, Department of Conservation Western Australia, Perth.

Dowling, R. 2001, 'Environmental Tourism' in Douglas, N. Douglas, N. & Derret (eds), *Special Interest Tourism*. John Wiley and Sons, Brisbane.

Faggetter, R. 1998, 'Making every visit count—interpretation in Victoria's national parks', in E. Hamilton-Smith (ed.), *Celebrating the Parks*, Australian Symposium on Parks History, Carlton South, Victoria.

Forestry Tasmania, 1994, *Guided Nature-based Tourism in Tasmania's Forests—Trends, Constraints and Implications*, Forestry Tasmania, Hobart.

Global Arts Link, 1999, *Exploring Culture and Community for the 21st century*, Global Arts Link, Ipswich, Queensland.

Haig, I. 1997, Viewing nature: Can a Guide Make a Difference?, Department of Outdoor Education, Griffith University, Brisbane.

Hall, C.M. & McArthur, S. (eds). 1993, *Heritage Management in New Zealand and Australia: Visitor Management, Interpretation and Marketing*, Oxford University Press, Auckland.

Hall, C.M. & McArthur, S. 1996, *Heritage Management in Australia and New Zealand: The Human Dimension*, Oxford University Press, Melbourne.

Ham, S. 1983, 'Cognitive pyschology and interpretation: synthesis and application', *Journal of Interpretation*, 8, pp. 11–27.

Ham, S. 1992, *Environmental Interpretation*, North American Press, Golden, Colorado.

Ham, S. 1997, 'Environmental education as strategic communication: A paradigm for the 21st century', *Trends: Park Practice Program*, vol. 34, no. 4, pp. 4–6.

Hammit, W.E. 1981, 'A theoretical foundation for Tilden's interpretive principles', *Journal of Environmental Education*, 12, pp. 13–16.

Hawkins, D.E. & Lamoureux, K. 2001, 'Global growth and magnitude of ecotourism', *Encyclopedia of Ecotourism*, Wallingford, Oxon, UK.

Heintzman, J. 1988, *Making the Right Connections: A Guide for Nature Writers*, UW-SP Foundation Press Inc., Stevens Point, Wisconsin.

Holloway, J.C. 1981, 'The guided tour: A sociological approach', *Annals of Tourism Research*, vol. 8, no. 3, pp. 377–401.

Horton D. (ed.) 1994, *The Encyclopaedia of Aboriginal Australia*, Aboriginal Studies Press for the Australian Institute of Aboriginal and Torres Strait Islander Studies, Canberra.

Howard, J. 1997, 'Interpretation down under: Guided activities at parks and interpretive centers in Australia', *Legacy*, vol. 8, no. 1, pp. 10–15.

Howard, J. 1997/8, 'Towards best practice in interpretive guided activities', *Australian Parks and Recreation*, vol. 33, no. 4, pp. 28–31.

Howard, J. 1998, 'Environmental education and interpretation: Developing an affective difference', *Australian Journal of Environmental Education*, vol. 14, pp. 65–70.

Howat, G., Crilley, G. & Milne, I. 1995, 'Measuring customer service quality in recreation and parks', *Australian Parks and Recreation*, vol. 31, no. 4, pp. 37–43.

Howes, M. 1998, 'Interpretation—issues and trends', in E. Hamilton-Smith (ed.), *Celebrating the Parks*, Proceedings of the First Australian Symposium on Parks History, Melbourne.

Hughes, K. 1991, 'Tourist satisfaction: a guided cultural tour in North Queensland', *Australian Psychologist*, vol. 23, no. 3, pp. 166–171.

Interpretation Australia Association—conference proceedings since 1992. The excellent articles in these proceedings are best accessed via the website (see contact details on page 294).

Johnstone, C. 1992, *What Is Social Value?*, Australian Heritage Commission, Canberra.

Johnstone, K. 1981, *Improvisation and the Theatre*, Eyre Methuen Ltd, London.

Karshner, R. 1993, *You Said a Mouthful—Tongue Twisters*, Dramaline Publications, Toluca Lake, California.

Knapp, D. 1997a, 'Back to basics: Interpreting to the lowest common denominator', *Trends: Park Practice Program*, vol. 34, no. 4, pp. 17–20.

Knapp, D. 1997b, 'The relationship between environmental interpretation and environmental education', *Legacy*, vol. 8, no. 3, pp. 10–13.

Knudsen, D., Beck, L. & Cable, T. 1995, *Interpretation of Cultural and Natural Resources*, Venture Publishing, State College, PA. USA.

Lewis, W. J. 1993, *Interpreting for Park Visitors*, Eastern Acorn Press, Conshoshocken, PA.

Linklater, K. 1976, *Freeing the Natural Voice*, Drama Book Publishers, New York.

Mackay, H. 1994, *Why Don't People Listen*, Pan Macmillan, Sydney.

Malouf, D. 1988, *How to Create and Deliver a Dynamic Presentation*, Simon & Schuster, Sydney.

Mastny, L. 2001, *Travelling Light: New Paths for International Tourism*, Worldwatch Institute, Washington DC.

McCallion, M. 1988, *The Voice Book*, Faber & Faber Ltd, London.

McKay, H. & Dudley, B. 1996, *About Storytelling—a practical guide*, Hale & Iremonger, Sydney.

McKercher, B. 1998, *The Business of Nature-based Tourism*, Hospitality Press, Melbourne.

Merriman, T. 1998, 'Certification program takes off', *NAI News*, Summer, pp. 1, 8.

Mills, E. 1920, *Adventures of a Nature Guide and Essays in Interpretation*, New Past Press, Friendship, WI.

Mills, H. 1999, *Artful Persuasion*, MG Press, Summer Park, Qld.

Moscardo, G. 1995, 'Total quality interpretation', in E. Beckmann and R. Russell (eds), *Interpretation and the Getting of Wisdom*, Conference papers of the Fourth Annual Conference of the Interpretation Australia Association, Interpretation Australia Association, Collingwood, Victoria.

Moscardo, G. 1996, 'Mindful visitors: Heritage and tourism', *Annals of Tourism Research*, vol. 23, no. 2, pp. 376–397.

Moscardo, G. 1999, *Making Visitors Mindful*, Sagamore Publishing, Champaign, Illinois.

Moscardo, G. 2000, 'Are we doing the best we can for international visitors?' Interpretation Australia Association newsletter. Issue 18 September.

NSW Heritage Office 1998, *Living with Aboriginal Culture*, NSW Heritage Office, Sydney.

Office of National Tourism 1996, *Projecting Success—Visitor Management Projects for Sustainable Growth*, Department of Industry, Science and Tourism, Canberra.

Oxford University Press, 1995, *The Oxford Large Print Dictionary*. Oxford University Press, Oxford, UK.

Parkin, N. 1969, *Ideal Voice and Speech Training*, Samuel French Ltd, London.

Pearse, A. & Garner, A. 1985, *Talk Language*, Camel Publishing Company, Sydney.

Pearson, M. & Sullivan, S. 1995, *Looking After Heritage Places: The Basics of Heritage Planning for Managers, Landowners and Administrators*, Melbourne University Press, Melbourne.

Peoples, D.A. 1992, *Presentations Plus*, John Wiley & Sons, New York.

Pond, K. 1993, *The Professional Guide*, Van Nostrand Reinhold, New York.

Punt, N.A. 1979, *The Singer's and Actor's Throat: The Vocal Mechanism of the Professional Voice*, Heinemann Medical Books, New York.

Queensland Department of Environment and Heritage 1996, *The Art of Interpretation* (videos and workbooks), Queensland Department of Environment and Heritage, Brisbane.

Regnier, K., Gross, M. & Zimmerman, R. 1992, *The Interpreter's Guidebook: Techniques for Programs and Presentations*, Foundation Press, Inc., University of Wisconsin, Stevens Point, Wisconsin.

Richardson, J. 1993, *Ecotourism & Nature-based Holidays*, Choice Books, Sydney.

Rodenburg, P. 1998, *The Actor Speaks—Voice and the Performer*, Methuen, London.

Saunders, R. 1989, 'Summary of interpretation techniques and their values', *Australian Ranger Bulletin*, vol. 5, no. 3, pp. 13–14.

Sawyer, R. 1970, *The Way of the Storyteller*, Penguin Books, New York.

Schimdt, C.J. 1979, 'The guided tour', *Urban Life*, vol. 7, no. 4, pp. 441–467.

Sharpe, G.W. 1982, *Interpreting the Environment*, 2nd edn, John Wiley & Sons, New York.

Sutherland, L. 1996, 'Interpretation and visitor services—An evaluation of policies and practices in Australia's botanic gardens', unpublished masters thesis.

Tannen, D. 1986, *That's Not What I Meant*, Virago Press, London.

Tilden, F. 1977, *Interpreting Our Heritage*, 3rd edn, University of North Carolina Press, Chapel Hill, USA.

Tourism Queensland 2000a, *Tour Operator Tool Kit*, Tourism Queensland, Brisbane.

Tourism Queensland 2000b, *Outback Interpretation Manual*, Tourism Queensland, Brisbane.

Turner, J.C. 1993, *Voice and Speech in the Theatre*, 4th edn, rev. Malcolm Morrison, A&C Black, London.

Upitis, A. 1989, 'Interpreting cross-cultural sites', in Uzzell, D. (ed.) *Heritage Interpretation*, vol. 1, The *Natural and Built Environment*, Belhaven Press, London, pp. 142–152.

Uzzell, D. (ed.) 1984, *Heritage Interpretation—the Visitor Experience*, Belhaven Press, London.

Uzzell, D. (ed.) 1989, *Heritage Interpretation, vol 1: The Natural and Built Environment*, Belhaven Press, London.

Valentine, N. 1993, *Speaking in Public*, Penguin Books, Ringwood, Vic.

Veverka, John A. 1994, *Interpretive Master Planning*, Acorn Naturalists, Tustin, California.

Weiler, B. & Davis, D. 1993, 'An exploratory investigation into the roles of the nature-based tour leader', *Tourism Management*, April, pp. 91–98.

Weiler, B. & Ham, S.H. 2001, 'Tour guides and interpretation', *Encyclopedia of Ecotourism*, Wallingford, Oxon, UK.

Western Australian Naturalists' Club, 2001, 'The development of nature-based tourism in Western Australia' in *The Western Australian Naturalist*, vol. 23, no. 1

Wolfe, R. 1997, 'Interpretive education as an under-rated management tool', *Interpscan*, vol. 24, no. 2, pp. 15–19.

SOURCES OF INFORMATION
ORGANISATIONS

These organisations are an excellent resource for Guides. Most of them have associated and affiliated state and regional organisations which can provide information at state, regional or local level.

Aboriginal and Torres Strait Islander Commission	PO Box 17 Woden ACT 2606 Phone: 02 6121 4000 http://www.atsic.gov.au/
Australia ICOMOS (International Council on Monuments and Sites)	Secretariat Faculty of Arts Deakin University Burwood Vic. 3125 Phone: 03 9251 7131 Fax: 03 9251 7158 http://www.icomos.org/australia/ Email: austicomos@deakin.edu.au
Australian Archaeological Association Inc.	PO Box 6565 St Lucia Qld 4067 Phone: 07 3365 2385 Fax: 07 3365 2359 http://www.australianarchaeologicalassociation.com.au Email: mailbag@australianarchaeology.com
Australian Association for Environmental Education	PO Box 205 Manly NSW 1655 Phone: 02 9976 5087 Fax: 02 9976 5347 http://members.iinet.net.au/~aaee/
Australian Broadcasting Commission	www.abc.net.au (excellent up-to-date resources on a range of topics and subject areas)
Australian Bureau of Statistics	St Andrews House Sydney Square Sydney NSW 2000 http://www.abs.gov.au

Australian Council of National Trusts	14/71 Constitution Avenue Campbell ACT 2612 Phone: 02 6247 6766
Australian Commonwealth government information	Excellent links and access to a wide variety of Commonwealth government information departments and services through the website: http://www.fed.gov.au/KSP/
Australian Garden History Society, The (AGHS)	Gate Lodge 100 Birdwood Ave Melbourne Vic. 3004 Phone: 03 9650 5043 or toll-free 1800 678 446 Fax: 03 9650 8470 info@gardenhistorysociety.org.au
Australian Heritage Commission	Australian Heritage Commission John Gorton Building King Edward Terrace Parkes ACT 2600 GPO Box 787 Canberra ACT 2601 Phone: 02 6274 2111 or 1800 020 625 Fax: 02 6274 2095 http://www.ahc.gov.au
Australian Institute of Aboriginal and Torres Strait Islander Studies (AIATSIS)	GPO Box 553 Canberra ACT 2601 Phone: 02 6246 1111 Fax: 02 6261 4285 http://www.aiatsis.gov.au/
Australian Museums and Galleries Online (AMOL)	http://www.amol.org.au
Australian National Training Authority	http://www.anta.gov.au/
Australian Outdoor Education Council, The	PO Box 1896 RGPO Melbourne Vic. 3001
Australian Storytelling Guild	Australian Storytelling Guild (NSW) Inc. PO Box Q274 Queen Victoria Post Office Sydney NSW 1230 http://www.home.aone.net.au/stories Email: gsoneill@ozemail.com.au
Australian Tourism Export Council	Level 2, 80 William Street Woolloomooloo NSW 2001 Phone: 02 9360 5255 Fax: 02 9332 3383 http://www.atec.net.au/
Australian Tourism Research Institute	http://www.crctourism.com.au/atri.htm
Australian Tourist Commission	Level 4 William Street Woolloomooloo NSW 2011 http://www.atc.net.au

Bureau of Meteorology	150 Lonsdale Street Melbourne Vic. 3000 GPO Box 1289K Melbourne Vic. 3001 Phone: 03 9669 4000 Fax: 03 9669 4699 http://www.bom.gov.au
Bureau of Tourism Research	GPO Box 1545 Canberra ACT 2600 http://www.btr.gov.au
Community Biodiversity Network	admin@cbn.org.au http://www.cbn.org.au/ (BioNet, EarthAlive, OceansAlive)
Department of Industry, Tourism and Resources	http://www.industry.gov.au Toll-free Publications Line for the Tourism Department is 1800 804 465
Ecotourism Association of Australia	GPO Box 268 Brisbane Qld 4001 Phone: 07 3229 5550 Fax: 07 3229 5255 Email: mail@ecotourism.org.au http://www.ecotourism.org.au
Environment Australia	John Gorton Building King Edward Terrace Parkes ACT 2600 GPO Box 787 Canberra ACT 2601 Phone: 02 6274 1111 Fax: 02 6274 1666 http://www.ea.gov.au
Institute for Earth Education	PO Box 41 St Agnes, SA Email: ieeaust@adam.com.au http://www.earthed.com/
Institute of Australian Tourist Guides	IATG National Office PO Box 664 St Ives NSW 2075 Phone: 02 9987 2705 Email: diazinaus@ozemail.com.au
Institute of Australian Tourist Guides—Area NSW	PO Box W128 Warringah Mall NSW 2100 Phone: 02 9401 1051 Fax: 02 9401 1050 Email: iatg@optushome.com.au
Interpretation Australia Association	Conference proceedings from each of the IAA conferences are excellent reading and a useful resource. Interpretation Australia Association PO Box 1231 Collingwood Vic. 3066 http://www.interpretationaustralia.asn.au/ (The IAA website provides links to Interpretation associations throughout the world, references and recommended resources.)

Museums Australia	PO Box 266 Civic Square ACT 2608 Phone: 02 6208 5044 Email: ma@museumsaustralia.org.au
Oral History Association of Australia	c/- Oral History Program State Library of NSW Macquarie Street Sydney NSW 2000 Phone: 02 9273 1697 Email: rblock@slnsw.gov.au
Professional Tour Guide Association of Australia Inc.	PO Box 34 Armadale North Vic 3143 Melbourne Vic. 3000 Phone: 03 9614 0806 Fax: 03 9614 8877 Email: ptgaa@aton.asn.au
Royal Australian Historical Society	History House 133 Macquarie Street Sydney NSW 2000 Phone: 02 9247 8001 Fax: 02 9247 7854 Email: history@rahs.org.au
Tour Guides Association of NorthernTerritory Inc.	PO Box 41795 Casuarina NT 0811 Email: banana@ocfa4.net.au
Tour Guides Association of Western Australia Inc.	Rob Johnston President Phone/Fax: 1800 688 644 PO Box 1104 Subiaco WA 6904 Email: dotnrobj@bigpond.com
Tourism Forecasting Council	GPO Box 1545 Canberra City ACT 2601 http://www.tourism.gov.au/Tourism/TFC/tfc.html
Tourism Training Australia	GPO Box 2493 Sydney NSW 2001 Phone: 02 9290 1055 Fax: 02 9290 1001 Email: reception@tourismtraining.com.au http://www.tourismtraining.com.au/ (It also provides contacts to State Tourism Training organisations which are excellent contacts for tourism-related careers and resources.)
Victorian Tourism Operators Association (VTOA)	PO Box 510 Collins Street West Melbourne Vic 3007 Phone: 03 9614 8855 Fax: 03 9614 8877 Email: vtoa@vtoa.asn.au http://www.vtoa.asn.au
World Federation of Tourist Guide Associations	http://www.wftga.org/

WHERE TO FIND ADDITIONAL INFORMATION AND REFERENCE MATERIAL

- Local government—some have historians, oral history programs, activities, archives and local museums; libraries with storytellers; and a range of programs, for example North Sydney Council—http://www.northsydney.nsw.gov.au
- Libraries—local, regional, state and national; universities, TAFEs and colleges
- Videos, DVDs and films—most major libraries including those in universities have a collection of videos relevant to the work of Guides
- Government departments
- Tourist information centres—local, regional and state
- Local special-interest clubs, for example naturalist, bird observers, plant study and historical
- Guidebooks
- Reference books—a range is available through libraries and bookstores, and second-hand bookstores
- Television
- Internet
- Personal experiences and those of friends and relatives—ask them what they like or what their latest political discussion was about
- Newspapers—various newspapers; most big newsagents carry newspapers from other states and other countries; same with magazines
- Special-interest journals
- Newsletters
- Special-interest clubs
- Leaflets and booklets provided by attractions and special-interest organisations
- Visit attractions
- Inflight magazines are useful as this is often what people might be reading before arriving in Australia
- Periodicals
- Listening to the radio, in particular the ABC
- Keep up with the times—try to incorporate recent events into your commentary
- Search out your local and regional area by contacting your local government or relevant state tourism and heritage-based organisations. Their information facilities include journals, conferences, lectures, workshops, walks, member events and excellent research opportunities. A number of them also have their own research libraries. You are strongly encouraged to join at least a few special-interest organisations. Support these organisations by promoting them on your tours to people who express relevant interests. Never abuse the privilege of a person providing you with information—often the organisations are conducted on a volunteer basis by people committed to the ideals and ethics. Honour and respect these organisations.
- Tourism with Integrity is produced by Commonwealth Department of Communications, Technology and the Arts and is available from Australian Council of National Trusts, PO Box 1002, Civic Square ACT 2608; email: acnt@spirit.com.au; phone: 02 6247 6799
- Tour Operator Tool Kit and *Outback Interpretation Manual*; Phone: 07 3535 5273; email: merryn.draper@tq.com.au
- Research—part of research is getting to know your local and regional area so you can provide some assistance to people and answer their questions regarding where to go for a few drinks after the tour, recommended restaurants, average prices of hotel and motel rooms, and so on. Get to know one-off and major events; for example, car races, street festivals, community parades and sporting events. It is also useful to find out about the area through oral histories, historical photos, attending other tours and visiting attractions.

Note: You obviously need to check the date of any references you use, especially guidebooks.

Index

Aborigines
   interpreting heritage 18–23
   places 23
   sites 21–2
   stories 265
accommodation 13–14
accreditation 6, 233, 251, 282–4
activity planner 285–8
'advance and extend' technique
   159
adventure tourism 275
advertising 250
affective learning 146
age of tourists 38–9
agencies 13
aggressive behaviour 215–16
airlines 12
alcohol 225–6
alliteration 193
American tourists 68
analogies 184, 195–6
anchors for nervous tensions
   89–92
anecdotes 183
art galleries
   guide program 53–4
   Interpretation in 49–52
articulation 96–7
assertive behaviour
   dealing with criticism 222–4
   dealing with persistent people
     222
   managing difficult situations
     with 215, 216–21
attitudes 41
attractions 13
audience
   see also presentations
   age 38–9
   analysing 38–44
   attitudes 41
   benefits of interpretive
     approach 6
   botanic gardens 77–8
   capturing attention 181–3
   communicating with *see*
     communication
   cultural background 40, 66
   customer service 208–12
   definition 2
   difficult *see* difficult situations
   ecotourism 231–2
   expectations 41, 42–4
   face-to-face interpretation 7
   focus on 83

Guide's influence on
   satisfaction 34
   hazards 143
   interpretive approach 5
   knowledge 41
   market 39
   motivation 42, 82
   nature-based tours 248–9
   needs 44
   relationship with 47–8
   researching 45–6, 119
   sensory channels 63
   socioeconomic background
     41
   stories 261–2
   tour evaluation 131–2
   tour planning 117
   types of 38
   zoos 107–8
auditory senses
   communicating through 63
   learning through 148
Australian Historic Themes 174
Australian Museums and
   Galleries Online (AMOL)
   website 7

baggage loss 226–7
ballads 264
barriers to communication 64
behaviour
   aggressive 215–16
   assertive *see* assertive
     behaviour
   problems with *see* difficult
     situations
   submissive 215–16
behavioural objectives of a tour
   117
body centre 83
body language *see* non-verbal
   communication
body piercing 62
botanic gardens, Interpretation in
   76–80
brainstorm tree 160
breath control 94–6
briefs 115–16, 121
budget tourists 41
buses 239
bush stories 271–4

cafés 14
camping-based tours 244
certification 282–4

character Interpretation 266–71
closed questions 74
clothes 61–2, 266–7
coach captains 239
coaches 13, 239–40
coastal tours 12
cognitive learning 146
commentaries
   see also presentations
   beginning 179–80
   building 169–81
   capturing the audience's
     attention 181–3
   context 169–70
   definition 168
   delivering 180
   designing 119–20
   end 179–80
   evaluating 180
   grammar 191–2
   information delivery 183–5
   language 189–97
   props 187–8
   relevance 185–7
   sequence 178–9
   stories in *see* stories
   structure 168
   techniques 192–7
   theme 172–8
   topic 170–1
   vocabulary 190–1
communication
   see also language
   Aboriginal cultures 20
   barriers 64
   definition 57–8
   effect of cultural diversity on
     64–9
   ensuring 64–70
   factors affecting 57–63
   forms of 56–7
   importance of method 59
   listening skills 70–3
   myths 64, 65
   need for 56
   non-verbal 59–63
   'premature speculation'
     69–70
   process 56–7
   sensory channels 63
   tour staff 239
conducting a tour *see* tours
conferences 15
confidence 83, 93
confirming 238